S0-BDL-570

EARLY CHILDHOOD EDUCATION SERIES
Leslie R. Williams, Editor

ADVISORY BOARD: Barbara T. Bowman, Harriet K. Cuffaro, Stephanie Feeney, Doris Pronin Fromberg, Celia Genishi, Stacie G. Goffin, Dominic F. Gullo, Alice Sterling Honig, Elizabeth Jones, Gwen Morgan

(continued)

Polk State College
Lakeland Library

Powerful Children

Understanding How to Teach
and Learn Using the Reggio Approach

Ann Lewin-Benham

Foreword by Howard Gardner

Teachers College, Columbia University
New York and London

The views expressed in this publication are those of the author representing her own interpretation of the philosophy and practices of the Municipal Infant-Toddler Centers and Preschools of Reggio Emilia

The content of this publication has not been officially approved by the Municipality of Reggio Emilia nor by Reggio Children in Italy; therefore it may not reflect the views and opinions of those organizations.

Published by Teachers College Press, 1234 Amsterdam Avenue, New York, NY 10027

Copyright © 2008 by Ann W. Lewin-Benham

All rights reserved. No part of this publication may be reproduced or transmitted in any form or by any means, electronic or mechanical, including photocopy, or any information storage and retrieval system, without permission from the publisher.

Library of Congress Cataloging-in-Publication Data

Lewin-Benham, Ann.
    Powerful children : understanding how to teach and learn using the Reggio approach / Ann Lewin-Benham ; foreword by Howard Gardner.
        p. cm. — (Early childhood education series)
    Includes bibliographical references and index.
    ISBN 978-0-8077-4883-1 (pbk. : alk. paper)
    ISBN 978-0-8077-4884-8 (hardcover : alk. paper)
        1. Early childhood education—United States. 2. Reggio Emilia approach (Early childhood education)—United States. 3. Child development—United States. I. Title.
    LB1139.25.L49   2008
    372.21—dc22   2008010258

ISBN 978-0-8077-4883-1 (paper)
ISBN 978-0-8077-4884-8 (cloth)

Printed on acid-free paper
Manufactured in the United States of America

15 14 13 12 11 10 09 08   8 7 6 5 4 3 2 1

For my husband
Robert Samuel Benham
Insightful and caring

Core List LK 1-11-10 B+T 51.00

Contents

Foreword

APPEARANCES CAN BE DECEIVING. In the middle ages, it was widely assumed that young children were just small adults—and, accordingly, they were so portrayed in works of art. Those who had the opportunity to attend school were expected to learn—and if they did not, the fault presumably lay within themselves. In the succeeding centuries, accounts of child development and learning slowly emerged. We accordingly acknowledge those pedagogues—Pestalozzi, Froebel, Montessori—who added to our knowledge of how children develop and identified those physical materials and adult actions and attitudes that are likely to help them learn better.

The science of child development followed its own course. Once Darwin's epochal ideas about the evolution of the species had become known, psychologists and so-called "baby biographers" put forth their own notions of the stages of human development—outlining the ways in which human children resembled and differed from their primate counterparts. A huge leap forward occurred when the Swiss psychologist Jean Piaget actually observed his own children with exquisite care and carried out pointed empirical investigations of what they did, and did not, understand. Piaget presented a portrait of human cognition that placed most of the agency for development on the interactions of the solitary "epistemic" child with the world of objects. In contrast, the Russian psychologist Lev Vygotsky called attention to the many ways in which culture as a whole, and the specific supports provided by older individuals, colored the pace, the contours, and the ultimate achievements of human development.

In the last 50 years—what might be termed the post-Piaget, post-Vygotsky era—empirical investigators have provided ample evidence of the fine grain of early childhood. On the one hand, we now know that even human infants possess an impressive knowledge of the world and of the means for making sense of it. By the end of the first year of life, infants already evince knowledge of the realms of number, of human intention, of the possible and impossible behaviors of physical objects—and, nod to Piaget, they achieve this with little specific tutelage on the part of adults. Consistent with the Vygotsky tradition, it is also clear that the quality and quantity of interactions with knowledgeable adults (and older children) play a determinant role in whether young children are assimilated into their community and whether, by the time of their entry into the primary grades, they are on the road to becoming life-long learners.

Nobel-Prize-winning physicist Murray Gell-Mann once remarked that, in the 21st century, the most valued intellectual possession will be a synthesizing mind. I take it that he meant that we are all deluged by information, much of it of dubious value. The skilled synthesizer can determine what is worth attending to and what can be safely ignored. Moreover, she can put it together in ways that make sense to her—else the synthesis will soon disintegrate. And, to the extent that she seeks to communicate, the synthesizer must be able to present the ensemble of ideas so it will make sense to others and prove useful in her own endeavors—be they either theoretically or practically oriented.

Ann Lewin-Benham has a background second to none in the theory and practice of early childhood. In the late 1960s she launched one of the United States' first public-school-based Montessori programs in the four poverty areas of Arlington County (VA). For 2 decades she served as the founding director of the Capital Children's Museum, and soon became a leader in the burgeoning field of children's museums. On the site of the Children's Museum, Lewin-Benham also launched Options School for inner-city children (and adults), to help them negotiate the rigors of higher education. And, most crucially for readers of this book, Ann Lewin-Benham set up the remarkable Model Early Learning Center.

At this Center, Lewin-Benham achieved the amazing feat of synthesizing theory with practice. Drawing on her knowledge of the science of human development, she developed a framework that was fully conversant with contemporary knowledge of how children develop. At the same time, deeply immersed in the most impressive practices of early childhood education, Lewin-Benham set up a school that brought out the full potential of young children living under difficult circumstances—in her evocative phrase, making them *Powerful Children*.

In my view, as in Ann Lewin-Benham's, the most impressive prototype of early childhood education of our time can be found in the small northern Italian city, Reggio Emilia. Over a 40-year period, pioneering theorist–practitioner Loris Malaguzzi and his dedicated colleagues choreographed an approach to early childhood education that is now admired and imitated all over the world. As a pioneer childhood educator herself, Ann Lewin-Benham recognized the power of the Reggio Approach early on, and has done as much as any American to bring it to the attention of educators. The Reggio Approach is central to the Model Early Learning Center and to the picture of early human development portrayed in these pages. And indeed, those interested in learning about documentation, assessment, projects, and group learning, in the Reggio mode, will receive an excellent introduction here.

Rooted as she is in theory, Ann Lewin-Benham is a master teacher and a master observer of teaching. In these pages we can follow her own thinking and that of her colleagues, as they set up a learning center that is truly meant to be a model. And we can delight in the detailed discussion of topics that take on fresh life in the worlds of every young child: the changing seasons, the aura of birthdays, the special meaning of verbal and graphic messages received from or sent to another child, the power of the physical environment within and outside the space that is school. As we read about Coco the cat, or the saga of "the turtle, the butterfly, and the moon," we are reminded that childhood is a world of sensory images, tactile sensations, potent odors, squeals of laughter and, in Malaguzzi's memorable phrase, "one hundred languages."

Like other products of cultural invention, education cannot simply be transplanted from one society to another. And the distance from an affluent bucolic Italian region to the turbulent realities of inner-city Washington D.C. is considerable. Nor does Lewin-Benham ignore the quickly changing conditions in the United States—the increasing pressures for accountability, the push to foist the methods and goals of primary school onto preschool, the powerful and often destructive forces of markets, media, and material consumption. Ann Lewin-Benham helps us to understand how the deep structure, the essentials of the Reggio Approach, can be maintained, even as many of the specific practices must be transformed—indeed, reinvented—if they are to take root in the quite different soil of the United States today. And she does not shirk from explaining the difficulties involved in such a transplantation process—and why, in the end, even the greatest skill and the highest motivation may not suffice.

Challenges notwithstanding, *Powerful Children* is a book that is garlanded with hope and optimism. Each new child constitutes a new world, and the ages from 2 to 5 remain "the magic years." Each new child provides a chance for the rest of the human species to show what we can do, how we can make the world wondrous for that child, and, in the process, increase the likelihood that the child will one day give back—by becoming a good parent or teacher himself or herself and by contributing to making the world better. In her practice and in her writings, Ann Lewin-Benham has made such contributions—and we are all in her debt.

—Howard Gardner
Cambridge, Massachusetts, January 2008

Acknowledgments

I AM GRATEFUL TO MY BELOVED HUSBAND, Robert Benham, who supports me by giving me time to pursue my writing. I appreciate beyond words Jennifer Azzariti, the MELC's Studio teacher and an innately gifted artist, who has the rare capacity to engage children deeply with the materials, tools, and intensity of an artist; she intentionally cut the time she could have devoted to building her career and used it instead to raise her sons, Louis and William. She generously shared with me her stories, personal journals, and vast slide collection from the MELC. I will always appreciate the MELC families and children, who accomplished so much so quickly; all their names have been changed to protect their anonymity. The MELC teachers—Genet Astatke, Wendy Baldwin, Deborah Barley, and Sonya Shoptaugh—were intrepid in making efforts to change; without them there would be no book. I am ever indebted to David Perkins, Reuven Feuerstein, Howard Gardner, and Loris Malaguzzi, whose brilliance informs my thinking. Likewise, I am in awe of the Reggio educators who have shown us all how a community, led by its teachers, can support the best possible early education. I thank educators Linda Tsantis, colleague and innovator, whose inspiration and knowledge have enriched this book; Connie Condrell, Alexandra Cruickshank, and Donna Rafanello, who commented on various chapters; and technology gurus Chris Grotke and Miles Fawcett, who reminded me of how 4-year-olds made a video of their cat. My appreciation to archimania, Inc., Memphis, Tennessee, for the floor plan of the Model Early Learning Center, and with gratitude I acknowledge the MELC teachers and Amelia Gambetti for the many images used in this book and on the cover. I am extremely fortunate to have Marie Ellen Larcada as my editor—enthusiastic, sharp-minded, humorous, and unfailingly available. My thanks also to Karl Nyberg for many careful, thoughtful readings. Finally, I thank the many administrators, teachers, students, parents, and others who have been in my audiences. Your attentive listening and thoughtful questions showed me what needed to be said.

Introduction

THIS BOOK HAS THREE PURPOSES: to give a voice to the powerful innate intelligences of preschool children, to provide a multitude of examples of classroom experiences that tap those intelligences, and to connect the dots between children's intelligences and preschool practices so that policymakers, educators, and parents will see clearly how they relate. In fulfilling these purposes I draw on three experiences: First was using the Reggio Approach with preschoolers and their families, all eligible for Head Start, in Washington, D.C., at the Model Early Learning Center (MELC). Second was the birth of my only grandchild, Sheppy Lewin, whom I have cared for days at a time since his birth on February 9, 2001. This grandparenting experience enabled me in my 6th decade to experience anew the incredible spectacle of human development. Third was writing my first book, *Possible Schools: The Reggio Approach to Urban Education* (2006). It tells the story of the MELC, which I founded in the late 1980s, and chronicles how we floundered in the first 2 years trying to establish discipline in the children and excellence in our practices. When we did, with the expert coaching of Amelia Gambetti, we were accredited by the Municipal Preschools of Reggio Emilia for exemplary use of their approach. I immediately followed the book's publication by lecturing frequently. Because my audiences varied from universities to civic organizations, I addressed persons with widely varying knowledge of human development—from graduate students in psychology to persons exposed only minimally through sound bites. Also I again began observing in widely varied classrooms. Through audiences' and teachers' questions, I have taken the pulse, as it were, of a broad cross-section of beliefs about children and learning. In the intersection of these experiences, I found the purpose of this book: to satisfy parents', educators', and policymakers' desire to know what actually constitutes excellent preschool practice.

I have three reactions to the experiences. First, despite the spate of recent research on infant and early development, the general public feels no urgency to provide quality early education. Second, with some notable exceptions, preschools remain much as they have been since I began in early education in 1963. Knowledgeable educators' dialogue about teaching techniques and content has improved, but in most classrooms actions have not followed words. What *has* changed are family work patterns—far more children are cared for out of their home for long hours and by persons other than family. Third, again with notable exceptions, teachers, teacher educators, and administrators from preschools to universities do not know how to change in order to bring best practices into the classroom. Many, however, are pushing elementary school methods into preschool—a dangerous trend.

By providing numerous specific examples of innovative, effective, research-based early education, I hope to help readers become aware of what their beliefs about young children are, to realize what shaped their beliefs, and to understand what is different and possible as the first steps toward change. I also hope to inspire people to *want* to change, to show what we should require of preschool and how the experiences I portray help children learn. So, throughout this book I will describe in clear word pictures how powerful early education works. The phrase I use to describe this kind of education is *significant work*.

THE BOOK'S THEMES

The book has four themes: (1) an explanation of significant work with examples and case histories in every chapter, (2) key features of the Reggio Approach, (3) explicit information about teaching principles that can be effected through significant work, and (4) descriptions of what children learn from significant work.

Key Features of the Reggio Approach

The Reggio Approach is widely considered to represent the best early childhood practices. The Approach is based on sociocultural theory and has evolved over many decades into robust examples of how that theory looks in practice. The central idea is that relationships that are mediated by thoughtful adults are essential to learning. We learn as a result of relationships among people (teacher/children, children/children, and children/parents) and through intentional teaching that mediates how we use the environments, tools, and materials that are particular to our culture.

I consider that there are nine essential features of the Reggio Approach.

1. Belief in children as powerful people, which means that teachers see children as people with rights, not needs. Therefore, even babies are engaged in experiences that are challenging and complex far beyond the norm.
2. Work in small groups, which means that teachers usually teach three to six children at a time, not the entire class. The purpose is for "the mix of personal differences [to] afford individual members the incentive to learn and to prove themselves through contributions that are authentically important to the group" (Wilson, 1998, p. 180). Small-group work is facilitated by the fact that every class has two teachers; moreover, by sharing their different perspectives, teachers become better observers and more responsive to children.
3. An *atelier* (artist's studio) and *atelierista* (artist/studio teacher) is in every school. Loris Malaguzzi, founder of the Reggio Approach, recognized the unique contribution that an artist, as an expert in the use of wide-ranging materials, brings to children's experiences.
4. Metaphor of the Hundred Languages, which means children's increasing ability to use many varied tools and materials. Humans' expressive capacity is vast; modalities range from math to music,

sonnet to shot-put. The idea is to engage children in a great range of different forms of expression.

5. Roles of time and space are interrelated. Because the environment is detailed so thoughtfully, teachers use it as a third teacher; therefore, children's engagement with anything in the environment is as valuable as their engagement with the teacher.

6. Extensive family participation involves families in aspects of the school's life as varied as furniture construction and fundraising. In parent meetings teachers discuss details of the children's experience with parents, who respect the teachers' expertise as fully as we do the doctor's or lawyer's. Teachers consider parents their full partners in fostering children's potential, and parents respond by becoming deeply involved.

7. Documentation, consisting of large photo-journal-like panels, covers school walls and shows words and photos of children at key moments in projects. Because documentation reflects pivotal moments in experiences, it is integral to projects, and children study documentation as a spur for what they do next.

8. A new complex role for teachers means they consider themselves researchers about children's development. They listen and observe more than they talk, and find the themes for projects in children's words and actions. They hypothesize, as scientists do: "I wonder what might happen if . . . ," and collaborate with children on projects that take unpredictable directions.

9. A system to support teachers is based on the belief that teachers' continuing development is as important as the children's. Continual teacher education is supported by knowledgeable professionals, reasonable hours and pay, and the community's deep respect for teachers' expertise.

Each feature of the Reggio Approach is described separately in Chapters 1 through 9. A cautionary note: In the Reggio Approach all features are inextricably related so, if you were observing a class, all would be in play and it would be hard to see one without the others. However, in order to clearly illustrate each feature, I highlight only one in each chapter.

In Chapters 2 through 9 I present projects in the MELC, either clusters that are related or one robust project. I explain each project's origin, evolution, and outcomes; show how the classroom environment supports it; relate the project to one particular teaching principle; and describe how it exemplifies significant work and impacts or reflects children's intelligences. An emphasis in each chapter is how the projects reflect a particular feature of the Reggio Approach.

What Is Significant Work?

Work is significant when it provokes young children to draw deeply on the vast store of innate capacities that are particular to humans. A multitude of capacities are hard-wired in the brain and become evident in the first years of life (Gardner, 1983; Pinker, 1997). More than 200 have been identified cross-culturally, studied, and summarized by anthropologist Donald E. Brown; to name just a few: movement, language, theory-making, singing, rhythm, empathy, the abilities to classify and understand metaphor, symbols, and analogies, and to collaborate and to intuit others' motives (Pinker, 2002). *Significant work* draws on these and many other capacities.

Significant work will engage a child in the way psychologist Mihaly Csikszentmihalyi describes *flow:*

> a narrowing of attention on a clearly defined goal. . . [being] involved, concentrated, absorbed, . . . the depth of concentration . . . [enabling us to] . . . become lost in the activity. (1993, pp. xiii–xiv)

Story of a child-in-flow: A Montessori classroom-behind-glass was an exhibit at the 1933 Chicago World's Fair. Visitors were astounded at the children's concentration. To test it, a child seated at a table was lifted, chair and all, turned completely around, and set down, without breaking her concentration. If the right stimuli and a supportive environment are present, you will see children-in-flow. They are engaged in significant work. Here are two examples involving children with whom I have worked.

Example 1: Reading. My grandson Sheppy was read to frequently almost from birth. His family wanted him to hear the fullness of the English language, its sounds, rhythms, and vocabulary. They read *Mother Goose*, Maurice Sendak's *Nutshell Library*, T. S. Eliot's *Old Possums Book of Practical Cats*, not necessarily books you think of reading to a newborn, but books abounding in rhyme, rhythm, and a great richness of words. I cannot show causality or prove a correlation, but Sheppy was very verbal very early. His family continued to read Big books and to discuss them with him, and he expressed Big ideas. Because Sheppy's parents rarely watched TV, Sheppy did so only at others' homes—although he did watch videos carefully screened by his parents. When Sheppy was 3 years, 9 months, his dad rented the video *20,000 Leagues Under the Sea*. Twenty seconds into it, Sheppy and his dad agreed: It was too scary. Books are less graphic, so we found the book at the library. Sheppy, riveted by the dramatic cover illustration, immediately wanted to hear the book and would not be diverted. Rather than embark on 400 pages with text well beyond him, I *read* the illustrations.

When I saw Sheppy 3 months later, I gave him both the unabridged and an abridged version. Immediately he reviewed the illustrations, then sat me down to read the 200-page abridged version. We read straight through, Sheppy as engrossed by the story as he had been by the illustrations.

In Chapter 12, Captain Nemo explains the origin of his stash of gold, recounting how the Spanish Armada, laden with gold, came upon British warships. Rather than lose his horde to the enemy, the Spanish captain sank his fleet, ultimately found by Captain Nemo. I asked Sheppy if, were he the captain, he'd have sunk his fleet. Solemnly and emphatically he shook his head: "No!" I inquired what he would have done. Extending both arms forward, he raised his palms in a gesture that clearly meant, "*Stop!*" and with deliberation and great emphasis said, "I would have paused the war. I would have said to everybody, 'You have to talk.'" Reading a book with big ideas and eliciting a child's reaction is significant work.

Example 2: Visual Perception. Louis, the son of my colleague Jennifer Azzariti, is 6 months older than Sheppy. Whenever I see Louis, he has made some incredible object: a sword and scabbard, a tricornered hat, a weaving loom, a birdhouse. His constructions are complex, made from varied materials, decorated with ribbons, feathers, paper streamers, paints, markers. When Louis was an infant, Jennifer collected oversize art books, atlases, magazines, anything with high-quality, colorful, detailed images. She positioned these around the room in Louis's line of sight so from infant seat, floor, or crib he would see something stimulating. Again, it is impossible to connect Jennifer's intentionality in providing excellent images for the baby, and Louis's prowess in making well-executed, highly decorated constructions. But like Sheppy's family, Jennifer had a particular intention, structured the environment, and stimulated the baby's visual perception, another example of significant work.

Qualities of Significant Work

Significant work of any type at any age has these qualities: It is intentional, highly articulated, purposeful and absorbing, responsive to a child's interest, and transcendent, meaning it has the potential to branch to numerous other rich subjects that are directly or tangentially related. Significant work is creative, complex, and original. And it stimulates one or more innate human capacities—in Sheppy's case, language and reasoning; in Louis's, visual, kinesthetic, and planning capacities. There are many examples of significant work in this book, most from the MELC after 1992–1993, when we began to adapt the Reggio Approach. Bookmark this page so as you read each example you can reread the qualities enumerated above. Significant work stems from a teacher's choice: Intentionally she or he decides to embrace a philosophy and undertake a set of practices based on a belief in children's enormous power.

Consider the following comparisons. They contrast work that is creative, complex, and original with work that is redundant, simple, and boring.

Creative. Significant work is creative. Picture a typical preschool bulletin board with self-portraits made from construction paper, yarn, and glue. The entire class cycles in groups, each spending about 5 minutes, until all complete the activity. It must be finished that morning because the curriculum calls for a different activity the next day and each parent expects to see her child's work displayed. The faces look alike, resembling one another but not the child who made it. They show no individuality, and at a glance you know they are by preschoolers.

In contrast, consider an MELC project called Representing Different Selves done by four children working as a small group. They had many conversations with a teacher about their faces, examined them in a mirror, felt them, and discussed each one's distinctive characteristics. They worked collaboratively, each child's work sharpened by the others' attention. The teacher encouraged the group, one-by-one, to describe their features in detail while she took notes. She read the notes to the group, then they scoured the classroom to find materials with which to represent themselves accurately. They spent over an hour on each of 3 days. The finished project had each child's color photo, verbal description, a piece of Plexiglas mirror, and five representations in different media: texture, tempera paint, #2 pencil, fine-line black marker, and pastel. The representations varied greatly, and a viewer easily could see each child's distinguishing features.

Complex. Significant work is complex. Consider this typical example: a stencil of a leaf, no particular tree, just generic serrated-edge, which children are to trace, cut out, color with a yellow, orange, or green marker, and decorate with plastic wiggly eyes (standard preschool material). What seems simple is actually difficult because few preschoolers have sufficient dexterity to trace the serrated shape, much less cut it; so the teacher has traced and precut enough for everyone. What's left for the child? coloring the leaf and pasting on the eyes. Like the face activity, the leaf requires just a few minutes, with the entire class cycling through in groups, working quickly so the curriculum stays on schedule.

In contrast, consider an activity in the MELC called Fall. The teachers engaged the children in dialogue about their excited reactions to the changes taking place outside, realized that color dominated their remarks, and selected the five children whose reactions were most pronounced. Each child chose a collection of small boxes, painted them in colors they themselves mixed to resemble fall, arranged and glued the boxes side-by-side, and chose a selection of fall objects, many they had collected outside. The challenge was to select objects that fit each box, matched its color and size, and conveyed the feeling of fall through texture. Their finished project included dried leaves, pine needles, grass, tissue paper, folded and painted strips of paper, buttons, and paper shapes they themselves cut. They had to simultaneously plan ahead and stay focused on attributes—color, space, texture, the feeling of fall—and the process of gluing. The project, which took most of a week, yielded a complex piece of work.

Original. Significant work is original. Contrast the following formulaic activity with the MELC activity described below: The teacher presents a model of an owl made from three paper plates, construction paper, glue, wiggly eyes, and crayons or markers. The children are told to copy it. Again, it involves precision beyond most preschoolers' ability, in this case cutting and folding. So like the serrated-edge leaves, the teacher actually prepares most of the work, with the children merely pasting on the eyes and coloring the wings. In contrast, the MELC children made something they called Cuckoo Bird using thin copper wire, feathers, straw, folded paper strips, photos of themselves, and messages they wrote in fine-line colored markers and pens (Chapter 8). The bird was over 3' long and 2½' tall, a bird like no one had ever seen.

Creativity, complexity, and originality distinguish significant work. They typify the projects I describe throughout this book.

CHAPTER OVERVIEW

The following descriptions of the book's chapters show how the book's themes —children's innate intelligences, the Reggio Approach, teaching principles, and significant work—mesh.

In Chapter 1, I describe the structure that must be in place before beginning significant work: First, a teacher must understand what he or she believes about young children and how those beliefs were shaped. I describe four major forces that shape beliefs about children—politicians, marketers, early educators, and researchers. If teachers hold diminished views of young children's capacities or use only teach/test techniques, it will hamper the ability to do significant work. Second, the environment must be prepared by attending to detail. For example, blocks can be augmented with collections of animals or people, with tubes, rope, and paper strips, or with found objects in interesting shapes. Items in the housekeeping area should be attractive and feel real, but still be child-sized; such items don't appear in preschool catalogues and will challenge a dedicated shopper. Materials must be sufficiently varied to attract children with different interests, and a great variety of books must be on-hand to extend each experience. Throughout I provide examples of detailed classroom design. Third, the children must be self-regulated: If they do not have the internal control to respect one another and classroom rules, it will be impossible to do significant work. The feature of the Reggio Approach highlighted in this chapter is the importance of believing, in Reggio educators' words, that children are "rich, strong, and powerful." Belief about children is the teaching principle, something we know matters, but don't necessarily connect with practice.

In Chapter 2, I tell stories from the MELC as its teachers began using the Reggio Approach—children's first exploration of color and beginning work with clay, glue, and paper. Most would-be Reggio-inspired teachers see arrival points, what a practice looks like well beyond its inception. The purpose for describing early work is to show departure points, what powerful practices look like as teachers are just beginning to use them. The Reggio focus is how to facilitate work in small groups, a structure that builds relationships and is essential for significant work. The teaching principle is the relation between theory and practice.

In Chapter 3, recognizing that seasons are staples of most early childhood curricula, I describe the MELC's Seasons projects. Typical seasons activities are formulaic, stereotyped, and predictable. Here I show how to build children's interests in seasonal changes into significant work—diverse, robust, and original. I explain the role of Studio and Studio teacher, which are integral to the Reggio Approach. The teaching principle is school readiness.

In Chapter 4, I describe the relationship the MELC children developed with Coco, the school's cat. This relationship was important in their learning to control their behavior, begin to pay attention to books, and tell stories. It was also the impetus for many early projects. I show how significant work with Coco evoked the children's use of a Hundred Languages, the chapter's Reggio feature. This phrase is a metaphor for helping children acquire facility in using a great variety of tools, materials, and skills essential to significant work. The teaching principle is self-regulated behavior and social/emotional competence.

In Chapter 5, I describe how the MELC celebrated birthdays, inspired by Reggio practices. Birthday celebrations help children extend their interest over long periods, and result in a curriculum that emerges from children's interests.

The Reggio feature is the integration of time and space. The teaching principle is what constitutes intentional curricula.

In Chapter 6, I explore the MELC's Communication Center, an area that spurred a huge interest in writing and reading. I describe how the Center was designed, its functions, and the great traffic in messages it generated—from the children to one another; to their teachers; to Coco the cat; to the turtle; to their families; and to children in other schools. I describe many related activities that emerged, their significance for pre-readers, and how they stimulated family involvement, the chapter's Reggio theme. The teaching principle is emerging literacy.

In Chapter 7, I relate one long project, Coco and the Turtle. The children's deep friendship with the turtle extended over 3 years. The story demonstrates children's empathy for other living creatures. I tell the story from the perspective of how the teachers documented it, and weave examples of documentation throughout in order to trace a clear path through this complex process, which is the Reggio feature of the chapter. The teaching principle is assessment.

In Chapter 8, I describe projects called the Easter Dove, the Cuckoo Bird, and the Nest. Many teachers are confused about how to start, continue, and conclude projects; that is, they do not understand project boundaries, when to dissolve or to maintain them. I unpack these complex projects so that teachers can see the structure and apply it to their own complex projects. The aspect of the Reggio Approach that I highlight is the teacher's role. Significant work results when teachers are researchers—listening, observing, and recording; designers—harmonizing time, space, and relationships; orchestrators—selecting children and moving projects forward; collaborators—building relationships with both children and peers; documenters—enabling children to reflect; and mediators—intervening with intention, meaning, and transcendence. The teaching principle is preschool teachers' role in relation to significant work.

In Chapter 9, I describe a project in which two children made a large clay bridge. I use the story to explain systemic issues like the teacher support that undergirds significant work. Support includes shared beliefs, on-going professional development, and other characteristics of the system that sustain the Reggio Approach. The teaching principle is professional support for teachers.

In Chapter 10, I briefly address issues in early education including teacher quality, assessment, special education, program/population match, and family involvement. Then I review standards recommended by major organizations like the National Association for the Education of Young Children and KIDS COUNT. Using these standards as a template, I refer to specific examples from earlier chapters in the book to suggest how standards could more specifically reflect best practices. Finally, I address policy implications and ideas for change in teacher education.

I hope my stories of young children's significant work inspire readers, motivate teachers to adopt the beliefs and use the practices that I describe, and help parents, administrators, and policymakers better understand what constitutes excellent early education.

CHAPTER 1

Beliefs, Classroom Environments, and Discipline

Nothing is so firmly believed as what we least know.
—Michel de Montaigne (ca. 1580)

S NAPSHOTS FROM THE Model Early Learning Center's (MELC) first 2 years showed: Six children scooping and pouring at the water table, and another six with a teacher making gelatin to explore red, the color-of-the-week. Red dominated a wall display—pictures of beach ball, wagon, rug, jacket, lollypop, and the word *red* in large letters. There were ditto sheets with outlines to color red. Four children were playing with blocks, three with trains; five were using sorting materials, five others were listening to the book *Curious George*, another to a book-on-tape. One was using a Montessori map, one was examining a basket of shells. Four were at loose ends, joining the block players, but quickly drifting away, taking something from a shelf, but promptly returning it. Three were bordering on disruptive. One staff member was directing the gelatin activity, another was reading the story, yet another was clearing breakfast remainders, and the fourth was half-heartedly watching the block builders. None seemed aware of the others' activity nor did they consult one another by eye contact or discussion. No one tried to engage the children at loose ends. These snapshots, typical of preschool, neither matched what we said we believed nor reflected the lofty mission statement in our foyer.

Superficially the snapshots look okay: a relatively calm, orderly environment, varied materials with cognitive content, choice by children, most putting their work away on their own, and no overtly disruptive behavior. *But*, except for the color-of-the-week, a banal activity, nothing extended from a prior to a future day. No activity, except perhaps the book, responded to something that deeply interested the children. Groups were together at random, not chosen intentionally by teachers. Contrast these with snapshots from Reggio schools, or the MELC once we adapted Reggio practices: An environment with incredibly beautiful work by children evidenced skills required for school readiness; challenging activities evidenced self-regulated children; passionate engagement evidenced an intentional curriculum; and significant work evidenced highly qualified teachers. You would see extensive reference to parent involvement, evidencing a home/school bond. You might guess the children were gifted (they were not), and could infer that the teachers believed in preschoolers' competence.

How we interpret the two sets of snapshots reflects our beliefs about young children. Belief is so firmly entrenched in behavior, the two are virtually indistinguishable. Cultural factors influence beliefs, in particular four powerful forces: politicians, marketers, early educators, and researchers. Here I explain their influence, then discuss two preconditions for significant work: how to attend to details in designing a preschool classroom, and how to help children become self-regulated. Well-detailed environments, self-regulated children, and, above all, teachers' understanding, articulating, and practicing what they believe, result in excellence.

BELIEFS THAT SHAPE PRACTICES

The views of others shape our beliefs about children's nature and our behavior as educators. In her Foreword to the book *I Compagni* Carolyn Edwards characterizes U.S. preschool education as "underfunded, fragmented, and squeezed in a political vise" (Corsaro & Molinari, 2005, p. xii). A first step to change this is for us—early educators, parents, caregivers, and policymakers—to understand what shapes our beliefs.

Politicians' Pronouncements

From the introduction of testing in the 1800s to No Child Left Behind, politicians have used school reform as a platform to garner attention. I recap some history here.

The First Tests. Horace Mann, politician and advocate of universal education, first introduced testing in Massachusetts public schools in the mid-1800s. He believed public schools had to be "controlled . . . and held . . . accountable to the public." Ever since "politicians have condemned public school as sitting on the precipice of failure," saying that "we need to measure, compare, sort, analyze, and categorize schools and schoolchildren in order to fix them" (Sacks, 1999, pp. 69–70). In Mann's era school headmasters were powerful public officials competing with other politicians for public acclaim. This made politicians strive "to put the headmasters in the worst possible light" (p. 71). School heads no longer have such clout, but politicians still call for testing "not just to discover how well schools or kids are doing, but rather to obtain external . . . validation of the hypothesis that they are not doing well at all" (p. 71). Politicians tear down schools so they can rebuild them, believing it will build their own image.

The American ideal of free and equal public education for everyone contradicts the reality of testing, which from its beginning has "segregated people in unequal schools or tracks" (Sacks, 1999, p. 71). Testing in the mid-1800s was used to sort huge waves of immigrants, and test design was influenced by eugenics, a then-popular belief that superficial traits—skin color, head shape, hair texture—equated with intelligence. Today most people find such beliefs "ill-considered results of unprecedented social and economic conflict that came with the expansion of industrial capitalism" (p. 32). Mann's initial test, "just thirty questions to cover an entire year's curriculum" (p. 71), hardly indicated anything. But politically motivated testing remains firmly entrenched.

IQ Testing Begins. In the early 1900s America imported Frenchman Alfred Binet's new, seemingly scientific IQ test. It merged with the idea of Stanford psychologist Lewis Terman that testing was a magic bullet to measure intelligence and became the Stanford-Binet. "Policymakers and the public [became convinced] that . . . [it] was a final, indisputable measuring stick of human performance" (Sacks, 1999, p. 27). It continues so today despite critics who, then and now, have proved that it lacks "the most fundamental element of science: a plausible explanation of cause and effect that might account for the observed data" (p. 21).

As a culture that loves quick fixes, we have accepted politicians' notion that it is efficient, once and forever more, to quantify someone's intelligence through testing. Never mind that tests are culturally biased, questions cover unrelated and largely meaningless subject matter, and no scientific basis links results to anything we now understand as intelligence. The politically introduced idea of testing has a stranglehold on American education, partly because it has evolved into a global industry that garners $40 billion annually (Ohri, 2007).

In Lyndon Johnson's Great Society, Title I school funding introduced the idea of a national norm and, in a twist that is still reverberating, started a national craze for accountability. The issue, in my opinion, is not *whether* we should account for children's progress, but *how*. Practices like teacher notes on validated rating scales, documentation as practiced in Reggio schools, folios of work across time that show a child's changes from September to June, and something like Jennifer's Magic List (Chapter 7) should suffice in early education. The public certainly has the right to expect positive outcomes from education. But testing won't bring best practices into effect and in fact seems to promote worst practices for young children. The subject is complex and worthy of its own book.

Age of Accountability. Accountability roiled education in George W. Bush's No Child Left Behind (NCLB), which I consider the most misguided education legislation ever passed. NCLB required testing for preschool and kindergarten, along with academic expectations and teaching via predetermined scripts. The result was that the worst practices from elementary grades—rote teaching to mainly silent and still children—were pushed into preschool. Such practices are particularly injurious to young children, whose brain development is still closely tied to movement, as neurophysiologist Frank Wilson (1998) describes for babies.

> It is in the child's earliest experiences in practical physics—watching, locating with both hand and eye, then intercepting moving objects—that the nervous system builds its own unique library of solutions to the computational problems presented by coordinated movement. (p. 103)

Manipulating objects helps preschoolers' comprehension. For example, notice how rote counting, "onetwothreefourfive," changes to true one-to-one correspondence *if* 3- and 4-year-olds can move objects as they count them. "In the transition [in the preschool years] from nonverbal to conventional calculation," research shows that objects and their inherent manipulability "play a key role" (Mix, Huttenlocher, & Levine, 2002, p. 110).

In a wicked fate for school children, but one with strong historical precedent, NCLB was tied to such massive federal funding for public schools that few systems were willing to flout the regulations, even when they drove good teachers away and ruined instruction by causing teachers to teach to the test and thus sacrifice understanding for right answers. As Sacks (1999) points out, we had good tests long before NCLB added several more layers.

> The lesson from history is that political motivations and the exercise of political power by those in positions of authority, rather than sound educational reasons, have driven the nation's use of standardized tests in schools. Indeed, whatever the perceived problems with the nation's schools, the answer has been almost always the same: more testing. (p. 70)

Cautions. School boards, administrators, unions—anyone who goes along with the teach/test paradigm—must understand that it is politically driven. In fact, after NCLB's first 6 years and expenditures of $6 billion, its own evaluations showed that the goal of its academic cornerstone, "Reading First"—to make every child literate by third grade—was not being met. In a lecture to a general audience, A. Grehan (2006) reported that, according to test results, NCLB instructional techniques made no significant difference in second and third graders' vocabulary or reading comprehension. Educators who know the history and understand the political bias in policies will be better equipped to argue effectively against politically motivated practices that they know violate children's best interests. Moreover, they will be alert to choosing practices not simply because they meet regulations, but because they further children's competence. The significance is that politically motivated acts impact teaching practices. Educators and parents who don't believe that tests adequately reflect children's competence need to read the history and join together to protest.

Marketers' Messages

Just as politically driven testing impacts teachers and schools, market-driven TV impacts children and parents. TV marketing so violates children that Kunkel, Wilcox, Cantor, Palmer, Linn, & Dowrick (2004), in a report by a task force of the American Psychological Association (APA), called the APA's position "unprecedented" (p. 22). The authors refer to APA's recommendation to restrict "all advertising primarily directed to audiences of children before the age of 7–8 years." APA recommended this after a comprehensive review of 173 studies of the effects of TV advertising on young children.

TV Advertising and Children. The facts are not unfamiliar, but, collected in a single document couched not in journalists' flamboyant headlines but scientists' careful language, they are shocking.

> Advertisers spend more than $12 billion per year to target the youth market. . . . Children age 14-years-old and under make $24 billion in direct purchases and influence $190 billion in family purchases. . . . [B]rand loyalty built at an early age may reap economic rewards over a child's lifetime. (Kunkel et al., 2004, p. 2)

The APA report documents several dangers. First, there are so many viewers of just-for-children channels that advertising on them is profitable. Thus, the amount and type of advertising directed at children is unprecedented and has influenced purchases significantly (Kunkel et al., 2004, p. 2). Second, there are unprecedented numbers and kinds of links between program and commercial content: On child-oriented Web sites ". . . boundaries between commercial and noncommercial content are blurred if not absent entirely" (p. 3). Third, in 1999, 26% of 2- to 4-year-olds and 39% of 5- to 7-year-olds had TVs in their bedrooms, thereby having access with no parental knowledge or presence. Finally, advertisers are present in classrooms through "posters, billboards, corporate-sponsored educational materials, ads and product placement in textbooks, and even traditional television commercials" (pp. 3–4). Consequently, "the average child is exposed to more than 40,000 TV commercials a year" (p. 4)—over 100 daily—most for toys, cereal, candy, or fast-food restaurants. Need we wonder why our children are obese?

Marketers make the ads "entertainment and enjoyable for their own sake" (Kunkel et al., 2004, p. 4). They associate products with "fun and happiness, rather than . . . provid[ing] any factual product-related information"(p. 5). Ads don't use words young children understand, but say things like, "some assembly required," or "part of a balanced breakfast"(p. 5)—creative terms to mislead children and obscure content unhelpful to sponsors.

Impact on Preschoolers. Preschool children lack two essential skills to defend themselves against such marketing: the ability to perceive the difference between commercial and noncommercial material, and skepticism. Research shows that under age 6 they do not understand manipulation of such mental events as beliefs, desires, and motives, and thus are unable to recognize ads' persuasive intentions. Under age 5 children miss the breaks between program and commercial, and often interpret ads as just a scene in the program. Whenever a commercial came on, Sheppy, who at age 6½ had rarely seen TV, asked why the channels kept changing. Even if they understand the purpose of ads as manipulative, they cannot yet recognize that this requires them to be skeptical. Skepticism develops not by TV watching, but as children age and cognitive skills grow.

Ads generate detrimental attitudes about life skills like understanding nutrition; having quality relationships with others, especially parents; and being wary of materialism. While the tobacco and alcohol industries claim not to advertise or promote their products to children or adolescents, evidence indicates otherwise.

> In June 1996, the liquor industry dropped its voluntary ban on radio and television advertising, and recent concerns have been raised about the . . . sweeter alcoholic drinks . . . that have effectively targeted the underage market. . . . The consensus . . . is that advertising and marketing contribute to youth smoking and alcohol consumption. (Kunkel et al., 2004, p. 11)

Ten percent of typical fourth graders have had more than a sip of alcohol (Donovan, 2007).

Finally, research confirms that

> Media violence promotes aggressive behaviors, attitudes more accepting of violence, increased hostility, and other antisocial outcomes . . . [as well as] fears, anxieties, and sleep disturbances. . . . The majority of violent media offerings with mature ratings . . . had marketing plans that explicitly targeted children who . . . were too young to see, hear, or play them. Consequently, such advertising typically appeared in venues frequented by underage children . . . such as Saturday morning cartoon shows. (Kunkel et al., 2004, pp. 11–12)

Aborted Legislation. The APA questions the fairness of targeting young children who are cognitively defenseless and therefore "uniquely vulnerable" (Kunkel et al., 2004, p. 14) to the effects of advertising. Acknowledging children's vulnerability, in 1977 the FTC asked Congress to intervene. But Congress sided with marketers and halted all funding for the FTC, forcing it to shut down. It resumed operations "only after Congress passed legislation rescinding . . . the agency's powers [to] regulate 'unfair' advertising" (p. 16). The FTC stuck to its position, but was powerless to take action.

Cautions. Teachers who understand marketers' influences can choose what images, books, and other TV-influenced products to ban from the classroom. They can better interpret children's ad-induced behavior, can explain the problems to parents, and can ask them to consider removing TVs from preschoolers' bedrooms, limiting the amount of TV, watching *with* preschoolers, and talking with children about what marketing is. They can offer lists of worthwhile videos—and indeed there are some—and encourage parents to substitute them for commercial TV. Unfortunately, so-called *educational* TV is influenced by market forces only slightly less than noneducational TV. Parents who understand how marketers manipulate their children may better resist children's nagging for needless or harmful purchases and pestering for TV time. The significance for teachers is to understand how TV influences cognition.

While TV may expand children's awareness of content (sometimes into violent, sexual, or other child-hurtful areas), if children watch TV with no adult mediation, they will not learn about the implications of the content. Worse, they will not learn to focus attention or selectively identify relevant versus irrelevant stimuli. TV cannot teach children to contemplate, personalize, and elaborate, cognitive processes that are essential to turn experience into learned behaviors, but *can* give children unsavory content to imitate (Feuerstein & Feuerstein, 2004). At those times when parents have no alternative but to allow the TV to babysit, providing a video from a well-chosen collection is an alternative to commercial TV.

Early Education Principles and Standards

The beliefs that pervade early education are evident from the principles and accreditation standards of the National Association for the Education of Young Children's (NAEYC). I address principles and standards below and conclude with implications and some cautions.

Principles of Developmentally Appropriate Practices. The pervasive belief among early childhood professionals is to use developmentally appropriate practices (DAP); DAP principles influence most early childhood practices. I briefly recap them here:

- appreciating childhood as a unique, valuable stage of life;
- basing work with children on knowledge of child development;
- appreciating and supporting close ties between child and family;
- recognizing that children are best understood in the context of family, culture, and society;
- respecting the dignity, worth, and uniqueness of each individual;
- helping children and adults achieve their full potential in the context of relationships that are based on trust, respect, and positive regard. (National Association for the Education of Young Children [NAEYC], 1996, p. 3)

NAEYC does not promote any particular practice. Rather it states general goals, such as all programs should help children become adults who:

- communicate well, respect others, and engage with them as members of a team;
- analyze situations, make reasoned judgments, and solve new problems;
- access information through various modes, including spoken and written language, and intelligently employ complex tools and technologies;
- continue to learn new approaches, skills, and knowledge;
- develop positive dispositions and attitudes;
- understand that effort is necessary for achievement;
- develop a positive self-identity and a tolerance for others with different perspectives and experiences (NAEYC, 1996).

NAEYC advocates that programs establish their goals in collaboration with families, and that teachers be knowledgeable about human development, learning, children's capacities and interests, and social and cultural contexts.

Five decades of research on child development underlie DAP core beliefs:

- the closely related nature of physical, social, emotional, and cognitive development;
- the orderly sequence of development;
- different children's developing at different rates;
- early experiences' affecting development;
- both nature's and nurture's importance in development.

NAEYC advocates that child care centers and programs create a caring community of learners, enhance development and learning, construct appropriate curriculum, use assessment, and involve families in reciprocal relationships. It advocates for staff preparation, adequate staff–child ratios, and the monitoring of program quality (NAEYC, 1996).

When formulated in 1987, the DAP did not advocate for sufficiently challenging practices or accommodate a diversity of cultures. Moreover, its statements were vague and self-referential. In 1997, responsive to the criticism and influenced by recent exposure to the Reggio Approach, NAEYC revised the DAP to suggest that teachers demand more of children (but not the wrong things), and not narrow the curriculum to easily measurable basic skills that diminish intellectual challenge and underestimate children's competence. The revised statements suggest using a validated curriculum, but do not endorse any particular one, such as Montessori, High/Scope, the Reggio Approach, or others (NAEYC, 1996).

NAEYC's Influence. With more than 100,000 members, NAEYC is *the* major voice in early education. It publishes hard-copy and on-line journals and each of its annual conferences are attended by thousands, where topics reflect wide-ranging approaches to early education and address myriad issues, from diversity to discipline, finance to food. NAEYC plays a major role in certifying caregivers through the Council for Professional Recognition founded in 1985. In 2006 NAEYC's new accreditation system for centers became fully operational (NAEYC, n.d.a). The process requires self-assessments validated by on-site visits. To qualify for NAEYC accreditation, centers must have a professional development plan for teachers, with additional training within 5 years (NAEYC, n.d.b).

Accreditation Standards. NAEYC's effort to set standards is noble; standards cover centers of all types and sizes, serving children from infancy through kindergarten. Ten standards are enumerated in about 672 criteria, including job descriptions, qualifications, and performance measures, as well as extensive criteria for health/safety. NAEYC says meeting its standards "represents the mark of quality in early childhood education" (NAEYC, 2008i). Here I discuss the tenor of the standards.

Lest anyone question whether the criteria are too specific, consider health/safety (NAEYC, 2008m, 5.A.; 2008g, 5.C.; 2008c, 9.C.06). I have visited well-regarded centers where the infants stayed in a windowless basement with filthy ductwork and pipes, visitors walked with outside shoes on carpeting where babies crawled, and edges of tape securing diaper-changing pads were black with grime. I live in a city where infants and toddlers are forgotten in day care vans and die from heat exposure. That said, to meet the health/safety criteria, I would have to hire someone whose sole job is monitoring compliance with criteria, not caring for children. Further, the emphasis on protecting children from environmental hazards (NAEYC, 2008f, 9.D.), while well-intentioned, may be beyond anyone's ability. Recall the lawyer who, on behalf of families whose children died from polluted water, prosecuted brilliantly and tirelessly but after 8 years still failed to convict two major corporations (Harr, 1995). I question the reasonableness of expecting schools to attack such issues. *Communities* must protect children from environmental hazards and shield schools from the burden of being environmental police.

I do not think that the MELC could have achieved accreditation. The amount of self-examination required to analyze our work in terms of hundreds of criteria would have derailed our effort to adapt the Reggio Approach. The deep problems are not that we disagreed with specific criteria—like labeling all the materials (NAEYC, 2008d, 2.E.03) or encouraging each kindergartner to write independently each day (2008d, 2.E.11)—or that we would have incurred heavy expenses to meet criteria for having "technology-based information management systems" (2008h, 10.B.03), "an ongoing monitoring system to ensure that all program goals and requirements are met . . . [, and] a data system . . . to collect evidence [of same]" (2008l, 10.F.05). Rather, the problems lie with the overall tenor: The criteria convey a top-down approach; most are derived from beliefs based on constructivist theory; and the process may engulf the practice. I shall explain.

Top-Down Approach: The standards emphasize accountability and are biased toward authority that is vested in curricula, program staff, and assessments. For example: "The *curriculum* guides teachers' development and intentional implementation of learning opportunities" (NAEYC, 2008e, 2.A.03, emphasis added). At the MELC, *events* guided the curriculum as it evolved from this intersection: teachers' attentive listening to children to discern their interests, and children's sustained interest (thoughtfully supported by teachers) in pursuing their own varied interests. Or, "*Program staff* inform families about community events sponsored by local organizations" (2008a, 8.B.03, emphasis added). At the MELC, information about community events came from both what parents brought to our attention and what we brought to theirs. And bring things they did, once they learned that we listened to their interests as attentively as we listened to their children's. Reciprocal processes are not reflected in the criteria. The criteria emphasize practices tied to assessment: "Teaching teams meet at least weekly to interpret and use assessment results to align curriculum and teaching practices to the interests and needs of the children" (2008b, 4.D.02). At the MELC, authority was vested in a complex system of relationships, and we used minute-by-minute observation to constantly align our responses to children's actions.

Constructivist Perspective: The constructivist perspective assumes that development occurs in naturally evolving stages. We followed a sociocultural perspective, which assumes that growth occurs from adults' intentional intervention in and mediation of children's experiences in small-group activities. Not one of the 60 criteria in Standard 1, Relationships, makes reference to the small-group structure that characterizes socioculturally oriented practice (NAEYC, 2008n), nor do the criteria in any other standards (2008j). Yet small-group structure is vital to foster children's development and is the essence of practices based on sociocultural theory.

Engulfing Process: A criterion states: "All components of program operation are guided by written policies and are carried out through articulated plans, systems, and procedures" (NAEYC, 2008h, 10.B.02). Accreditation relies on achieving mastery of 80% of the 672 criteria codified in NAEYC's policies and procedures. The danger is that joy, spontaneity, innovation, novelty, and complexity are sacrificed because they are difficult, if not impossible, to codify. If policy statements and procedures manuals (2008h, 10.B.) do not call for *it*—however inspiring and educational *it* may be—teachers will not attempt *it*, directors will not approve *it*, boards will not sanction *it*, and the community will not accept *it*. Consider: Aesthetics is not mentioned once in any criterion, even Standard 9, Physical Environment (2008k). The standards might make children safer, the environment cleaner, the curriculum more fully articulated, but they are unlikely to nurture the human spirit.

The NAEYC is well-intentioned and has demonstrated its interest in being responsive to early childhood practitioners. Time will surely refine the accreditation process. In the meantime, I empathize with center directors—some who spoke to me in confidence, others who spoke out at lectures—who find the process cumbersome, more punitive than supportive, and, in the words of one, like "a plane being built as it's flying."

Implications. NAEYC must offer something for everyone, because caregivers range from untrained moms who may be school dropouts providing in-home care to center directors with Ph.D.s (NAEYC, n.d.c). Principles and standards establish a baseline, but without examples it is difficult to grasp what is advocated. Neither the DAP nor the standards lend themselves to designing or outfitting classrooms, defining specifics of practice, or succinctly stating your beliefs about young children. Yet the DAP and the standards are necessary because low-quality care is a national problem. Only a third of teachers in child care centers have a college degree (NAEYC, n.d.c). "Cosmetologists must attend as much as 2000 hours of training before getting a license, but thirty states allow teachers in child care centers to work with children without any training in early childhood development" (Children's Defense Fund, 2002, p. 55). The public does not seem to care: Proprietors of Memphis day care centers were under state investigation for improper use of funds; their problems appeared in headlines daily for 2 years. But neither letters, editorials, op ed pieces, nor news commented on the quality of care—in a city where, between 1997 and 2003, eight children died by being left in day care vans (Malkin, 2003). Were the DAP and standards universally in place, children would not die in vans and newspaper coverage that misses the point would not be so worrisome.

Cautions. NAEYC critics need to understand that NAEYC's effort to set standards is laudable. But being everything-to-everyone had caused best practices to become invisible. If NAEYC could operate high-quality model centers to exemplify best practices, it might show policymakers and caregivers what constitutes excellence. If it could advocate to raise caregivers' salaries commensurate with other professions, that would improve teacher quality significantly.

The theory on which DAP rests is the constructivist theory: that naturally occurring stages, not teacher interaction, drive development. NAEYC leadership may have moved beyond this; the revised principles and new standards give a nod to the sociocultural perspective. But practitioners, for the most part, continue to follow constructivist principles. Constructivist and sociocultural theory differ on the role of the teacher. Piaget stressed natural development as the factor accounting for "general structural change in children's thinking, and Vygotsky stressed the social side highlighting the transforming impact of dialogues with expert partners on children's naturally formed concepts" (Berk & Winsler, 1995, p. 109). Piaget's theory virtually eliminates teacher intervention, which Vygotsky's theory considers essential in children's learning. Teachers need to understand the impact of these distinctions on their teaching.

Researchers' Multitude of Studies

The Piagetian/Vygotskian dichotomy is one example of how research on human development confounds commonly held beliefs about young children. In the late 20th century research burgeoned, driven partly by new technologies that made brain functions visible and partly by the critical mass of researchers working in new areas like neuroscience, psycholinguistics, cognitive psychology, genome research, systems theory, and evolutionary biology. Globalization and technology made boundaries around the world permeable to sociologists and anthropologists, prompting vast increases in studies of diverse cultures, present and extinct.

Theories of Development. A framework that I use to think about human development is David Perkins's (1986) description of three kinds of intelligence: (1) innate systems in the brain which most consider impervious to change; (2) knowledge that accretes gradually, is difficult to affect directly because it is vast and domain specific (geology, English lit, economics), and accumulates throughout life; and (3) metacognition—thinking about one's thinking. This latter *is* accessible and is where, Perkins believes, educators can make a difference.

Perkins's framework positions individual psychologists' works as well as branches of psychology vis-à-vis one another. For example, Howard Gardner's Multiple Intelligence theory (1983) and Steven Pinker's work on linguistics and the nature/nurture question (1994) represent aspects of intelligence that are innate: We are born with capacities that are manifestations of powerful, complex systems in the brain and are seen universally in all humans. In contrast, behaviorist theory attributes learning to responses produced by external stimuli, and doesn't account for what goes on in the brain. It provides the rationale for the teach/test paradigm, which, simply put, says: I do *this* to you and you do *that* in response. In schools this begets drill, memorization, and regurgitating facts. Although behaviorist theory has been discredited as an explanation for how we think, it is entrenched in a constellation of school practices. Despite continuing controversy—at times bitter—over its value, its legacy persists.

In stark contrast, developmental and cognitive psychology have yielded basic research on discrete, specific aspects of how we think and learn. These branches of psychology, along with sciences like neurophysiology and cybernetics, provide ever-increasing information on thinking, learning, and related aspects of human development. Names stand out like Jean Piaget, the first to work with children, not animals, and Lev Vygotsky (Chapter 2), who anticipated the cutting edge of today's sociocultural theory. Research in the new mind sciences crosses many disciplines. Many brilliant scientists are pushing the frontiers of our understanding of human cognition as they study highly localized functions in specific parts of the brain, or interpret behavior in terms of new understandings of brain function. For example, psychologist Reuven Feuerstein's theories and vast practical applications have pushed the frontier for noninvasive ways to improve brain functioning.

The Relationship of Researchers to Educators. It is hard for laypersons to follow developments, much less distinguish significant from unscientific research. This problem is complicated by the gap between theory and practice, the disjunction between lab and classroom, and the difficulty of assembling a cohesive picture of what the research means. Moreover, scientists, educators, and the general public all use different languages.

I believe theory and practice rarely unite because a particular kind of genius is necessary to integrate them. Early education is fortunate to have had four—Pestalozzi, Froebel, Montessori, and Malaguzzi. All developed robust philosophies and substantial practices. Pestalozzi was a model of a reflective, caring, progressive teacher. Froebel advocated the importance of play and developed many toys we take for granted, such as blocks, sewing cards, nested cubes, and mosaic tiles. Maria Montessori developed what she called *materialized abstractions*, blocks and such that enable children literally to handle abstract concepts like size, shape, and color. Her materials cover wide-ranging areas—geography, geometry, biology, coding speech (writing), decoding print (reading), arithmetic functions. Beyond developing materials, Montessori individualized instruction, prepared well-organized classrooms, and showed how to help children regulate their behavior.

Like Montessori, Loris Malaguzzi, progenitor of the Reggio Approach, acknowledged every child's unlimited potential, the necessity for a beautiful environment, and the importance of listening intently to young children's thoughts. His innovation was the ability to create schools—laboratories actually—to test ideas about human development. He and his followers used their own astute observations of children's immense capacities to evolve a social framework as the basis for learning. Those who engage Malaguzzi's ideas find echoes from leading epistemologists, philosophers, psychologists, educators, designers, scientists, and all the arts. Having an artist in every school is one of his several major innovations. Reggio schools' progressive classroom practices, extraordinary parent involvement, and commitment to documentation as the way to show "children's learning paths and processes" (Rinaldi, 2006, p. 68) are hallmarks of the Reggio educators' many innovations. The numerous Reggio schools have endured for nearly 50 years, further testimony to their founder's genius.

Cautions. Research is significant because it highlights weaknesses in current understanding and possible new directions to overcome the weaknesses. But research may use language and techniques, like statistics, that are unfamiliar to many. The research is voluminous and some is focused narrowly on aspects of development that are localized to particular brain functions or behavior. This research is hard to generalize or interpret in practice. Moreover, different research may report contradictory results. Thus, research may be more confusing than helpful to practitioners.

Summary: A Welter of Ideas

The phrase "blooming, buzzing confusion," which William James mistakenly thought represented infants' minds, better represents the mass of information on early education. Is an idea a fad or does it reflect solid philosophy? What are the belief peddler's qualifications? Like connoisseurs seeking choice morsels, we must selectively choose what influences us. Hard? Very! Can it be done? Yes! Teachers can make informed choices to bring performance into accord with scientifically valid views of how children think and learn. My personal bias is for the Reggio educators' succinctly stated belief that children are, from birth, "rich, strong, and powerful." Early educators also must honestly assess their classroom design and whether their children are self-regulated, topics that conclude this chapter.

DESIGNING AN ENVIRONMENT

In early education the environment *is* the curriculum. Reggio teachers "structure the environment to reflect their belief that the 'environment is a third teacher'" (Lewin-Benham, 2006, p. 14). Whether children fly around the classroom as superheroes, imitate aliens, or create vehicles with Lego® and small motors depends on available stimuli, teachers' mediation, and relationship with their classmates.

Part of a Reggio teacher's role is designing the environment, which means selecting stimuli, providing mediation—directly or indirectly—and orchestrating relationships. Designing preschool environments requires experience most teachers do not have. Thus, the environment in many early childhood classrooms is not likely to provoke significant work. As I portray significant work throughout this book, I will describe how a well-designed environment contributes. In the following examples consider one basic principle: *Design is detail.* The individual examples seem trivial, but in the full tapestry of a classroom, each detail matters—greatly!

Example 1: Enticing Parents

We had difficulty involving parents in the MELC. The first breakthrough came when we requested photos from home, recorded children's stories about how the photos reflected their family, and had them draw what the photo meant. With the first photo, story, and drawing, we began a panel. That is, we laid out the material, with no extraneous decoration, on a large illustration board that we hung on the wall. Just seeing one family's story immediately motivated others to send their photos. Laying out and hanging a panel is designing—choosing a discrete subject, eliminating distracting material, selecting typefaces, titles, brief descriptions, and photos to tell a story. Studying the panels stimulates children to think about their thinking (metacognition), and well-designed panels evidence high-quality teaching. Panels also engage families in emerging literacy activities: Children love seeing themselves in the stories on the panels, and the stories become a vehicle for the children to tell stories by *reading* the panels to family members.

Example 2: Expanding Materials

We needed to greatly increase the materials, but realized that items in cardboard boxes or the storeroom would be out-of-sight and therefore unused. How could we store materials visibly, attractively, and accessibly? The solution was adding shelf units to the Studio, writing letters with the children to their families requesting materials and glass jars (to use as storage containers), and involving children themselves in sorting and storing the materials. As we sorted materials with different small groups, we discussed how each might be used, eliciting and playing the children's ideas off one another. As we stored the full jars with the children, they learned where they could find the materials. Storing materials is designing—redefining the space to make storage visible and accessible, and identifying suitable containers. Involving children themselves in procuring builds literacy. Sorting and storing build numeracy. Understanding where to store materials builds children's ability to use the environment purposefully, which is necessary for self-regulation. Additionally, the process drew families into school activity. Good design that realizes disparate goals is another mark of highly qualified teachers.

Example 3: Encouraging Movement

Children need to expend physical energy. Yet, playground time is not always possible: It might interrupt significant work; the day might be rainy; most children might be working when only some need vigorous activity. We felt it was unreasonable to make many accommodate few. The solution was to build indoor apparatus for climbing, crawling, and jumping that would be available any time and safe with minimum supervision. It gave rambunctious children sanction to be physical whenever *they* needed. Creating or choosing apparatus is designing. Highly qualified teachers base their designs on observation of children's development, in this case, acknowledging that preschoolers' need for strenuous physical exertion doesn't follow schedules.

Design choices are endless and run the gamut from selecting wall color to picking particular pencils. These examples suggest merely three of myriad ways in which teachers who are designers can modify environments to children's benefit.

HELPING CHILDREN BECOME SELF-REGULATED

As the MELC began, we experienced discipline problems that threatened to sink the school. Four children exhibited extreme behavior problems, which meant that chaos, not calm, reigned. Three successive directors failed to get a handle on the problem. Finally, Connie Condrell, an experienced Montessori teacher finishing a Ph.D. in clinical child psychology, tackled the problem. Using Montessori techniques combined with psychological know-how, she taught us how to help children become self-regulated.

Connie took firm command, established procedures, taught the staff techniques, imposed rules for everyone, and defined roles. She gave the staff daily notes on the prior day's results—what worked, what didn't. Behavior fell into place in 6 weeks. As master teacher she knew strong class management techniques and spoke with authority no teacher possessed. As long-time school director she could assess the potential in teachers, assistants, and aides. As clinical psychologist she knew discipline techniques unfamiliar to teachers. During Connie's first weeks it was typical to see her firmly holding two children at once: a 3-year-old on her lap and an older child by his waist, drawn tightly to her to restrict his hitting, kicking, or punching. She was calm, loving, tough, and firm. The children knew she meant business and they settled down. The teachers emulated her behavior and adopted her techniques.

Simultaneously, Connie worked with us to redefine roles. Following a strict Montessori regimen, teachers were to teach, and assistants, title changed to classroom manager, to maintain discipline, ever-vigilant for disruptive or unsettled children. The manager redirected them until they became engaged: Would you like to use the pegs or the blocks? If children couldn't choose, the manager chose for them, firmly: Let's use the pegs. If they failed to settle, the manager removed them from the room. The aide prepared meals, helped children to the bathroom, and the like.

Four Simple Rules

Connie instituted four rules all preschool teachers know: Use your quiet voice. Use your walking feet. Keep your hands to yourself. Put your things away. How these rules are implemented determines the tenor, discipline, and order of a class. If you ask children to use *their* quiet voices, you must use *yours*; you cannot shout across the room: "Alex! I hear you!" but must walk purposefully, *while he is yelling*, and softly but firmly command him to speak softly. Likewise, you cannot race across the room, but must move no faster than you want the children to move. Managing the tone was the classroom manager's job. While the teacher gave small-group lessons, the manager made sure other children followed the rules. The policy implication is the necessity for two adults in early childhood classes.

Connie implemented rules rigorously, modeled behaviors with utmost consistency, and insisted staff do so. That was the key to self-regulation. It is hard to imagine a group of preschoolers more undisciplined than the MELC's. The four out-of-control children set a high-pitched, frenetic tone that the others copied. Audiences laugh when I explain that the four rules provided the solution! In the abstract we all know that children internalize adults' behaviors. Practicing this is not so easy.

Emphatic Management

The classroom manager job description used strong words like "must," "enforce," "never" and many imperatives: "Do," "Use," "Go," "Take the child . . ."—specific guidelines in emphatic language. Teachers rarely are trained to be emphatic, give directives, or use imperatives. All took a positive form—*Do*, not *don't do*—so children had clear pictures of what we expected, without negatives or criticism. These words and the above techniques settled the MELC. To begin significant work, teachers must honestly assess their class. Do children use loud voices? run? leave materials out? hit? If so, they must learn to regulate these behaviors *themselves*, to develop the *internal* control to monitor their own behavior. They learn this from teachers' behavior and consistent use of words, which children copy in private speech, telling themselves what to do so they gradually become able to self-regulate (Berk & Winsler, 1995). Children who are not self-regulated cannot do complex projects. From then on if behavior began to deteriorate, we reinstituted the roles of teacher, classroom manager, and aide, and the children quickly settled down.

Vast research exists on unfocused, impulsive, and disruptive behavior that is typical of preschoolers, and on distinctions between normal and severe or frequent disruptiveness. Research shows that change

> often must begin with fairly directive efforts to reduce . . . inappropriate behavior. Giving specific instructions and requests, keeping expectations for task-oriented and social behavior clear and highly consistent, following through to make sure the child complies, and praising the child for attending and cooperating. (Berk & Winsler, 1995, p. 96)

High-quality teachers practice these techniques.

A GOAL: SIGNIFICANT WORK

I believe that early childhood teachers are passionate—in their desire to work with young children, love of young children's nature, and belief in their tremendous capacity for learning. But I also believe some do not know how to engage children's powerful innate intelligences, which produces a conundrum: motivated teachers who are ill-prepared to be effective. The problem is complicated by humans' language instinct, our amazing ability to assimilate new words, not merely multi-syllabic tongue twisters but words that represent powerful concepts and refer to entire sets of beliefs. Psycholinguist Steven Pinker (1994) says because of our instinctive language ability "simply by making noises with our mouths, we can reliably cause precise new combinations of ideas to arise in each other's minds" (p. 1). When teachers speak fluently about educational practices, we assume they know what they're talking about. But fluent speech is not the same as bringing concepts to life with children. Following many language mavens into their classrooms, I found their practices looked nothing like their words.

In this book I am explicit about practices teachers must adopt in order to do *significant work*. To recap, significant work involves doing complex projects in many media, sustaining projects over a long time, designing and managing an environment rich with materials, drawing parents deeply into a school's life, and giving children every opportunity to form relationships by working collaboratively in small groups. Teachers who do this will exceed standards and their work will exemplify best practices.

At the root of this book is my belief that not all experiences are equal, that what young children do matters in what they ultimately want to do and can do with their lives. Examples of significant work—in this book, in the Reggio schools, in some preschools striving to adapt the Reggio Approach, and in a few other high-quality classrooms—show that young children can solve complex problems, develop skilled performances, and form relationships well beyond what is generally expected of preschool-aged children. I advocate that teachers thoughtfully design the classroom environment and ensure that preschoolers become self-regulated as essential steps before beginning significant work. Above all, teachers must examine their beliefs about young children. Reggio educators' work is shaped by their belief: Young children are *rich, strong, and powerful*. Shining throughout the stories in this book are teachers who became highly qualified at tapping young children's power and engaging their varied, immense capacities.

CHAPTER 2

Where Theory and Practice Meet: First MELC Projects

Human learning is best when it is . . . given over to constructing meanings rather than receiving them.
—Jerome Bruner (1996, p. 84)

OST TEACHERS TRYING THE REGGIO APPROACH read descriptions in books or see presentations at conferences of robust, successful projects—arrival points long after beginning to use the Approach—not beginning stages. The early work described here shows departure points, frustrations, how insight occurred unexpectedly. The basis of Reggio teaching is to work in small groups and structure relationships that make significant work possible. The teaching principle is how Lev Vygotsky's sociocultural theory looks in practice.

I had observed in Reggio classes on a dozen different visits, taken many photos, heard lectures, and shared them with the teachers so we had an image. Barely aware of what we were doing, we plunged ahead, recording conversations but not understanding them, having isolated experiences we did not know how to connect. The Reggio Approach is theory-based, not formulaic; that is, you start with a question—who *might* use the blocks (theory), not with a list—who *will* use the blocks (formula). Theories begin, What if . . . , Suppose. . . . Reggio practices follow the Vygotskian perspective: Learning is an endeavor in which children are challenged and deeply engaged with teachers in ways that are "participatory, proactive, communal, [and] collaborative" (J. Bruner, 1996, p. 84). For example, teachers use yesterday's notes of children's conversations as suggestions for today's activities, but may not follow the suggestions if children's responses lead in other directions.

In 1992–1993 we used the word *sociocultural*, but understood neither Vygotsky's theory of how teacher intervention affects children's development nor its implications for our roles as teachers. We were unaware that among preschool philosophies the Reggio Approach is probably the fullest example of sociocultural theory and "is highly compatible with Vygotsky's ideas" (Berk & Winsler, 1995, p. 140). There were so many things we did not know. In this chapter I describe how our work slowly came to reflect major principles of sociocultural theory.

BEGINNING A REGGIO-INSPIRED PRACTICE

Our space, the teachers' natural tendency toward thoughtful mediation, and our shared vision set the stage. But we groped as we tried to figure out how to mesh our own beliefs and our children's culture with the demanding practices we were attempting.

We started with these assets: ample space, no constraining lesson plans, and a shared vision. In a tumultuous 2½ years with wildly out-of-control children, we'd finally learned to help them become self-regulated, calm, keep materials in order, and respect one another. Now our immediate concerns were: How to take notes and of what? How to tell what was significant and what wasn't? What was the Studio's role? What determined which children would work on which projects? What did it mean to *negotiate* the formation of groups and the subject of projects? We did not know what it meant to orchestrate, collaborate with, or mediate children, or how to launch projects based on relationships among children's ideas, their peer groupings, the school's materials, and ourselves.

Evaluating Assets

Our environment, our dispositions, and our vision were assets. But how to use them effectively?

Our Environment. Our school was organized, free of clutter, and interesting—many varied spaces, long halls, nooks, large windows. White walls, quiet floor coverings, and abundant natural light made it aesthetic from the first. We had a separate Studio and resources aplenty—pens, papers, markers; Montessori maps, unifix cubes, unit blocks; ample space, enough adults. With no lesson plans, we had long, open periods to pursue interests with individual or small groups of children. We understood the difference between externally imposed discipline and self-regulation, which is the basis for social-emotional growth and essential for small-group work. Children must be able to control asocial actions, choose materials on their own, concentrate, and put materials away before teachers can leave the class on its own while working with a small group. The environment was calm because our children were for the most part internally controlled, so we could give them great leeway.

Ourselves. We mediated as necessary, sensitive "to the difference between doing things for children and letting them do things for themselves" (Berk & Winsler, 1995, p. 43). Without using Vygotsky's words *zone of proximal development*, we understood there was a "distance between what children can accomplish during independent problem solving and what they can accomplish with the help of an adult or more competent member of the culture" (Berk & Winsler, 1995, p. 5). Within clear limits we respected children's rights to move, talk, sit where they pleased, choose friends and activity, change activity, drink water, use the bathroom—whenever they wanted. We believed evolving activities, not preplanned lessons or predetermined products, should guide activities.

Vision. Most important we had a vision. Even before the 1992–1993 school year, my slides from Reggio and descriptions had roused the teachers' enthusiasm to try something different. Because they were go-getters by nature and eager to try something new, they would do anything necessary to realize the vision.

A tribute to Maria Montessori: In my mid-20s I trained for 9 months in the rigorous tradition of the Association Montessori Internationale with a demanding, inspiring British woman, Margaret Stephenson, herself trained by Mme. Montessori. I taught, then trained teachers. My beliefs in organized environments, open-ended time, choice by children, and self-regulation were shaped by those experiences.

Groping with Concerns

Where to start? There was so much we didn't know!

First Commitments. Our first commitments were: Pay attention to every aspect of the environment, don't allow clutter, establish order, maintain everything immaculately, even watering and grooming many plants. Eliminate teacher/aide hierarchy by seeking everyone's perceptions and involving all adults in everything—recording children, attending staff meetings, discussing problems, meeting with parents. Do all work in small groups. Attempt projects. Record what children say and document experiences. Because teachers made notes from the beginning, we have records of our earliest attempts. We had moments of despair, breakthroughs, and new starts as the teachers tried to practice something with no working model and little guidance.

First Questions. Immediate concerns were: the difficulty in listening, responding, and taking notes simultaneously, and figuring out what a project was. Challenges were: how to care for the environment and to collaborate with one another. New children's lack of discipline and some older children's need for more self-restraint meant that the need for self-regulation kept cropping up. Managing behavior, we found, required certain procedures with new (or unself-regulated) children and different procedures with returning (or self-regulated) children. New children needed to learn the four basic rules (Chapter 1); returning children needed continual emphasis on understanding how to use the increasingly complex environment. Most difficult was the degree of uncertainty we felt in general. After a lot of staff turnover and a careful selection process, we had found teachers—Deborah, Genet, Jennifer, Sonya, Miss Wendy—who were open to learning a new approach and, as it developed, were intuitively good mediators. You can watch them become more intentional as their understanding and skill with the new practices grew. The following stories show us wrestling with these challenges.

Understanding the Cultural Surround

Choosing what to put in preschool classrooms is a conscious, deliberate act. Everything is there for a purpose. The teachers were uncertain how to make these intentional choices. In a memo she sent me, we can see Jennifer struggling with this question: She had cleaned easels and shelves, removed everything from the Studio she wouldn't need immediately, and gathered and organized materials for the light table. She had punchlists of tasks unfinished from summer's renovation, purchases requiring my signature, and questions about caring for the environment. How should she keep the environment not just clean and organized but *prepared*, so it would lead the children? How could she anticipate questions they might ask and materials they might need? She guessed this related to projects, but wasn't sure how. What kinds of questions should she ask the children and when? She had preliminary thoughts about projects—perhaps leaves or spiders? self-portraits? They could do a lot with faces—change them with Mylar masks, make them from found objects. She wondered whether making clay balls and worms was a project. She remembered particular Reggio slides—containers with typical regional/cultural items such as sheaves of wheat, collections of pasta, local glassware. She wondered how we could reflect *our* region and culture. Should she put beautiful photos of black-eyed peas and collards in the Dining Room? Should she hang images of cornrow and Afro hair styles? Should they investigate traditional African fabrics? (J. Azzariti, personal communication, October 1, 1992).

After 15 years of studying the Reggio Approach, new answers still emerge to these big questions. Their significance is the impact of the culture at large, of the immediate environment, and of human relationships on children's learning. In preschool, environment and relationships *are* the curriculum. If you understand this, you will find unregulated children, disorderly environments, a paucity of materials, abc/123 curricula, and scripted lessons painful because they deter the expansion of children's minds and constrict cultural influences. If children's bodies thrive because of what they eat, their minds expand because of what they use—the materials their culture offers—and how their peers and adults use those materials with them.

Learning to Listen and Take Notes

Listening to children's ideas is the basis for projects, and note-taking is basic to listening. Learning to take notes is challenging. Learning to read notes is as difficult as learning to read a foreign language.

Recording Techniques. Reggio teachers listen so intently, they actually place tape recorders among small groups of children to capture what they say. Each MELC teacher devised her own note-taking method, initially mainly handwritten. Somehow, while actively conversing with children, the teachers managed to write long, verbatim transcripts. Miss Wendy's record of her first conversation about Coco the cat is handwritten, covering three-and-a-half 8½" x 11" sheets edge-to-edge. Her notes on other Coco projects that fall and winter cover another 31½ pages. She reflected years later: "It was hard. I had to write and listen and be concentrating on those children and thinking what I would say next all at once" (W. Baldwin, personal communication, January 25, 2007).

What Do the Notes Say? Teachers-in-training are taught to journal, to take notes on classroom goings-on or particular children's actions. But the focus is not necessarily on listening to what children are saying in order to use the notes as the basis for what to do tomorrow. This was one of our early difficulties. The teachers knew that projects begin by listening: What truly interests the children? Which ideas are rich enough to pursue? They also knew the answers to these questions were in their notes. But the answers were not always apparent. When they saw two interests that *were* clear, they pounced on them as the first projects—the children's fascination with Coco, the cat, and their endless absorption with wooden trains. Miss Wendy, the teachers agreed, would follow the interest in Coco; Sonya, the trains that the children heard at the station nearby.

Learning to Read Notes. The teachers unfailingly read their notes aloud together every day afterschool. When Miss Wendy read her Coco notes, everyone heard potential for several projects: how cats behave, how to treat Coco, how to observe him. Train projects emerged from the careful notes Sonya made of her observations. Sometimes she acted immediately on the children's interests, like their desire to visit the train station *that very day*. Other times reading her notes led to related projects, like drawing the sounds trains make, which she decided on after reading in her notes that the children imitated train sounds while playing with the trains. Jennifer kept notes in a daily journal of children's activities; it jogged her memory about which children had used which materials. As she read her notes she realized which children she should bring to the Studio—because they had never used a particular material, or were ready to do something more challenging. Working in small groups enabled the teachers to listen and observe the children closely. They found that each observed different things about the same child. Gradually, as the teachers learned to trust one another (an often-painful process), they became able to challenge one another's observations, notes, and interpretations. They learned

> how to state their opinions, explain their choices, and be receptive to better choices; how to be confrontational without being destructive; how to disagree without triggering rancor; how to accept criticism without being defensive; how to acknowledge mistakes without making excuses or blaming. It was a huge breakthrough when they . . . [realized] that criticism can strengthen one's own performance . . . [and yielded] individual control to group process. (Lewin-Benham, 2006, p. 100)

But a year passed before they learned how to use their notes fully—to quote a child to himself as a way to rekindle interest, keep him focused, or spur his memory; to see possibilities for new projects or continuations of started projects. It was frustrating to do all that work, and not understand how to take advantage of it. *Not* taking notes would have been easier, but to their credit all did.

CHILDREN'S FIRST EXPERIENCES

Some early experiences actually were projects—trains lasted 3 weeks; Coco projects (Chapter 4) spread over months. It was easy to find projects involving

FIGURE 2.1.
Gels on
window
in hall to
dining room

Coco; his doings interested the children immensely. Some first experiences, like colors, were happenstance. Others were missed opportunities.

Color and Light

Early Fall 1992. Jennifer put colored gels on south-facing, sun-filled windows in the long hallway to the Dining Room. As the teachers predicted, the children were very excited.

October 7: Gels on Window Panes. Tiara walked down the hallway, looking from floor to windows and back.

SONYA: "What did you see?"
TIARA: "Blue light."
SONYA: "How'd it get there?"
TIARA: "It slided there."
SONYA: "Where did it come from?"
TIARA: "Out the window. . . . All the rest of them gone!"
SONYA: "Where'd they go?"
TIARA: "I don't know."

October 8: No Sun! Dark and rainy. Going to breakfast ZeZe looked at the floor and gasped: *"Oh my God!* Aaaaah! The colors off the floor!" Looking at the window to be sure the colors were still there, then back down: "Aaahh! The color not on the floor. They gone!" Knowing nothing of the relation between sunlight and shadows, he was disoriented. Renowned psychologist Reuven Feuerstein, whose work has significantly advanced sociocultural theory and practice, says feeling disoriented is an essential prerequisite for learning, that to learn we must notice that something is different from what we expect, and be bothered by the difference: "The origins of reflective thinking lie in perplexity, confusion, or doubt" (John Dewey, 1933, cited in Feuerstein, Feuerstein, Falik, & Rand, 2002, p. 144). ZeZe was confused!

November 10: Overlapping Gels. Jennifer added gels to the Studio's south window and placed a small tray with colored gels on the windowsill. She conversed with ZeZe, whose excitement about the colors hadn't waned.

> ZeZe: "Why don't the teacher ever put green on the window? I like green."
>
> Jennifer, selecting a green gel, placing it on the pane, and pointing to a green shadow: "How about this?"
>
> ZeZe, ecstatic, shouting: *"Green!!!"*
>
> Jennifer, indicating the tray: "You do it."
>
> ZeZe, *very* excited, holding two gels against the pane: "I know how. My mommy gonna like this! I'm so crazy." Then, observing the green shadow on the floor: "YAY! I did it!"
>
> Jennifer: "Look at all the colors on *you*! Look at the easel!"
>
> ZeZe, seeing his gel's shadow on the easel: *"Ooo-oooh!"* Putting a red gel on the pane: "Watch this. If it do this . . . ," sliding the gel up, "and," adding a blue gel, "put this up there." To Jennifer: "Can you hold it up tight? Over there. Thanks. Don't let me mess my thing up. That's good. *That's purple!* Ooooh!"
>
> LaShay, watching unobserved: "Hie! Yesiree!!"
>
> ZeZe, talking to the purple: "I see you color." Looking at the easel and separating the gels: "I see you blue." Rapidly moving gels around: "Now I see *you*, yellow."
>
> Jennifer: "It doesn't look yellow to me. It looks blue."
>
> ZeZe, his gels sometimes landing on top of one another: "No it don't. It look yellow. It orange. Now it red. She red, light red. Oh my God!"
>
> Jameana, having joined the group: "I see red everywhere! I see a red dog."
>
> ZeZe: "Oh my God! Oh my God!" Looks at the gels: "Wow! Oh my God."
>
> Jameana: "Oh my God! Everywhere is pink."
>
> ZeZe, combining green and yellow: "Look what I did! The place is *blue*!"

Experiences lasted 6 weeks. This was a breakthrough project in which the teachers effectively integrated environment, material, children's interest, and their own intervention. They thought the gels might be interesting, not suspecting color mixing would result. Fifteen years later, notes leap off the page with the children's excitement. Eliciting children's excitement and extending their interest in natural effects, like sun and shadows, nurture a disposition to observe and experiment. "According to Vygotsky, higher mental functions originate in the activities and social dialogues in which children participate" (Berk & Winsler, 1995, p. 153). The significance is that, unintentionally, the color experiences provided a powerful stimulus for activity and dialogue.

A Year Later: Color Everywhere. In 1994–1995 color was the focus of 16 separate intentional projects: Jennifer read the children similes they'd used in discussing color—"Blue is like trying to catch a fish out of water"—and asked them to transpose them into drawings. The teachers engaged children in theory-making about colors. The children discussed why the sky is the way it is, debated about how the sun moves across the sky, how its movement affects colors, and what would happen if, one day, the sky broke. They disagreed over who makes color in the sky and struggled to convey their ideas to one another. The conversations were long, many spurred by teachers' reading their own words back to them. It became common practice for any teacher to use whatever was relevant from another teacher's notes. Conversation had become the bedrock of all experience.

Conversation is one of the primary means of human interaction, a basic language function. In Vygotsky's theory language is "the 'tool of the mind' . . . , the most frequently and widely used human representational system" (Berk & Winsler, 1995, p. 21). In time the teachers began to listen for repeated words or

Figure 2.2. Miss Wendy conversing with small group

ideas which helped them tease a strand out of the tangled skeins of words. In analyzing their recordings together, if different teachers had recorded similar words, it might suggest a child's real interests. If quoting a child's own words back to him rekindled his interest, bingo! If the teacher reported this to her colleagues, if they tried and it worked, if it happened again, a focus began. Then, they could record what was related from one day or week to the next, and begin to see where ideas might lead. When they discussed these ideas . . . with the children, and found that it did extend their interest, it suggested the direction for a project. And, if the teachers asked "What should we do next?" and the children responded enthusiastically, they were off! (Lewin-Benham, 2006, p. 45)

Missed Opportunities

Because initially we did not know how to analyze which experiences had potential to be extended, or how to fan sparks of interest into projects, many notes reflect experiences that fizzled.

Not Knowing How to Listen. Latricia, arranging flowers in November: "How full do we fill it?" Smiling broadly: "I got two sponges so the water won't drop." To herself: "Beautiful, Latricia. Two this time. The most beautiful flowers I've ever seen in my life. Water is everywhere around here. I have to mop the floor. Are they drinking? If they don't get no water, they'll die. The flowers must be sayin': 'I want some drink before I die.'"

Had the teachers known how to read notes, they might have extended this experience by having children draw pictures of vases, create found-object arrangements, find flowers in books and magazines, experiment by watering some flowers but not others, discuss life and death. But not knowing how to reflect with children on experiences or use reflection to provoke a project, this experience went nowhere.

Misunderstanding Notes. Teachers' daily notes chronicled who did what with whom. For the morning of March 5 the intern Bonnie's notes read: Miss Wendy worked this morning with [seven children]. They sorted marbles, practiced walking around the environment, sitting in chairs, using the bathroom, and hand-washing. Bonnie continues:

> Reginold and Kamreal worked with me in the house learning exactly where things belong and procedures for cleaning up. Lorian, leaving the magnetic marbles, joined them.
>
> LaShay and Jameana worked in the dress-up corner with Alex. Later Alex worked with Tesha on concentration cards. Donnell, Akil, and Alonzo B. spent the majority of the morning together in the Lab on the computer. Donnell read them a story in the Library. [Three] worked on trains for some time. [Five] worked with an intern in the water hole. [Four] continued working on helicopters.

Bonnie's account makes dull reading, shows no relation to prior happenings, and doesn't hint at anything to follow. The teachers saw no projects in it.

A New Focus. Later that week Amelia Gambetti, retired Reggio teacher and renowned consultant on their practices, made her first visit. She suggested doing a project on the environment: discussing with small groups of children each area of the environment. Bonnie's notes showed which children worked in which area. The environment project meant taking those children back to the area, discussing its purpose, what to do with the materials, whether materials from other areas could be used there, how many children could work there, how to straighten the area when finished. Together teacher and group debated rights, rules, and responsibilities. In this way children eventually learned the function and how to manage every area in the school.

Bonnie's notes also showed which children chose to be together, useful for learning who prefers whose company. The notes showed who was drawn to, or competent in, an activity, useful if you want children to teach one another: ZeZe, I noticed how carefully you use the headphones; can you help Brandi select a tape and use the headphones carefully? From these perspectives, Bonnie's notes are rich with potential. The right questions pop notes into focus. A theory is a way to question. From the socio-cultural perspective it is important for children to choose their friends and activities, and for adults to provide "sensitive and contingent assistance, facilitating children's representational and strategic thinking, and prompting children to take over more responsibility for the task as their skill increases" (Berk & Winsler, 1995, p. 32).

AWARENESS DAWNS

Jennifer told visiting educators it took 2 years for the Studio to develop.

> When I started there were not even paints. We sat around on Amelia's first visit explaining what we were going to do. I was lost. That experience led to a dialogue between me and the other teachers. We began to work on the problem of how to establish communication between us. The Studio had tools and materials to make repairs, so teachers started coming: "Jennifer, this needs to be fixed." Now, they [teachers, parents, children] use all the materials well. Now I know the Studio is for everyone, an open place, a resource for other teachers and children. The Studio and I have come a long way. (J. Azzariti, MELC Day presentation, February 21, 1995)

The MELC teachers were determined. Their own struggles, experts' words, and the particular culture of our school gradually led to breakthroughs, eventually enabling them to trust one another, to form small groups successfully, to increase the complexity of projects.

Early Studio Work

Early in the fall Jennifer introduced clay, glue, and paper. Materials were new to the children, their hands unaccustomed to manipulating.

FIGURE 2.3.
Children
tearing
clay off
block

Clay. Jennifer shunned commercial and home-made dough, preferring sculptors' low-fire clay. She gave each child a good-sized hunk, challenging them to remove pieces and work them into balls and snakes. Early work was simply whatever their fingers could manage. Gradually, as they developed competence using their hands and as Jennifer's teaching became more intentional, they learned to slice, push, pinch, roll, pound, smooth, and shape. If you believe that only 3-R-related activities have value, consider this: Legible writing is possible only if your hands are competent. More important, research connects development of speech to using the hand (Wilson, 1998, p. 50). Neurophysiologist Wilson says, "At about one year, the thought–language nexus is becoming a hand–thought–language nexus" (p. 195). Preschoolers' hands are their most important tool; refining use of the hand helps children transform mental images, plan, follow logically related steps, and accomplish objectives that are significant in their culture. In sociocultural terms,

> Creating diverse symbolic representations of classroom activities and concepts *through artistic means* exemplifies Vygotsky's belief in the use . . . of cultural symbol systems as the major route to higher mental functions. (Berk & Winsler, 1995, p. 145, emphasis added)

Sometimes, children made specific objects. Jennifer encouraged them to sculpt Coco from clay, constantly urging them to look carefully, compare what they observed to what they produced, and make their sculpture resemble Coco. Just 8 weeks into clay work when asked to sculpt Coco, these 4-year-olds could represent the space a 3-D object occupies and correctly detail the surfaces: Donnell covered his "fur" with striations, close together and parallel; LaShay and Tesha made indentations in the paws, not too accurate but recognizable. All evidenced careful observation, intentional comparison, and concerted effort to reflect reality. The significance is that careful observation is one of the pillars of cognition; without it, higher level thinking is not possible. The pieces reflected the Vygotskian principle of teachers' scaffolding children's thinking.

Glue. At the beginning Jennifer used glue as a medium in itself, not for its adhesive property. Miss Wendy noted some children's discomfort: They didn't like feeling it on their hands and kept running to the sink to wash it off. Some children react that way to paint, instinctively finding it dirty. The teachers provided long periods of repeated experience so children would become familiar with the properties of materials—their texture, smell, consistency, and behavior. Such familiarity is significant as the foundation for understanding the physical world (Hawkins, 1974). If we want children to do more than watch TV, talk on cell phones, and use Game Boys™—to be proactive members of their culture—preschool is the time to lay foundations for higher level thinking that develops through what Vygotsky calls "cultural tools" (Berk & Winsler, 1995, p. 5) and Reggio educators call "a Hundred Languages."

Paper. Even common material like paper needs introduction. You can change paper endlessly: crumple, cut, tear, bend, curl, roll. Within a year the children would perform all these operations as they used paper to realize various ideas. But first they had to explore its properties with no purpose other than experiencing its behavior. Later they would find a huge range of functions is possible—wrapping gifts, shaping paper planes, folding origami, writing messages.

Mediation. Typical preschools adhere to the Piagetian idea of "readiness," a theoretical position that leads to markedly different teacher behavior than sociocultural theory.

> Because Piaget's theory stresses the supremacy of development over learning, the teacher's contribution to the process of acquiring new knowledge is reduced relative to the child's. . . . [The child] tak[es] responsibility for change in a social environment that *refrains from interfering with natural development.* (Berk & Winsler, 1995, p. 103, emphasis added)

Vygotskian theory acknowledges the role of development, but the primary emphasis is on relationships between child and environment, including the

FIGURE 2.4.
Coco's fur
and paws in
clay

people. Feuerstein goes further, believing that learning "cannot occur without the individual being exposed to and affected by [mediation]" (Feuerstein, Feuerstein, Falik, & Rand, 2006, p. 101).

The MELC teachers' tendency was to collaborate with children by scaffolding their problem solving. Each medium—paper, glue, and clay—has inherent problems and possibilities. Teachers structured "the task and surrounding environment so that the demands on the child at any given time [were] at an appropriately challenging level, and constantly adjust[ed] the amount of adult intervention to the child's current needs and ability," what Vygotsky calls the Zone of Proximal Development (ZPD). In confronting each problem the teachers fostered self-regulation by "allow[ing] the child to regulate joint activity as much as possible" (Berk & Winsler, 1995, pp. 29–30). All the while, the teachers set an emotional tone of warmth and responsiveness, and the children gradually built cognitive capacity.

Cultural Factors

Several sociocultural factors set the stage. They constituted the MELC's milieu.

Motivation. The teachers were highly motivated, driven by their own nature and a powerful vision of the possible. The groundswell of interest in Reggio schools barely had begun, but we sensed it was the future. Furthermore, we were part of the same institution as Capital Children's Museum, a plucky organization with tremendous cachet. The MELC's ambitious staff was not content to remain a nascent entity perched on the fifth floor of the successful museum, but wanted equal stature, a desire fed by the media, which featured the MELC, from its inception, on TV and in print. In October 1993, with our Reggio adaptation barely begun, *Child* magazine named us one of the 10 best U.S. preschools. And we were adapting an approach from the preschools that *Newsweek* magazine in 1992 named *the* best in the world.

Leadership. My leadership was a factor. I had initiated many programs, so knew how much time is required to get underway and how much more to mature. I was patient. As the MELC's Director I maintained relationships that were its lifeblood—contracts with D.C. Public Schools, line-item funding in the U.S. Congress, private donations. I procured resources from furnishings to funds, materials to members of advisory boards. I also assured that teachers were relieved from administrative work.

Breakthrough

By February 1994 the teachers' spirits were waning; they felt they did not know how to go *deeper*, their word for needing to know more. Visiting Reggio, I consulted with Carlina Rinaldi and Tiziana Filippini, seeking answers to the teachers' questions. "To every question they heard one answer: It depends!" (Lewin-Benham, 2006, p. 63). It was a watershed. We either would stay muddled without knowing enough to move forward, or would get help.

I persuaded Amelia to come for a weekend. She left the teachers energized. In the following 3 months transcripts of children's conversations tripled the number in the prior 6 months. Sonya developed a robust project about removing the Freedom Sculpture from the U.S. Capitol along many new dimensions. Miss Wendy developed Pollution and Ambulance 9-1-1 as major projects. Jennifer developed a new understanding of her role, how the Studio relates to work throughout the school, and how she, as Studio teacher, related to the other teachers.

Jennifer began to realize that her role was not *to teach children art*, but to use her knowledge of diverse materials to enrich the dialogue between children and among children and teachers and to stretch each child's personal style of exploration. She became aware that she should build a master/apprentice relationship, use her expertise to help children learn difficult skills, and enrich teacher collaboration by providing the artist's *different perspective*. As Jennifer's understanding evolved, she realized she needed to be involved in goings-on throughout the school, not only the Studio.

A principle of Vygotsky's theory is that all uniquely human, higher forms of mental activity are derived from social and cultural contexts and are shared by members of those contexts because mental processes are adaptive. They lead to knowledge and skills that are essential for success within a particular culture (Berk & Winsler, 1995). As the teachers adapted a more thoughtful way to help children think and learn, their teaching skills increased significantly.

Sociocultural theory takes into account widening circles—home, school, community, nation—and the different cultures and particular symbols of each: Gestures and facial expressions bond mother/child dyads; systems structure schools; history unites communities; religions, food, and jokes bind (or separate) nations. Increasingly the MELC teachers were integrating cultural symbols from widening circles into the children's experiences. As peoples of different cultures increasingly mingle worldwide, it will be a decided asset if children have formed the ability to collaborate in small groups.

SOCIOCULTURAL THEORY IN PRACTICE

Vygotsky's main ideas, outlined by Berk & Winsler (1995), are recapped here as they relate to the MELC's early activities.

Two Aspects of Development

Development occurs both *naturally* as "biologic growth and maturation of physical and mental structures" take place, and *culturally* as children learn to use cultural tools. "Human consciousness . . . emerges from engaging in cultural activity" (Berk & Winsler, 1995, p. 5). The MELC teachers built on what the children already knew and how they behaved—their physicality, talkativeness, clinginess—to begin to engage them in activities. Since all activities involved learning culturally relevant skills, the children's natural process of development was furthered by the MELC's sociocultural emphasis that we see throughout this book: extensive conversation, mutual respect, and challenging, culturally relevant projects carried out collaboratively. The group always profoundly affects the individual; the MELC teachers consciously exploited this phenomenon.

Lower and Higher Mental Functions

Lower functions are shared with other animals. Higher functions, which are uniquely human, "systematically reorganize lower mental functions" (Berk & Winsler, 1995, p. 5). Recall ZeZe's first reaction to colors when he simply responded to a stimulus (lower function), and how 6 weeks later he intentionally used colors to achieve an effect (higher function). Recall the children's initial clay work, barely breaking off a lump (lower function), and 6 weeks later, with their teacher's scaffolding, faithfully representing Coco's features (higher function). We see children's thinking capacity grow because teachers use conversation, intentional teaching, tools, and materials—all culturally relevant—as vehicles for learning.

Cultural Development

Concept formation, social interactions, and all other behaviors appear twice, first "on the social or interpersonal plane and then on the individual, or psychological plane" (Berk & Winsler, 1995, p. 5). That is, higher mental functions originate on the social level and "are eventually internalized" (p. 5). Recall how the teachers recurrently engaged the children in learning to use the environment. This helped them self-regulate by instilling the capacity to select work, use materials thoughtfully, and maintain them in orderly fashion. Many teachers never begin small-group work because they don't know how to teach a small group and manage the other children at the same time. The MELC teachers structured the environment, then gradually built children's understanding of the structure. As their understanding grew, the children became able to use and maintain the complex environment themselves.

Cultural Variation

Different cultures emphasize different activities and use different tools. As a result, higher mental functions "vary across cultures" (Berk & Winsler, 1995, p. 5).

> Early childhood professionals have a long tradition of regarding what the young child knows and develops as personally rather than socially constructed—a tradition that flows from Piaget's [work]. . . . The Vygotskian view is unique in that thinking is not bounded by the individual brain or mind. Instead, the "mind extends beyond the skin" (Wertsch, 1991a, p. 90) and is inseparably joined with other minds. (Berk & Winsler, 1995, p. 12)

> According to socio-cultural theory, "forms of thinking assumed to develop universally in early and middle childhood *are much more a product of specific contexts and cultural conditions than was previously believed.*" (Berk & Winsler, 1995, p. 18, emphasis added)

The MELC children's paucity of experience using paper, scissors, markers, glue, clay, and other materials was culturally determined: Their homes had neither materials nor parental guidance in using them. Thus, their skills on entering the MELC compared unfavorably with those of children from homes that abound in *stuff*, where highly educated parents instruct their children early in many activities that economically deprived children first experience in school—the use of paper and writing implements, card games like concentration and go fish, and lots of book reading. However, consistent with Vygotskian theory and as a result of intentional teaching, in only a year the MELC children surpassed others their age, thus eliminating culturally induced variation in mental function. They had daily instruction in how to use clay, paints, papers, and the MELC's other varied materials. The teachers engaged them many times a day in conversation, read books to small groups or one-on-one, and played alongside them as expert collaborators. The results were evident in the growing originality, creativity, and complexity of their work.

Understanding Development

Understanding human behavior depends on seeing "how it formed developmentally" (Berk & Winsler, 1995, p. 5). We develop because of the evolution of specifically human capacities, the role of a continually evolving culture, our individual life history, and our growing competence with specific tasks. This rich heritage accounts for children's power that is the cornerstone of the Reggio belief system that the MELC teachers embraced. Awareness of the different aspects of human development helps teachers better understand their role as mediators in children's developing competence. As tasks increased in challenge, recall Jennifer's constantly urging children to observe, compare, and incorporate the properties of various materials, all capacities that, over eons, humans learned to exploit. Watch throughout the book how the teachers *play* the children's natures in everything they do.

Role of Education

"Learning and development are neither separate nor identical processes, . . . [but] combine in a complex, interrelated fashion such that *instruction leads, or elicits development*" (Berk & Winsler, 1995, p. 104). Reggio practices are complex in how they intertwine with children's learning, sometimes leading, sometimes following, always intentional. Throughout this chapter we see the teachers struggling to learn these practices. Each teacher, for different reasons, was highly motivated and willing to invest whatever energy was needed to succeed. They believed in schooling as a process, not just to socialize, but to help children acquire diverse and significant skills.

Zone of Proximal Development

A hypothetical ZPD is a dynamic region between "what [children] can accomplish during independent problem solving and what . . . [they] can accomplish with the help of an adult" (Berk & Winsler, 1995, p. 5). Even in their earliest attempts using Reggio practices, the teachers worked alongside the children, observing, questioning, pushing them to observe, compare, analyze, and express their thoughts fully in both language and other diverse modalities. Perhaps most striking in Reggio practices is the skill with which children transform ideas to words, words to drawings, drawings to 3-D, theories to working models. Moreover, they learn to select the materials and tools best suited to each form of expression, and the friends with whom to work. We see this beginning throughout this chapter as the teachers learn to mediate children's efforts.

Importance of Language

"Language, the primary cultural tool used by humans to mediate their activities, is instrumental in restructuring the mind and in forming higher-order, self-regulated thought processes" (Berk & Winsler, 1995, p. 5). Think of the cat sculptures. The children made them after many discussions with the teachers about all aspects of Coco so that he became not just *cat* but an entire constellation of ideas, first in words, then in other media brokered by words the children now *owned*. Children absorb new words as effortlessly as whales ingest krill. When ZeZe saw the colors in the Studio and began overlaying gels, Jennifer's question, "Where do you think they came from?" had an explosive effect! Words have power over actions.

Children will ponder the farthest reaches of the universe, whether manifest in a moving column of ants or gathering storm clouds. In socioculturally oriented classes, teachers notice those ponderings, enter children's conversations, and feed their ideas, not with vocabulary-controlled stories, but with libraries' vast publications and all of the culture's *stuff*. Then they help children interpret their ideas, drawing on one another's different strengths and perspectives and using the culture's varied tools and the wide-ranging media of human expression—clay, cloth, symbols, sticks, wire, words. Our ability both to absorb our culture and to shape it is our heritage—whether forging new technologies or ministering with the most heart-easing words. Sensitive adults' conversing with small groups of children about wide-ranging ideas and about using materials to express those ideas ensures children their birthright—the capacity to act on thoughts and achieve goals that their culture recognizes as significant.

CHAPTER 3

The Studio's Role in School Readiness

Dialogue among students, studio teacher, and materials "strongly informed . . . our way of being with children."
—Loris Malaguzzi (in Edwards et al., 1993, p. 68)

SEASONS ARE STAPLES OF EARLY CHILDHOOD CURRICULA, but activities are often formulaic with predictable outcomes. Yet, seasons have inspired soaring creations in dance, music, painting, and literature, and penetrating investigations in science. They dominate our lives with concerns about summer droughts or winter blizzards. Children find season changes dramatic. The MELC teachers captured that drama in diverse, robust, original projects, some of which are shown in this chapter. The aspect of the Reggio Approach featured here is the role of the Studio (*atelier*) and Studio teacher (*atelierista*). The teaching principle is learning school-readiness skills.

The word *atelier* means workshop or studio, usually an artist's. The *atelier* is, physically and conceptually, the center of a Reggio school, an embodiment of these beliefs: There are, at least, a hundred languages—sound, movement, materials—in which children can express themselves, and school must help children learn to use these languages skillfully. Practice using the Studio's rich stock of materials gradually increases children's skills, eventually leading to amazing competence with many media and fluency in many modes of expression. The *atelierista*, or Studio teacher, adds the perspective of a different discipline—one rich in understanding how materials behave—to the school's dialogue. Studio and Studio teacher foster collaborative work in small groups, honing many competencies, preparing children for school.

FALL EXPERIENCES

Children react intensely to fall's vibrant colors, crunching sounds, and moldering smells, their excitement reawakening adults to autumn's sensory assault. Because the teachers tried to see everything through children's eyes, they were alert to these reactions and used them as the impetus for projects.

Making Collections

September 1993. Remembering the prior school year, children brought handfuls of acorns. The teachers recognized this as the beginning of a project. By mid-October children were talking together or with the teachers about leaves, colors, sounds, and smells and bringing fall objects daily. They commented: "Leaves are falling off trees." "Different color leaves are on the ground and trees." "It's colder and we have to put on jackets." "Squirrels are eating nuts." They noticed everything. Teachers made fall objects and children's comments about them into a panel. *Reading* the panel sparked further questions about fall, which the teachers collected and used in conversations with several small groups.

Language skills are essential for school readiness. Research shows: "Children from low-income families are more likely to start school with limited language skills" (KIDS COUNT, 2005, p. 2). Question/answer, the staple of classroom discourse, is part of White children's experience, but not, according to Heath, low-income Black children's. Heath said:

> More than 50% of . . . [white parents'] utterances . . . [are] interrogatives, most . . . used to train children in knowledge about the world. . . . When [Black] adults . . . ask children questions, . . . [they] were of a very different sort than the ones White teachers posed (Heath, 1983, 1989, cited in Berk & Winsler, 1995, pp. 16–17)

Extensive school-style Q&A prepared the MELC children for grade school.

In the Studio Jennifer laid out carefully organized seeds, pods, leaves, stems, and twigs she'd gathered or the children had brought. On the light table she arranged other fall-colored collage materials—translucent gels, cellophane, tissue paper. Some children made collages. Others observed leaves, then drew them with black or colored pencils or fine-line pens. Drawing and gluing refine movement and observation, important cognitive skills that would be amplified in increasingly challenging activities.

In mid-October the children and teachers wrote a letter asking parents to help collect signs of fall. Tiara's mother nodded: "Oh! We go out and gather things this weekend." Nineteen bags were returned Monday, 30 by Wednesday, all bursting, some with unusual treasures. Sonya and Miss Wendy divided the children into groups to examine and talk about each item so they could establish logical ways to store the materials. Sorting leaves by color, shape, and size was a huge endeavor that continued for weeks. It required judgment and astute visual discrimination, careful observation, focus, and persistence to sort and store the enormous collection. These are school-readiness skills, preparing the children to understand basic mathematical concepts like classification, and reinforcing the self-regulated behaviors essential for the independent work that success in school demands.

Doing Projects

For weeks the Studio was alive with fall activity: conversations, using the light table to outline leaves, drawing and coloring leaves, increasingly complex

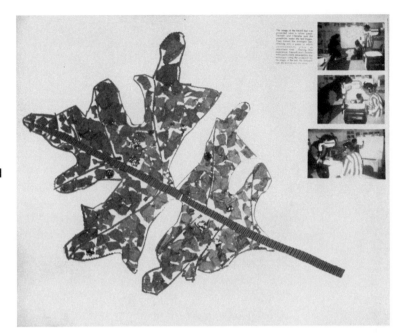

FIGURE **3.1.**
Huge leaf,
cardboard
and crushed
leaves

collages. Fall materials still poured in, parents as immersed as children. Two children made an elaborate fall diorama in a shoebox—miniature, lifelike figures against a realistic background. On October 28 nine families joined an outing to the National Arboretum; in small groups the adults crunched through leaves as the children ran through tall grasses, then sketched trees. It was a golden day, relived in many conversations and a slide show, parents as eager as children to see their images.

Changing Scale. Jennifer projected a child's drawing of a leaf, the children amazed by its huge size. Two traced it using black pens, then outlined its perimeter and veins in wire, and filled the spaces with corrugated cardboard and paper. It required persistence and cooperation. They were awed by making something so beautiful. Jennifer varied the activity by having children study the fall panels to remind themselves of the colors, then mix paint in those colors and paint their huge projected leaves. Seeing their fascination at working in huge size, the teachers offered all older children the option, which they eagerly accepted. Scaling is a sophisticated measurement tool used in art, math, and science, one of many experiences that exceed standards for early childhood programs. The children's eagerness reflected their positive attitude to learning.

Choosing Materials. November 2. Jennifer organized materials for groups of children to work on fall weavings, paintings, or collages. Sonya crushed a huge number of leaves, which, stored in jars, added a material of wonderful texture, color, and aroma to the Studio's well-stocked shelves. Working with

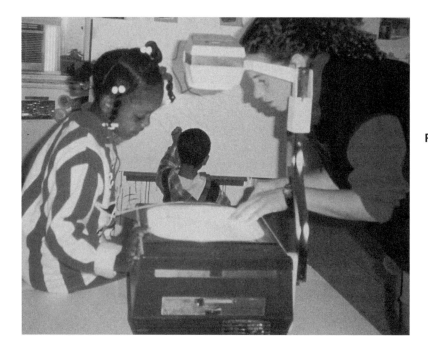

FIGURE 3.2.
Setting
an image
on the
projector

Jennifer, three 4-year-olds made the collage-sculptures described in the Introduction. It was challenging: choosing from the Studio's great assortment, focusing simultaneously on color, texture, and size to represent fall abstractly. Projects required increasing representational skills—making collages from the tiny bits and subtle hues of crushed leaves, dealing with balance and symmetry to construct a fall mobile, wrestling with perspective to draw the collection of glass jars, discerning how best to fulfill a purpose. Quatesha's ideas about what everyone made, dictated to Sonya, narrated a fall panel. Older children compared the four seasons and had many theories about the differences. One supposed there were "a hundred seasons in Italy."

Teacher training offers little guidance on how to meet the Early Childhood Education standard that projects should continue and grow in complexity. Here we see seasons full of projects showing continuity. Teachers' collaboration and thoughtful attention to what children said brought big ideas to fruition. Children participated actively, asked questions, and used increasingly large vocabulary, essential grade school behaviors. The teachers hung eight large panels; two portrayed the full sequence of fall activities. The others, blank for now, awaited winter and spring. Each season's bounty—leaves, sticks, blossoms—was used in weavings, small sculptures, paper structures. In theories, poems, drawings, and paintings children expressed their observations and proposed reasons for seasonsal changes.

Sculpting. In Spring 1994 Giovanni Piazza, the *atelierista* from La Villetta Preschool in Reggio Emilia, visited. He challenged the teachers to work *bigger*. That lead to the tree sculpture. Against the ceiling Jennifer hung a huge limb that she and the children draped in papier mache and wire, a prominent, complex construction that stimulated imagination and that they dressed anew each season. It stretched the length of the panels on seasons, tying them together symbolically, an analogy for change. Using analogy is a thought process unique to the human brain. Feuerstein says, "Analogic thinking . . . is basic to cognitive functioning . . . and implies establishing a . . . rule that connects items" (Feuerstein, Feuerstein, Falik, & Rand, 2002, pp. 424–425). Many projects prepared the children to notice and use analogies, giving them a cognitive leg up. The significance was, by year-end, the children observed seasons astutely, saw diverse uses for natural items, and matured in their ability to speak, write, draw, and think.

Discriminating Among Materials

On November 19 a group of children made a mural, mixing the paint in fall colors. It was large, detailed, and striking. Such results do not just happen. They are the culmination of other activities—relationships among adults, children, families, and the environment; the role of a Studio and Studio teacher; and the materials.

FIGURE 3.3.
Painting an image that has been projected and traced

Exploring Properties. As artists, Studio teachers see unique relationships among color, shape, and form. They understand how materials behave: which paint leaves dense strokes, which barely a trace; which wire is facile enough for small-scale, which for sturdy constructions; which glues bond best with which materials; what materials achieve specific effects. The MELC children were not limited to a typical preschool vocabulary of construction paper, crayons, and paste, but knew paper, for example, as a material with an infinite range of weights, textures, colors, striations, transparencies, and finishes. They experienced how paper and wet materials interact: what slides off paper's surface, what beads, what is absorbed, how paper and water affect each other.

Exploiting Varieties. While the children were noticing fall, collecting evidence, and classifying it, Jennifer was structuring experiences in the Studio to help them acquire the language of materials. She did this by preparing numerous exercises solely to explore one particular material. Each week different small groups tried the under/over pattern of weaving, poked, pinched, and gouged clay, coiled and bent paper. They experimented making paper into strips, bridges, curls, or pleats. They folded, crumpled, glued, wove, crossed, rolled, twisted, or marked it. They layered it in stacks, cut it into shapes, or tied it.

Another week the activity might be on the light table. Jennifer would preselect items in a particular color range—perhaps many shades of green, or a palette reflecting the season. Materials were clear, translucent, or reflective, each behaving differently when light was projected through them. They glued layers of tissue paper and acetate to observe light through many colors, or filled tiny clear plastic bags with leaves, seeds, and pods to observe light's filtering effect.

Between October and February Jennifer introduced a great range, 15 materials in all—wire, corrugated paper, pen, ink. Other teachers introduced music, water, movement, chalk. The teachers observed that after just one demonstration children adopted a technique and applied it spontaneously when it suited a task, exemplifying the human tendency for adaptive behavior. The other teachers also learned the techniques, so new media and skills became part of everyone's repertoire.

Developing Skills. Because most cannot yet read or write, preschoolers use materials as the means to express themselves. Experience aggregates. The facility a child gains by manipulating scissors prepares his fingers to squeeze the glue bottle with just enough pressure to let a drop emerge or, if he needs it, a stream. Mixing paint or using many shades of green attunes the eye to observe subtle color distinctions. Saturating a brush or merely tipping the bristles trains the hand to make refined movements. Each material requires different coordination of brain, eye, and hand. The fall mural reflected the various skills the children had acquired thus far and their teachers' own growth: Jennifer's understanding that children can have the fullness of nature's colors, not the limited palette of materials produced for preschool; Miss Wendy's knowing they could have anything in the public library, not just limited-vocabulary readers; Sonya's realizing children's own questions are far more profound than any in teachers' guides. In seasons all the teachers saw an unlimited range of sensations and awe-inspiring beauty, the reflection of eternal struggles with extremes, the joy of warm spring sun, the tingle of crisp fall air. They helped children harness these sensations to wonder about nature or make something of quality. The children felt satisfied with their accomplishments. As experiences accumulated, they learned increasingly subtle distinctions, honing observation skills that prepared them for grade school, and acquiring practical knowledge that prepared them for life.

WINTER EXPERIENCES

Winter 1995 was vengeful, with heavy snow, ice storms, and school closed for many days. For the children it was a wonderland. The teachers fully exploited winter's textures, colors, and effects.

Discussions Set the Stage

January 4. Miss Wendy's conversation with a small group recognized that a new season had begun. Three days later Jennifer had a surprise on the light table—materials for winter collages. The next week she asked the children to make drawings about winter. A huge storm intervened; school was closed for 9 days, and there were extreme ice storms and snow 2 feet deep. The children talked about nothing else. The teachers developed questions to discuss with them about winter and trees. For days Genet held conversations with different groups.

Speaking precedes literacy. The huge emphasis on conversation provided lots of experience hearing and using language. Conversation enlarges vocabulary by putting words in context. Context envelops words with meaning and prepares children to form new concepts. Expanding children's ability to express their thoughts by enlarging their vocabulary is the most important school-readiness skill preschool can provide. Engaging children in conversation and listening to them with total focus are the most effective ways to expand children's language. The MELC children were learning to stay focused on topics and to expand words into ideas, ideas into theories, theories into debates.

January 31. Miss Wendy gathered four children to make winter collages. First she asked, "What are these?" having the children simultaneously touch and name rocks, beans, and paper, which Alex and Brandi identified; Angela added trees, shells, and glue. When Miss Wendy asked their color, the children chorused "White!" They decided the items resembled snow, and snow meant winter. Symbolic representation is a high-level cognitive skill "requiring systematic and accurate data gathering . . . [and] internal representation . . . in a visual/spatial" form (Feuerstein et al., 2002, p. 213).

Miss Wendy asked why leaves fell off the trees.

ALEX: "It was because the trees were cold."
BRANDI: "The wind blew them off."
MISS WENDY: "What can you do with the white items?"

A welter of thoughts, detailed descriptions, long conversations, and ideas for complex projects emerged.

Projects Become More Diverse

More snow days! Back in school the children were full of stories—how they played in snow and slipped on ice. *Everyone* became involved in winter projects—creating trees, making weavings, writing poems, ice skating, collaborating on a winter sculpture, describing theories about how snow forms, and representing theories in three dimensions.

Verbal Descriptions. February 1. Miss Wendy gathered three children to describe winter trees they'd drawn:

QUATESHA: "It doesn't have leaves. . . . They fell off because the wind was . . . so strong in winter," making a connection between cause and effect, a problem-solving skill.
FRANK: ". . . If it's cold outside, they [the leaves] fall off. If it's winter they have to blow . . . ," connecting cause and effect in the form of a proposition.
ALEX: "No clothes on, leaves are their clothes. They're naked. That means it's cold . . . ," drawing an analogy and implying a proposition: If trees are naked, then it is cold.

Cause and effect, analogies, and propositions are higher level cognitive skills. Learning to express these in preschool is significant; it prepares children to think when they reach grade school.

FIGURE 3.4.
Winter
trees

Weavings. The following week, Jennifer prepared unusual looms for winter weavings—wires stretched between two sturdy sticks—and a winter palette of materials—some lengthy, glistening, and white; others hard and transparent; still others soft or bumpy. She asked the children to imagine how to augment the collection. How you launch children on a project determines whether the result is pedestrian or creative. An assignment to write "What I Did Last Summer" yields different results than an assignment to write a story by completing the sentence: "Summer's torrid heat sapped all my energy until . . . " Before beginning, Jennifer and the children talked about the qualities of snow and predicted what might happen when they wove on the light table. Prediction causes you to think about possibilities and form mental images. The children considered which materials could be pulled under and over, and observed patterns of weavings and how they filtered light. These are significant experiences: Selection of materials requires understanding the constraints of a process; pattern is a basic mathematical concept; observing the effect of light sets the stage for wondering how light behaves. Problem solving, math reasoning, and observation are important school-readiness skills.

Poems. *February 10.* Snow still covered the ground. Cold hung in the air. Miss Wendy asked six children: "What reminds you of winter?" and suggested they answer in a poem. Terrell: "You have to repeat the same words, because that's what you do in poems." Their poem began: "Winter snow, winter snow . . . " Another read:

> Snow is white.
> When it's cold
> Snow becomes ice.
> There was a lot of snow,
> It was crazy.
> Snow melts.

Their writing showed the children were beginning to make conscious choices of particular words and realize the constraints of poetic expression.

Theories. The teachers cleared a shelf for books about blizzards, which the children consulted frequently. Sonya and four children discussed their theories of how snow falls, then they drew their theories. The drawings, like their words, were complicated and machine-like.

> DeMarcos (age 5): "You got to pull all the handles fast. . . . Sometimes it takes a while to come out. The first machine has a snowflake in it. . . . The snowflake comes out and makes snow."

Tiara's description went on and on. The central thoughts were: "Handles make it start up and the snow comes out. They have a little hole in the machine and they put all the snow in the bag in the machine."

As the children examined one another's drawings, it became clear they wanted one theory. Two days of debate followed. Throughout, the teachers talked among themselves and with the children about the process of reaching agreement by choosing which ideas to combine into one theory. They decided: "God's mother made a computer," and built a model. By this time they were experienced in discussion and sustaining complex projects. They created a shelf for the model and made a book about it.

Drawing an idea makes it easier to discuss. For example, if a child, talking about a train, says, "The engine makes it go," you don't know what the child understands. Words mask imprecise thinking. Drawing demands more precision, a model even more. It was difficult to understand what they knew about snow formation when they said: "Sometimes it takes a while . . ." or "rain turned into snow." The model was tall and rectilinear, and looked like an apartment building with windows, suggesting the children might have thought snow came from tall places. They heaped white cotton balls on top and covered one of the tall sides with white paper. When Jennifer asked whether they wanted something on the sculpture to move, they became very excited. She rigged a sort of pulley system with a basket that actually could be raised, lowered, and lifted off a hook. Jennifer said: "You pulled a string and things fell down! It was complicated, very literal, but it really worked" (J. Azzariti, personal communication, February 2007). It satisfied their idea that God made snow. Theorizing draws on prior experience, prediction, understanding cause and effect, and analysis—all higher level thinking skills that will be required in school. Transformation, turning words into drawings and drawings into three dimensions, is also a high-level skill.

The snow machine project showed how much the children had to learn. As a result the teachers added more books on weather, clouds, and snow formation to the school's library, and concurred that they needed much more discussion with the children about their ideas. The teachers themselves needed more scientific knowledge to scaffold the children's understanding with better questions. This was one of their first experiences transposing theories into tangible form and they knew they had a lot to learn about supporting children's theories, especially on complex subjects like weather formation. Children don't limit their questions to topics with easy answers. More nuanced discussions about snow formation would wait for another winter.

Wire. Ideas come constantly and evolve unpredictably. Winter 1995 was so snowy and icy it was a frequent topic of conversation. The children noticed how differently we move in winter. Two were interested in ice skating. So they went. Considering how to document the experience, Jennifer suggested wire because it is flexible and could represent bodies that land in strange positions! Also, the children had not used wire much. A harvest of wire sculpture resulted. Cemetria drew a profile of herself skating, glued it on felt, then cut it out and framed it in wire, a complex process. She proudly showed the finished figure at morning meeting. Terrell, thinking about making his sculpture, admired Cemetria's greatly, but wanted to wait. Jennifer agreed he could begin the following week. People often need time to think before tackling a challenge. At the MELC there was always time. Sculpting in wire required them to think analytically about how their bodies orient in space. Orientation in space is an essential cognitive function. Knowing up, down, front, back, right, and left is essential to follow instructions: Write your name on the upper right-hand corner on the back of the page.

Sculpture. In February the teachers were still enlarging the collection of magazines and books about winter. They discussed newspaper clippings about snowstorms with the children, adding any that reflected children's experiences to documentation panels. On February 23 they revisited the huge tree limb still dressed for fall. Ronald, Ceola, and Paula gradually transformed it with new materials—today silver foil that they shaped into objects to hang like frozen leaves, another day silver glitter to represent ice and snow, still another day glassy beads to represent icicles. They used materials and techniques they'd learned making a winter mobile. They worked 4 weeks in all. Sustaining activity over time prepares children for cumulative tasks in grade school. Winter projects were more complex than fall projects, evidence of the children's increasing skills and a hallmark of significant work. They finished transforming the limb early in March, along with the first hints of spring.

SPRING EXPERIENCES

The children talked about flowers they expected to see. The palette changed from winter's stark colors to spring's warm hues. Projects increased again in complexity.

Conversations Lengthen

At the end of March several children found the tulip magnolia on the playground in bloom. Excitement spread. A large group gathered underneath, staring up in wonder. The teachers divided the children into groups to talk about the changes. Ronald: "The grass is growing, the leaves are coming out, flowers be everywhere!"

In other conversations the children talked about how many more birds and animals were on the playground—squirrels, worms, bugs, butterflies, flies, bees. Willie theorized: "In winter all the birds went to New York City because they could find food there. Now they are coming back to see all of the pretty flowers." The younger children thought the animals had hiding places for the winter but could be outside now because it was warmer. They also compared winter and spring clothes—"now not even a coat." Their theory-making and comparisons evidenced the growing range of associations they were making.

Older children talked excitedly about riding bikes, running in the park, or taking walks to see flowers and trees. Since the wind was blowing, they could fly kites. Last year's panels reminded them of other things to do, like seeing cherry trees or playing ring-around-the-rosie under them. Anthony mentioned planting a garden; several talked about the cabbage, tomatoes, and other vegetables in their grandmothers' gardens. After spring vacation parents, accustomed now to taking part in school doings, sent seeds and seedlings.

Literature portrays childhood as a joyful time when children romp in sunny fields and commune with animals and plants. Television has robbed many children of such pleasures and left adults cynical. Watching children excited about standing under a blossoming tree, hearing them theorize about animals, and experiencing delight in nature provide a gentler aura to childhood.

Drawing Proliferates

March 23. Frank, age 5½ , excited: "We're going to see the cherry trees!" A large group went with three teachers. Cherry blossoms were barely visible but tulip magnolias were in full bloom along with tulips. The children played in the magnolia petals, reveled in the sunlight, and talked about trees.

QUATESHA: "A cherry is something that grows off a tree."
FRANK: "Look at the trees. They're naked!"
QUATESHA: "'Cause it's not summer. When it get warmer, the flowers will bloom."

The following week the cherry blossoms peaked! A smaller group brought pencils, paper, erasers, and clipboards to sketch them. All chose trees they liked, then sat down together to draw other trees that were still stark. At school, they glued on tissue paper flowers, turning drawings of bare branches into blossom-laden trees.

If you've never seen Washington, D.C., during the cherry festival, it is hard to conceive. Farther than the eye can see is a canopy above where branches intermingle, a carpet of blossoms below. Frank: "Me and Lorian were trying to jump to get them. I told Miss Sonya I wanted one and she reached up and got me one." Two teachers and ten children played there—chase, hide-and-go-seek, ring-around-the-rosie. They hugged trees and decorated themselves with blossoms. On the Capitol's north side they settled near a bevy of red and yellow tulips, smelled the flowers, gently touched the petals, carefully felt the texture, had lengthy discussions about the sensations, then drew. Brandi and Cemetria made Polaroid photos to show the others at school, not wanting their friends to feel bad about missing anything. The photos guided more drawings.

Chalk and Glue Effects

Older children loved the wind and recalled seeing kites in a museum exhibit. They made paper and pen sketches, adapting what they saw with their own designs, noting how the kites were made, and predicting how they would fly. A kite festival soon would take place and they would go. But when they saw their kite drawings on the documentation panels, they looked lifeless. The children understood why—there was no wind! Howard and Jennifer discussed the problem. Howard remembered swooping his arms while rubbing chalk over the chalkboard. *That*, he decided, looked like wind. When they added swooping chalk streaks behind the kites, they *did* look as if they were sailing. The children were becoming analytical: considering the relationship between a kite's design and how it would fly; reflective: observing that something was wrong with the kites' appearance; resourceful: solving the problem with symbolic representations.

With spring fully arrived, the winter sculpture looked out-of-place. Several children made it a project, removing materials that resembled ice and snow. With pink, green, and white tissue paper they made cherry blossoms, gluing them to strips of acetate, which became blossom streamers.

LORIAN: "Crunch these things up, they gonna be flowers. I'm gonna put all different tissue paper flowers on there . . . a whole bunch. This is the mother branch, this is the father, this is the baby."

She spoke in full sentences, correctly using the verb "is."

The children chose appropriate materials, learned how to shape them, the best glue to attach them, and how many to glue to transform winter into spring. Effortlessly they evaluated possibilities, evidencing knowledge of the properties of materials and displaying skill in using varied techniques. Quatesha: "The cherry blossoms are pretty. They are white, they smelled good. It feels like I'm touching one. The blossoms go down to the tree trunk." Everyone admired the spring branch.

The Complexity of Murals

Jennifer projected a slide. For 2 days, many children traced the colorful flowers and leaves, coming and going informally, working as long as they liked, some more than an hour, others several minutes. It would be their first mural. The next week two children mixed paints using the slide's colors as a reference. As they painted the traced shapes, they talked about the background: If it were green, how could a green leaf or green butterfly show up? That was a big problem!

The children worked all month. When the mural was hung, Tesha led her mother to the studio: "Oh, you've finished your mural and they've put it up!" Tesha beamed. Murals are big projects requiring the ability to foresee the outcome of several interim processes, each hidden by the next. This requires children to form mental images and visualize results many steps ahead. "People cannot retain or transmit . . . information . . . without the help of representations" (Perkins, 1995, p. 287). They are part of the bedrock of thinking and vital for understanding increasingly difficult grade school subjects.

When the tulips bloomed and the full class saw slides, photos, and their friends' drawings, a few insisted on seeing the tulips more closely, so they went to the Capitol. Later they asked to make a mural of the field of tulips. They discussed techniques with Jennifer, deciding to trace the flowers from a slide, then use tissue paper and mix water and glue to create stems and flowers. The older children, who were more skilled, traced and prepared the outlines. The younger children prepared the tissue paper and glue. After 2 weeks they moved the mural, half-finished, into the Big Room where other children, working with Deborah, a teacher, water colored the tulips, using slides as their color reference. Then, it went back to the Studio where others added more tulips. It was a major collaboration involving half a dozen processes, several groups of children, and 3 to 4 weeks. Younger children's vision and abilities were stretched by working alongside older children. The complex techniques, their insight about who could handle which tasks, the changing groups, the long time span, and the beautiful result made this project significant.

The Many Aspects of Collages

The children had many discussions about spring colors and arrived one morning to find a table in the Big Room covered with small squares of tissue paper. Jennifer demonstrated how to twist them into bows. As they made bows, they talked about what they could do with them and selected quite a large clear box that together they managed to fill. The minute it was full, they set it on the light table, satisfied with the effect and their collaboration.

The next morning another surprise awaited—large-scale quadrille paper on which to draw or glue the bows and other materials Jennifer had assembled in a palette of reds, pinks, yellows, greens, and purples. The work took days, with different children joining. Collaboratively they covered nine to ten papers with geometric designs, bows, drawings of flowers, their many impressions of spring. Their title, "Representing Spring," was significant: a word connoting symbolism that described a symbolic work. Another morning, Sonya placed a bouquet of large-petaled rubrum lilies on the light table. The children copied them in huge tissue paper and paint collages. The significance of these works was their many aspects—the variety of techniques, the range of skills, and the aesthetic results. They correlated to school readiness by requiring planning, focus, hand skills, stick-to-itiveness, cooperation, and enthusiasm.

The Drama of Shadows

The teachers projected slides of the Capitol grounds. In front of the screen the children became birds, flying over treetops. They played under cherry blossoms and huddled like tulips. At the end of April when the teachers projected slides of their spring excursions, the children brought a kite they'd made from poster board and theater gels to "fly" in a vibrant blue sky over cherry blossom images. In May they made a bird puppet as a prop, then posed challenges: Place the bird's shadow on a cherry tree; make the kite fly above the tulips. The powerful play of light, body, sculpture, color, and image was dramatic, bringing the full joy of spring into the school. It was significant because the children themselves had become inventive in using many media. Their confidence that they could handle complex tasks prepared them for school.

ROLES OF THE STUDIO AND STUDIO TEACHER

Seasons projects drew heavily on Studio and Studio teacher. In this section I discuss their inseparability and relation to Seasons projects.

The *Atelier*

A Studio is rich in materials and what children make from them. No medium or form of expression is foreign to an *atelier*. Diana School's had series of photographs titled "A Dialogue of Feet" and "Motility of the Mouth."

La Villetta's had elaborate water wheels and an intricate wind machine. You would be as likely to find a professional set of drums as a row of easels or both, the tools of a master carpenter, or a computer with a wide range of software. While studios are chock-full of materials, they are not cluttered; the potpourri of "stuff" is orderly. Studios look playful, but have a serious purpose—for children's big ideas to meet respect, encouragement, and expectations that even bigger ideas are afoot. Every studio is different in its particulars because it reflects the interests and skills of its *atelierista*, the artist who runs it.

The *Atelierista*

An *atelierista* is an artist or crafts master whose expertise with tools and materials provides a different perspective on the meaning of activities and the directions they might take. *Atelieristi* figuratively *live* in the *atelier*. They work with children and teachers, utilize parents' skills, orchestrate activities, and bring studio-type thinking to projects. Because *atelieristi* are not responsible for a class, they are available to work throughout the school. As artists *atelieristi* are expert with a wide range of diverse materials, tools, and instruments: paper, clay, wire, metal, paints, chisels, camera, brushes, guitar, horn, pulleys, gears, electric drill, power saw.

Atelierista and classroom teachers meet together frequently, spontaneously and planned, as colleagues engaged in scientific research. They discuss possibilities: What might happen when children use different materials to confront problems? What if children try to express their understanding of a crowd of people by making crowds out of paper? cardboard? clay? What if children find their classroom has disappeared under a layer of butcher paper? What if children try to represent pencil drawings in a different medium—wire, clay, or sound? Or, clay figures in pencil? Hypotheses are enriched because of *atelieristi's* expertise and are tested using diverse media that reflect *atelieristi's* broad experience.

The Relationship of *Atelier/Atelierista*/School

The spirit of suggestion is contagious, the possibilities endless. Children, teachers, and *atelierista* all chime in, one's ideas buoyed by the groups', a rich mix, as Malaguzzi said: a "big mess, a minestrone," supported by adults who understand the importance of listening. Ideas spread through an entire school, expanding and propagating. Teachers set the stage, expectant, predicting what might happen, brainstorming conditions necessary to support the predictions, hypothesizing what is most likely to happen, preparing the environment so it *provokes* the possible into the actual. Sometimes sparks from a single child affect the entire school. Parents become involved, forming a community of interest and experience.

> The *atelier* has protected us not only from the long-winded speeches and didactic theories of our time (just about the only preparation young teachers receive!), but also from the behavioristic beliefs of the surrounding culture, reducing the human mind to some kind of "container" to be filled. . . . Most of all it is a place for research. We have studied everything . . . forms and colors . . . narrative and argumentation . . . symbols . . . mass media . . . sex differences. (L. Malaguzzi, cited in Edwards, Gandini, & Forman, 1993, pp. 68–69)

When children transform observations into concrete form, they provide pictures of how they are thinking. This forms the basis for a conversation and a reciprocal relationship among children, teachers, and material.

STUDIO: PREPARATION FOR SCHOOL SKILLS

All year there had been activities involving shape and color. Genet and small groups frequently conversed about shapes, then canvassed the school or took walks outside to find them. They cut shapes in the Studio or, using Montessori Metal Insets, traced shapes in the Big Room. They analyzed the shapes of letters, and photographed shapes that looked like letters. They also analyzed color, in 16 separate activities in 1993–1994—beyond those discussed in this chapter—with color as the sole focus, refining the children's perceptual skill. By any measure, the work was beautiful and original. Unless you observed them working, it was hard to believe children produced such complex things.

The significance, however, is not what the children produced, but what their works reflect about their increasing cognitive capacities. In March Terrell wants time to think before sculpting the wire of himself skating; he is assessing his own ability before starting a challenging project. Gardner (1983) would call this intrapersonal intelligence. In spring Lorian observes, "The sky is very great. It's blue and the flowers are white"; she is evidencing increased visual perception and focused attention on stimuli. In May Galeesa steps aside to let Tesha and Cemetria trace flower outlines; she has learned how to collaborate. These skills are important for school success.

In mid-March before spring arrived, Miss Wendy and a group made cardboard sculptures from an array of paper materials. They began, as usual, by discussing the materials—their textures, thickness, whether you could bend, fold, roll, or cut them. They compared different kinds of glue. The challenge: Roll the cardboard and papers into tubes and form them into a sculpture. One problem was how best to glue paper to cardboard, something the children decided to do. Another problem was keeping the tubes from unrolling, something everyone found difficult. The finished piece, which they agreed to make collaboratively, was intricate: a grid of interlocking cardboard, like box separators, five rows tall by five columns wide, and in each compartment a tube differently configured from paper and cardboard. It was a regular geometry of form and texture and a subtle blend of color.

With their Studio teacher's astute eye and the Studio's vast resources, the children were mastering difficult techniques and learning the potential of many materials. They were developing the ability—in processes we continue to develop throughout our lives—to express abstract ideas in myriad ways, to think about their own thinking, and to understand the dynamics of collaboration. Their work was significant—conceptually rich and competently executed.

CHAPTER 4

The Concept of a Hundred Languages

With no possibility of boredom, hands and minds . . . engage each other with great, liberating merriment.
—Loris Malaguzzi (in Edwards et al., 1993, p. 68)

MY MONTESSORI CLASSROOM INHERITED a huge black rabbit, dispossessed for chewing through its family's electrical wires and washing machine hose and flooding the basement, twice. Thicket ran free in the classroom when children were present. Several had begun school under a cloud of sadness, two carrying particularly huge burdens. They would do nothing but hug Thicket, day after day for hours. When Thicket had enough, he'd take off, fast, straight across the classroom, and wrest his way under a cabinet. The children, who respected one another's rights to work on mats, walked *around* them. Thicket ran straight across, scattering concentrated work. Then you'd hear, "Bad rabbit!" But the children gave him lots of leeway, and many calmed inner struggles by stroking Thicket.

Years later, with much troublesome behavior in the MELC, I heard of a new litter of kittens and brought a kitten home. Its temperament seemed suitable for children, so in April 1993 I asked the teachers: "How about a kitten?" They stared at me dismayed: "The children would kill it!" I told them Thicket stories and explained my neighbor would welcome the kitten if things didn't work, and they decided to try. As with Thicket, many children soothed their problems holding the kitten. The cat, whom we named Coco, became the impetus for many projects.

Coco stories illustrate the idea of "a Hundred Languages," Reggio educators' poetic words to describe children's innate drive to explore and their capacity to become facile with many materials and tools. These early experiences show how, from the beginning, the teachers understood the importance of a prepared environment and significant work. The teaching principle is how children learn self-regulated behavior and develop social and emotional competence.

WHAT TO LEARN FROM A CAT

Initially the kitten was simply there, a small white animal with irregular black patches who mainly stayed out of the way. In June 1993, readying the environment for fall, the teachers assigned Coco his own mailbox with name, symbol, and photo just like the children's, one for each, where they communicated by sending and receiving an endless stream of messages to one another. By fall he was almost full size. Donnell summed it up: "Looka Coco! He gots *big*!" Coco became the subject of extraordinary drawings, photos, and clay studies, star of a video and slide show, and topic of a book. Interest in Coco spurred conversation and, as the subject of many discussions, Coco was the impetus for the children's expanding language capacity. Perhaps most important, Coco spurred social and emotional competence.

Basic Content

The MELC children expressed their ideas about Coco in both conversation and materials. As they learned how to treat the cat, they became more self-regulated.

Conversing. Some early experiences left no visible trace because they involved only words. Like all conversations, discussions about Coco were recorded and analyzed by the teachers in order to understand the reasons for their experiences: Why are we doing *this*? Why have we chosen *these* children? "Like playing ball with a baby who has to learn the process of back and forth . . . , it is not easy for a teacher to keep a conversation focused. . . . Studying conversations is time-consuming and exacting" (Lewin-Benham, 2006, pp. 44–45). Daily the teachers had intense discussions, questioning what conversations revealed about children's capacities, choices, and skills using materials.

November 2. The first project-like Coco activity began, called simply: "Coco the Cat Project." Six children became acquainted with Coco, observing and discussing him with Sonya, and drawing their perceptions.

November 5. Miss Wendy had a conversation about Coco with LaShay, a 4½-year-old, and Donnell, a 3-year-old.

> LaShay: "You're holding the cat too tight!"
> Donnell: "I am not!"
> Miss Wendy: "What would you like to know about the cat?"
> Donnell: "Is he running? How can we catch him? He fast, real fast."
> Miss Wendy, rephrasing Donnell's question, emphasizing how to entice rather than catch Coco, thus showing empathy, a basic social/emotional skill: "Yes, he runs fast. How can you get him to *come* to you?"
> Donnell: "No! No! No he not! He just want to go to sleep."
> LaShay, echoing Miss Wendy: "What would you like to know about the cat, Donnell?"
> Donnell: "Ha! Ha! He fast!"
> When Miss Wendy asks LaShay what *she* wants to know, LaShay replies: "They hurt his feeling."

Donnell and LaShay explain that many children have been running all over the school after Coco trying to catch him, that Renee put Coco down *hard,* that Derrick chased him. LaShay said children were pinching his ears, pulling the black and white hairs on his head, and "messing with his eyes," trying to pry them open. Miss Wendy asked how they thought that made Coco feel. "Mad!" said LaShay, describing how Coco bit her finger. LaShay hadn't cried because Coco just had little teeth, but it hurt her feelings, something they discussed at length. LaShay acknowledged that she was holding Coco too long and too tight. Miss Wendy asked if they liked playing with Coco, and both children promised not to chase or run after him.

Discussing this conversation at their afternoon meeting, the teachers realized the rich potential to build the children's social and emotional skills by discussing Coco's feelings, how to care for a pet, and the relevance to their relationships with one another. They rehung Coco panels from the previous year to make space for new panels. That same day Tiara and Frank discussed parts of the human body and studied eyes by making black and white photographic prints. These activities would find their way into Coco projects.

Reading. *November 9.* Miss Wendy asked Donnell whether he would like to read her a book about cats and offered him four choices. He picked *Kitten on Vacation,* which had a cat that looked like Coco. Page by page in a one-on-one session, Miss Wendy questioned and Donnell described. Miss Wendy repeatedly asked what body part Coco used and what was similar about Kitten and Coco, and provided lots of information. When Donnell referred to the cat's "fingers," Miss Wendy supplied the word *paws.* She also supplied the words *ironing board, bench, mountains, wall, license tags,* and praised Donnell for words he knew, like *horse* and *circle.* Donnell continued calling the cat's paws "fingers." When he referred to a picture of a "monster," Miss Wendy gave him the correct word, "fish," and had him summarize the book. Donnell's limited vocabulary shows how much content he had to learn and the importance of one-on-one attention focused on a book.

November 12. Miss Wendy asked whether LaShay would like to read her a book. She also picked *Kitten on Vacation.* Her vocabulary was much larger so Miss Wendy needed to provide only a few words. Both children lacked general information—that cats don't like to get in water, that on vacations you can see beautiful things.

The importance of reading and discussing books one-on-one cannot be overemphasized, especially for children who are underexposed to content and vocabulary. The MELC's huge emphasis on conversation continually built the children's language capacity. Language is essential for emotional control. "According to Vygotsky, the primary goal of private speech is not communication with others but *communication with the self* for the purpose of *self-regulation,* or guiding one's own thought processes and actions" (Berk & Winsler, 1995, p. 37, emphasis in original).

Observing and Comparing

November 15. Jennifer took Donnell, LaShay, and Renee to the Studio. They made hand- and footprints of themselves and pawprints of Coco, a dramatic experience, and discussed differences and similarities. When Jennifer questioned what a cat's feet are called, the children instantly responded, "Paws!" owning the new word. But it took many questions to focus the children on the differences between hands, feet, and paws. Finally Renee explained, "Cat's paws are smaller than mine." Jennifer exclaimed, "Excellent observation!" When Jennifer asked how many toes Coco had, LaShay said five, but the children's attention waned. Jennifer noted there had been a lot of excitement for one day. Not pushing children when interest has waned gives them time to consolidate an experience. Pushing for answers they don't have makes them feel incompetent, undermining efforts to build emotional strength.

Two days later Miss Wendy questioned each child one-on-one. Donnell carried on, comparing the cat's size to his sister and cousin. Miss Wendy refocused him on paws and he noted, "My feet bigger than Coco paws," using the correct word and adding: "He got claws that scratches." Renee was more focused and had lots more to say, recognizing that Coco's paws would never be as big as her hands, concluding: "He's a kitty cat so he has claws and I am a girl and I have fingernails." LaShay came right to the point, Coco's claws would never get big like her fingernails: "He's a cat!" Feuerstein says making comparisons is basic for cognition. It implies focusing on detail, attending to two things simultaneously, drawing on schemata, and finding a way to express conclusions (Feuerstein et al., 2006). This early in their development, Donnell could name only size, and even LaShay could muster only size and fingernails as comparisons. These anemic responses show the children's lack of ability to elaborate, a mental function that reflects what "verbal concepts are part of an individual's repertoire . . . [and can be] mobilized at the expressive level" (Feuerstein, et al., 2002, p. 139).

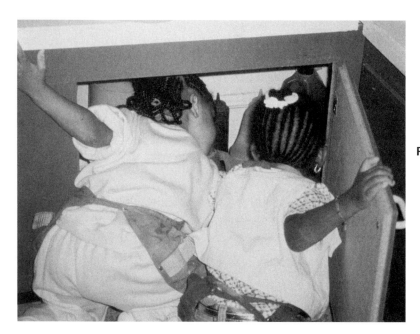

FIGURE 4.1.
Searching
for Coco

FIGURE 4.2.
Coco
in the
cupboard

PROJECTS: A CAT'S HUNDRED LIVES

The MELC children usually worked on several things at once, including projects and other activities. While they accumulated facts about cats and made comparisons between cats and children, they also observed and described the human body, explored materials, and continued having conversations. Projects, like comparing paw- and footprints and studying their own bodies, taught them the parts of the body.

February 15. They began a big project that continued until the end of April—photographing Coco. It started with a discussion about where Coco went during the day, and photographing him in his different haunts. When they developed their photographs, they were very concerned that parts of Coco's body were missing; heated discussions ensued over what you can and can't see when a photo is cropped. The children were beginning to defend their own point of view.

Discussions expanded and focused on Coco's feelings, why he ran away, what they could do about it—again analyzing what it means to be empathetic. They illustrated their ideas with the photos they had taken. Documenting Coco had become their favorite project. The year-long emphasis on verbal description built a cognitive basis—new schemata—for combining words and images. In June they made toys for Coco—tubes with dangling feathers, fabric, and beads. LaShay said, "They had to be pretty so Coco would enjoy chasing them." Then they photographed themselves and Coco playing with the toys. The documentation shows that by June they had added the languages of materials to words and images.

Coco the Video

In February four 5- and 6-year-olds made a video of Coco, a lengthy project requiring the expertise of the museum's animation staff, tremendous focus, and self-control. Chris Grotke, Head of the Animation Department, recalls:

> The MELC had some children who barely participated. Only Coco captured their attention. With new Hi-8 cameras, light enough for children to hold, we felt invincible: "Give us those kids." We sat in a circle in the school's storeroom—kids, cameras, cat. First we taught them the lens was like "eyes" and the microphone like "ears." We showed them how to press the start/stop button, and aim at the subject. For days we followed the cat around with the camera.

> ***Machine Basics.*** Chris, playing the children's tapes: "Do you remember what these are?"

> > DONNELL: "Tapes."
> > CHRIS: "First we're gong to rewind the tape. Do you want to push the buttons?" When the children saw their faces on the monitor, they couldn't stop laughing.
> > CHRIS: "What's happening in this picture?"
> > RENEE, dissolving in laughter: "That's Coco!"
> > LASHAY: "Ha! Ha! Ha! Look at me!" Chris stopped the tape to focus their attention. He demonstrated how to use the dial to move the tape back and forth, then gave each child time to do so. It required tremendous self-control.
> > DONNELL, twirling the dial: "Look at this! Coco is going real fast." Chris explained how to move the tape fast and slow and find particular pictures.
> > LASHAY, fascinated, to Coco's image: "I'm going to make you come back again."

They learned that, in order to control the machine, they first had to control themselves.

> ***Editing Techniques.*** Chris recalls:

> We hoped the children could edit the tape, but ran into trouble. It was like asking someone who doesn't know what a sentence is to write a paragraph. As they reviewed their footage, we noted which scenes they liked most. Sequencing was harder, the moving images on the monitor distracting. Finally, we decided to print an image per "scene." That did it! It was calmer, too, without the competing monitor.

Miles Fawcett, video assistant, recalls spreading the images all over the floor and assembling them, like a book. Chris encouraged Donnell to choose a picture, find another one, decide whether it should be the same as the last or different, come before or after, be small or large.

> Donnell: "*Big*! I like the one where he was running down the hallway! Put that in! And another just like that!"
> Chris recalled: "The sequences we ordered with the children guided us so we could make the final edit to their specifications."

They were learning that editing means searching through many images to find just what you want, and, once you've chosen, sequencing to get a particular result. The process requires forming a mental image, then reasoning how to make a video conform. At the end of the session Chris explained that he and Miles would put their selections on tape and, at the next meeting, view what they made. All four children cried: "Coco!" They understood what the effort had been about.

The Viewing. Miles explained they would see their video and offered them popcorn.

> LaShay, excited: "That's me holding Coco. That's you, Tesha. That's Donnell."
> Renee, delighted: "That's *Donnell*!"
> Donnell, enthusiastic: "That's *Coco, Tesha*, and *Renee*."
> LaShay: "I *love* that cat. The popcorn is good." Miles asked if they wanted to show the video to their classmates.
> LaShay, adamant: "No! They might take it home." Stymied by her antisocial response, Miles asked again.
> LaShay demurred, but finally said, "Okay," succumbing to the social pressure. When Chris asked whether they liked it, their answer resounded: "*Yes*!"

An Audience. Chris recalls:

We decided to have a big opening. We rolled the huge monitor onto the elevator and wheeled it into the classroom. The filmmakers sat in front in special chairs. We announced: "These filmmakers put great effort into making a video called 'Coco the Cat'; this is the world premiere, a special occasion." The audience paid close attention, fascinated. At the closing credits when the music started, they bounced in their seats. First a few, then all, jumped up and started dancing. Some hugged the filmmakers; others hugged the giant TV. Miles recalls they were ecstatic!

After, the teachers reported that the four children were doing better. One led the class in song, which surprised everyone. A couple went on to do still photography. What was most interesting was seeing that children—whom others might have given up on—could do well when the subject interested them. It was like the Reggio principles coming to life before our eyes.

I recall a steady stream of experts on learning coming to talk with us. We were immersed in theories and ideas like flow, multiple intelligences, and mediation. We took it seriously, trying to use the ideas in our work with children. It was like a masters program. Only years later did we realize what we had been exposed to.

Images in the video wobbled from small hands holding heavy cameras. The ceiling appeared too often, as happens when someone short aims at something above him. But the imperfections paled before the reality that preschoolers had completed a video production, scaffolded, of course, by experts. Throughout history that is what learning to think has been—guidance by knowledgeable adults in step-by-step processes that produce whatever a culture consumes. The more complex the process and the more thoughtful the guidance, the more the children learn. The collaboration was an unusual example of lessons in social competence.

Coco at the Vet

March 12. Coco stepped out a window onto the roof where he covered his coat in tar. Miss Wendy explained that Coco could become sick if he licked the tar; it necessitated an emergency visit to the vet. Miss Wendy reported that Coco's visit went well, and now he needed to be with us. It was the prelude to a major adventure called, as the documentation was titled, "A Big Happening in the Cat Project: Our Visit to the Vet."

The Operation. March 24. Renee, LaShay, Donnell, Miss Wendy, and Ms. Francis from the maintenance staff took Coco to be spayed. On the way Miss Wendy asked whether the children knew where they were taking Coco. Renee and Donnell chorused: "To the doctor." LaShay added: "To get a shot." Miss Wendy reminded them that yesterday during morning meeting they talked about Coco needing an operation so he would not become a father. Ms. Francis asked whether the children had seen all the cats running around the street with nowhere to go and told the children that we didn't want Coco to have kittens he couldn't care for. Miss Wendy assured them that we loved Coco, that he would be alright but maybe a little sleepy and might not want to play, and that the doctor would tell us how to care for Coco. Empathy and social/emotional competence were hallmarks of the project.

At the vet's office, Miss Wendy told Dr. Smith why they were there, and requested that he also check Coco for ear mites. Dr. Smith invited the children to watch the examination. Miss Wendy told them to watch closely so they could report to their classmates. Small groups on field trips were always encouraged to think about including the other children.

Dr. Smith: "I am going to give your cat a shot. I am trying to get all the ear mites out so you can see them under the microscope. I am holding him so he can't move while I work on his ears."
Donnell, with trepidation: "Is he going to get a shot *now*?"
LaShay, alarmed: "Oh no! He's going to get a shot!"

THE DOCTOR'S ASSISTANT: "Stand back. He may jump and make noise."
COCO: "Meee—*ow!*"
DONNELL, empathetically: "Coco sad."
RENEE, interpreting Coco's feelings: "Poor cat, he just want to go to his cage."
LASHAY, concerned: "Are you going to give him a band aid? . . . Everyone be quiet so Coco can go to sleep. Look at him. He is going to fall asleep."

Miss Wendy suggested they ask anything they wanted to know. They asked about things in the room and, when the doctor put a solution in Coco's eyes, commented sympathetically that Coco was crying. Back in the waiting room Miss Wendy asked what they felt about the experience, very aware of the strong emotions.

RENEE, knowingly: "I think it hurt 'cause Coco was crying."
LASHAY, matter-of-factly: "He went to sleep with his eyes open."

Fifteen minutes later when the doctor said they could take Coco, they clamored: "Is he still sleeping?"

LASHAY, coddling: "Coco, I got the tape recorder down here on the floor. Can you say hello to me? I smell alcohol on you. I am going to take you to the car."

Miss Wendy asked whether they wanted to visit the vet again. They chorused eagerly: "Yeah, yeah!" Including children in intense, emotional experiences builds emotional competence.

Discussing. *Fifteen days later, March 27.* Miss Wendy suggested that LaShay, Donnell, and Renee tell Tesha about the trip to the vet.

RENEE, beginning: "There was needles and alcohol on the table. The doctor put something in Coco's eyes to make him cry. Coco got his nails cut."
LASHAY, elaborating: "No, no! He cried because he didn't want to go to sleep. It took him a long time to go to sleep. They keep on messing with his ears."
TESHA, sympathetically: "Coco my cat."
DONNELL, emphatically: "They gave him a shot in his butt. I got a shot in my butt when they took my teeth out."
RENEE, thoughtfully: "Coco going to have an operation so he can't be a father. I think he can be a father to one kitten. Don't you think so, Donnell?"
DONNELL, vigorously shaking his head "No" at a concept he could not comprehend: "Uh uh. He *not* a father. That's *Coco.*"
RENEE, reflectively: "Ear mites, ear mites. That's what it was."
DONNELL, with certainty: "Uh, uh. They in his ears."

LaShay, to clarify the confusion: "Stop! Stop! No! No! It was all that black stuff. They took it out with a Q-tip."

Tesha: "Ha, ha!"

Miss Wendy, concerned at the inappropriate response to the cat's plight: "Tesha, tell me what you are laughing at."

Tesha, revealing she didn't know the word *mites*: "That mouse."

Renee, adamantly: "No, no! Ear *mites*!" And she launched into a long description, relating every detail of the office environment, evidence that emotional experiences make strong memories.

Donnell, concerned: "Coco couldn't walk."

LaShay, confidently: "Yes he can"

Donnell, emphatically: "No he *can't*. He slept in the storage room. They chase him."

LaShay, remembering: "He was sick. They say Coco got to rest when we get back to the school. The next day I couldn't find Coco. Maybe the lady came and took him away."

Renee, contemptuous at such an unlikely scenario: "You are silly."

Donnell, reassuringly: "He's in the storage room, right in there."

Throughout the experience the children showed empathy for the cat, understanding of the visit's importance, and ease in their relationship with one another. Their discussions show their competence in expressing wide-ranging emotions.

Drawing. Tesha changed the subject: "I want to draw." Miss Wendy concurred. It was a good time to draw what they'd seen at the vet's office.

Renee: "I am going to draw everything I saw."

Donnell, LaShay, and Tesha: "Me too!"

The children commented as they drew, talking to no one in particular. Renee's running discourse showed excellent recall and narrative ability.

This is my operating table right here. The doctor and the other lady right here looking in Coco eyes and ears for ear mites. You know that lady with the long hair, this is her desk right here. She didn't get up from her seat. She just talk on the phone all the time.

Renee went on and on.

Did you see the scissors, Miss Wendy? The doctor took all the black stuff out of Coco ears. Just looking for ear mites. She put the stuff on the tissue. I couldn't see no ear mites. Coco didn't like that. The lady said, "Do Coco live at school?" She's so silly! . . . She said, "Thank you for coming. Bring Coco back to see us and take some of the papers from here." This is my needle. Needles hurt, don't they, Miss Wendy?

Renee interrupted herself to reprimand LaShay: "What are you making? Don't look at mine!"

LaShay: "I don't want it to look like yours. This is my operating table. Coco right here laying down on the table. The doctor right here. I got a big table.

Tesha: "This is *my* operating table. Coco right here. The doctor here. I want to make two drawings."

Donnell: "This is my big operating table and Coco. He sleep. The doctor give him a shot in his butt. Coco don't have ear mouse."

Renee: "Ear *mites*."

The vivid details in their drawings and discourse revealed their own feelings: They didn't like shots or the strangeness of the doctor's office. They projected their feelings onto Coco accurately and empathetically.

Re-enacting. *April 21.* Donnell, LaShay, Renee, and Tesha staged a puppet show about the trip, electing Donnell to play the doctor; LaShay, the assistant; and Renee and Tesha, students. Coco was played by a puppet. They took turns holding Coco down, remembering how he squirmed. They used one of the hallway tables as the operating table, setting it up with tissues, alcohol, and an artificial needle. Like their drawings and narrative, their dramatic play faithfully recalled the detail of an intense experience and their feelings about it.

At their May 3 staff meeting the teachers reviewed the many Coco projects, planned the documentation, and considered who should transcribe the children's conversations, select their drawings or other work, write text, and design the layout. From then on Coco's trip to the vet was their favorite panel.

A Year Full of Exploration

An explosion of work in many media followed the numerous introductory explorations—words in endless conversations and discussions of pictures in books; portraits drawn in pencil, pen, marker, pastel, paint, and collage; found objects. The children had learned to use still camera, photo-printing equipment, video camera, editing equipment, and computer. They'd experimented with paint, light, shadows, and wire. They'd incorporated wide arrays of natural materials and manufactured items in varied productions. They had woven. They had used diverse papers—flimsy colored tissue to sturdy corrugated cardboard. Coco projects required many media. Their hands were beginning to sort materials, their minds to classify them. Familiarity and facility with materials is what Reggio educators mean when they say that children learn to "speak" a Hundred Languages.

MORE COMPLEX PROJECTS

As 1994–1995 began, new families were introduced to Coco at orientation. When Amelia Gambetti, our Reggio consultant, arrived, she brought Coco presents made by the children at La Villetta, the Reggio preschool where she had taught for 20 years. In November Jennifer and Amelia condensed some of the Coco panels and regrouped them to make way for documentation about

FIGURE 4.3.
Photo
of Coco,
close up

FIGURE 4.4.
Drawing
of Coco,
close up

new Coco projects. The reduced panels kept previous experiences alive. Reading the panels, the teachers realized they had not spent enough time helping new children learn about Coco, as Miss Wendy had done in Fall 1993 with Donnell, LaShay, and others. Also, they noticed that the youngest children would follow Coco around the school or, failing to see him, would search him out. So, in early December they divided the new children into two groups to talk about Coco, an introduction that stimulated new Coco projects. He may have become a fixture to the teachers, but was a source of wonderment to new children.

Using Diverse Media

Projects were documented in a panel titled "The Importance of Coco: A Character in Our School," the children's photographs, comments, and drawings clearly showing their love for Coco. There were two themes: a history of Coco's episodes, and the particular way Coco moved. The teachers realized movement was a rich topic by itself or for another video. Projects increased in variety.

Documenting Cat and Turtle. The longest Coco project was the saga of Coco and the turtle, which began when the school was unexpectedly given a turtle. A friendship between cat and turtle flowered under the children's watchful eyes and to the teachers' amazement (Chapter 7). The teachers had not expected that Coco would be as prominent a character as the turtle. By January 1995 the project was in high gear. Angela and Cemetria produced a sequence of drawings showing Coco jumping into the turtle's box. Angela began, drawing the box with its top on. They passed the drawing back and forth, each girl altering it to make the next, closely attuned to the sounds—Coco's jumping, the turtle's scratching. Others set the story of cat and turtle to music, which demanded intense self-control and total cooperation, evidence of self-regulation. Absorbing as the project was, it did not eclipse other Coco activities.

Sculpting Coco. February. Jennifer undertook a video project, taping first two boys then two girls modeling Coco in clay. The video revealed the difficulty of making a clay figure stand up. They worked over an hour, each child with a unique approach for how legs support a body. Terrell first created four legs, noticed how thin they were, and commented that the body would "squish" them, which they did! Discouraged to the point of tears, he insisted on continuing, and finally with great perseverance got the thickness right. Meanwhile, Alex, bending two front legs together, made a cat with only two legs and a body, and commented, "Standing up like a man." Tesha also had trouble making four separate legs. Galeesa solved the problem by propping a bowl under Coco's head, calling it a dish of food, and announcing, "He's eating." The children were persistent and stuck to the challenge, marks of children who are self-regulated.

On March 3 Glenn and Tamika decided to make a life-size clay sculpture. Glenn began with the head, using a lump of clay the size of a golf ball, but quickly realized it would have to be much bigger. Coco was lying on the light table. Tamika began the body, closely watching Coco as artists watch live models. They built it, under Jennifer's careful guidance, by piling coils of clay and smoothing each layer. It took a week. The final steps were adding texture to resemble fur, and attaching the legs. Sonya noted that it was much easier to sculpt Coco lying down in 3-D than to draw him in 2-D, and how helpful it was to have Coco right there. The sculpture was amazingly lifelike, showing young children's capacity to observe detail and the facility they can acquire when they have guidance in the use of real tools and materials. Most important is how successfully the children mastered the huge challenge. It begs us to think about what we ask of children, whether we challenge them enough, and what we believe our goal is: Readying them for first grade by teaching the abc/123 curriculum? Teaching them not to hit or horde but to apologize and share? Or helping them develop social and emotional competence through intellectual challenges and real-life conflicts?

Coco in Image and Word. The cat was endlessly interesting. The children talked about Coco spontaneously—his feelings; new favorite places he found for himself, like the light table; how smart he must be since he could open doors when he wanted to get into a room. On May 5, the teachers asked whether the children wanted to make portraits of Coco, then use two languages—drawings and words—to describe him to one another. It revealed how well the children knew Coco, how differently each child viewed him, how much their vocabulary had expanded, and how socially and emotionally competent they had become. In June, working closely with the teachers, they used their words and drawings to produce a 25-page book about Coco titled *The Many Images of Coco.* Also in spring the teachers assembled a slide show about Coco; watching and discussing it became a favorite activity. The children's increasing skill with the English language was evident in their astute comments, increased vocabulary, and improved grammar.

Thicket had a one-room-plus-bath classroom, about 1,000 square feet, a typical rectangle. Coco had three times as much space, with nooks galore, and the children discovered that, like all animals, Coco had favorite places. In the Environment project as the children toured every area, defining what happened in each, Latricia asked why Coco stayed in particular places. Sonya explained, "Coco likes a *familiar* place that he can call home"—like the light table that was warm when lit or the Dining Room at mealtimes. His favorite was a director's chair covered in black canvass. Wherever the chair might be, Coco sought it out, white cat on black complementing his own coloring, a fact that did not escape the children. The generous space added to the cat's allure: He might be anywhere! New children, less accustomed to his ways, could search him out, and those inclined to mischief could chase him down long halls. However, the frequent discussions about how to be Coco's friend—which they very much wanted—helped them learn not to chase and to regulate their behavior. And, as the caveats in conversations about how to treat Coco took effect, he found increasing peace in the environment.

THE HUNDRED LANGUAGES OF CHILDREN

Carlina Rinaldi (1992) says that language, and graphic languages particularly, play an important role in children's development. Malaguzzi (1991) knew that

> Children are born "speaking" and speaking with someone. The fact that words are lacking for a year does not stop their insuppressible, vital, eager research to build conversational friendships. The strong desire to communicate is the basic trait of children. (p. 14)

The Reggio schools first became known from the exhibition titled "The Hundred Languages of Children." But there is no specific number; there could be a hundred or a thousand languages. Far more languages exist than we use. Children possess the potential to use many of them. The question underlying the use of any language is: Do you think well?

Making Thoughts Visible

Complex systems in the brain enable children to learn to speak. Motherese "attract[s] . . . attention, mark[s] . . . speech as opposed to . . . other noise, distinguish[es] statements, questions, and imperatives, delineate[s] . . . sentence boundaries, and highlight[s] new words" (Pinker, 1994, p. 284). Other languages, like drawing, are equally important to communication, but not commonly used in our culture. When children draw, they don't copy, but actually reinvent the object, often becoming the object as they draw it. Three-year-olds make the sounds and movements of trains, the lack of correspondence between scribble and actual train of no consequence. The goal of drawing is to share your thoughts—expressed in pictures—with your peers and parents or teachers, *illustrating your own point of view*, literally providing a picture of how you are thinking. "In the transition from the infant who is not cognizant of the products of his pen to the child who cares deeply about whether a mark has been made, a crucial realization has come about. . . . [It] is one of the first indications to the child of his own efficacy" (Gardner, 1980, p. 24). Elliot Eisner (2002) says, "Representation stabilizes the idea or image in a material and makes possible a dialogue with it . . . [allowing us to pay] . . . attention to relationships and attend to details" (p. 6).

The Group's Influence

When small groups form to draw together and teachers intentionally involve themselves in the children's work, drawing becomes a reciprocal process between oneself and others. Rinaldi (1992) says reciprocity is basic to all Reggio practices and is a main reason for learning to express yourself in a hundred languages. Eisner (2002) says that viewing children's art in

> social rather than individual terms . . . [shows] . . . that what they learn . . . is not simply . . . about dealing with a material; it is also a function of what they learn from others . . . social norms, models for behavior, opportunities to converse and share one's work with others . . . situations . . . which . . . can be crafted by the teacher. (p. 93)

Varieties of Expression

Languages, as used by Reggio educators, is a complex term. It encompasses the human capacity to speak, write, and manipulate words to express a limitless number of ideas in myriad ways *and* to manipulate entire systems. Gardner calls them intelligences; Feuerstein calls them modalities—numbers, musical tones, symbols, or physical movement like gesture and facial expression. Languages encompass the extraordinary variety of materials humans have employed for utilitarian and expressive purposes—obvious things like paper and mark makers (paints, inks, pencils), fabric, found objects, and feathers, and less obvious things like the skin, bone, stone, and cave wall that early humans employed for writing surfaces. Languages include intangible things like light, shadow, emotions, and relationships. Facility in languages also means using the tools that shape and attach materials—scissors, punch, hammer, chisel, ruler, stapler, tape, glue. Among the Hundred Languages are negotiating relationships, managing social situations, expressing emotions rationally, and showing empathy. It is mind-expanding to contemplate the range of expressive options available.

SIGNIFICANT WORK/FLUENT EXPRESSION

Malaguzzi frequently was asked to define creativity.

> Today the times do not seem to be favorable to creativity. . . . [It] seems it can only exist in high places, in the hands of specialists who are working abstractedly on it. I am convinced that each one of us possesses creativity, every working day, not only on Sundays. (L. Malaguzzi, Question & Answer at Diana School, Reggio Emilia, March 6, 1992)

The definition of creativity is elusive. The idea makes some people uncomfortable, as if, like Peter Pan's shadow, it might fly off unpredictably. Such people are more comfortable with what they can quantify than with intangibles like beauty or originality.

Children are ultimately creative. Each child actually creates for himself language and movement. While there are consistent outlines for children's progress from infancy onward, each individual's path is unique as is each child's relationship with materials—drawn strongly to some and barely to others. Yet every child has a romance with some type of material and some form of expression. The more varied the materials, the more intense the romance and the richer the experience. Sheppy received his first LEGOS® at age 2½, a pirate ship with several hundred pieces. He and his dad assembled it, Sheppy sometimes losing interest. At 4½ by himself he assembled vehicles with several hundred pieces, following schematic instructions easily and more accurately than his granddad or I. When just 6, he devised over 48 original vehicles and no longer wanted kits: "I'd rather make my own creations." Together we spent 4 hours classifying his large collection. As I handed him pieces, he'd say, "That's an axel because it has a connector." Or "That's a hinge; it has a different function." He had learned these distinctions as many experts do—through intense focus, long hours, and experimentation, having an idea then realizing it, acquiring the LEGO® language.

The MELC teachers were learning how to read and feed children's interests in diverse materials. So Coco, himself unusual in a school, was rendered in increasingly expressive ways in an expanding number of media—by school year 1995–1996 in clay sculpture, video, pen and ink drawings, photos, a book, a slide show, paint, music, and of course words. Each rendering was at least credible if not downright amazing, a significant, creative piece of work.

The ability to use so many modes of expression gives children a feeling of power. Those who lack competence in one area have alternative means of expression. Those who produce work that others admire develop self-confidence as they see others' respect for their work. Those who collaborate on projects build social competence. Those who overcome fear and anger, express empathy, or comfort others become emotionally competent. Children's work in varied modes reveals how each is thinking, enables adults to see what each has learned, and provides the basis for a dialogue.

Children's play is rehearsal for life, whether they imitate precisely what they have seen, improvise, or elaborate. In playing they make use of whatever is in the environment to scaffold themselves. It is our choice whether they support themselves with power rangers, karate chops, laser fights, and TV figures, or with open-ended materials that can be used in numerous ways. What they use influences what their intentions will be, how they express meaning, and whether they act empathetically. The environment we prepare is the raw material from which, with our collaboration, children derive purpose, construct ideas, and develop emotional competence.

CHAPTER 5

Toward Better Preschool Practices

An environment is a rich network of possible situations in which adults envision relationships that will facilitate children's work.

—Loris Malaguzzi
(Q & A, Diana School, March 6, 1992)

I N THIS CHAPTER I DESCRIBE HOW the MELC celebrated birthdays, inspired by Reggio birthday celebrations. Birthdays extended children's interest in staying with the same activity for many days or longer. Parties evolved as teachers' interests changed. A cornerstone of birthday celebrations was how teachers used time and space, the Reggio feature of this chapter. The gifts the children made were creative, complex, and original, evidence that their work was significant. The teaching principle has two aspects: techniques and curriculum, which together constitute practices. In this chapter we see a content-driven curriculum and techniques in which teachers actively listen to children, sometimes leading them, other times following their lead in a true collaboration.

HIGHLY ARTICULATED PRACTICES

Teaching techniques vary from *laissez-faire* to highly restrictive, and may be based on behaviorist, constructivist, or sociocultural theory, each of which implies a different technique. The technique called *intentional* teaching, as explained by Klein & Knitzer (2007), "is *directive* without using drill and kill strategies; . . . is fun for young children and promotes positive peer and teacher interactions." Teaching is intentional when teachers are sensitive, focused, and collaborative, and provide experiences requiring children to think in increasingly complex ways. Thus, intentional teaching addresses both technique and content.

Intentional Teaching

Intentional teaching is different than either free play or drill/kill. Free play is generally undirected, with little teacher intervention. Children imitate one another or what they see at home, in school, on the street, or on TV. The younger they are (ages 2–3), the more their play accommodates objects to what they have in mind—the broomstick becomes a horse, the rectangular block a car. From 3 on they generally use objects according to their design—housekeeping dishes are food servers, not building units or hats; puzzle pieces are not weapons, but form pictures. Intentional teaching means that teachers belong in play areas to scaffold thinking, introduce new content and concepts, and foster social/emotional growth. But research finds

> a great number of missed opportunities related to play . . . [and] children were denied the opportunities to develop social skills in their group and interactive play activities . . . [which] were never elaborated and soon deteriorated into rough-and-tumble activities. (Shin & Spodek, 1991, p. 6)

Play deserves the hallowed place it occupies in the views of many psychologists and educators, and children's non-school hours would seem ample for play. Sadly, long extended hours in day care, television, and rushed family schedules have cut into the time children once had for play. Concurrently, research on the social aspect of learning has revealed a new role for school playtime, proving that teachers' intervention in play fosters the development of content, concepts, and higher level thinking. But teacher education is silent on *how* teachers should intervene. This void deprives teachers of the know-how necessary to use play in the complex ways implied in sociocultural theory. Malaguzzi (cited in Rinaldi, 2006) said:

> We need a teacher who is sometimes the director, sometimes the set designer; sometimes the curtain and the backdrop, and sometimes the prompter. A teacher who is both sweet and stern, who is the electrician, who dispenses the paints and who is even the audience—the audience who watches, sometimes claps, sometimes remains silent, full of emotion, who sometimes judges with skepticism, and at other times applauds with enthusiasm. (p. 73)

In contrast to play and the kind of teaching Malaguzzi describes, drill/kill techniques prescribe detailed instructions for teachers' questions and children's responses, and program virtually every minute following teacher guides. Children are expected to be quiet and motionless. Teachers do almost all the talking and use external rewards, not internal control, to make children comply.

Finding a balance is difficult because teachers may not know what constitutes meaningful content or effective techniques. The first teachers hired in the MELC did not know how to listen to children, ask questions, hold conversations, or help children become self-regulated, four skills that enabled us to find a balance between *laissez-faire* and directive teaching and to turn *laissez-faire* responses (like those in the beginning of Chapter 1) into intentional teaching.

An Intentional Curriculum

Birthday celebrations are one example of myriad preschool activities that, in both content and teaching technique, exemplify intentional curricula.

The abovementioned characteristics and the following parameters, all seen in MELC birthdays, expand the definition of intentional curricula:

1. An activity grows out of problems that teachers, parents, or children are experiencing.
2. Parents collaborate extensively with teachers to develop ways to solve the problems.
3. The school environment—time and space—is structured to support the activity: Spaces are full of intriguing, well-organized materials, and time is flexible so activities can last however long is necessary to conclude a cycle of work, sometimes minutes, but typically hours, days, or weeks.
4. Groups of two to six children, never the whole class, define and undertake highly specific problems in close collaboration with teachers, and persist until the problems—all of which require different and increasingly sophisticated skills—are solved.
5. Teachers regularly discuss the purpose with children so they always have a goal in mind. But particulars of the outcome are open to new ideas throughout, even up to the activity's end.
6. Work is highly social, depends on relationships among children, and relies on children's increasing social and emotional competence. Children, with teachers, define goals, work through problems, and complete projects with a spirit of supportive collaboration and great sense of fun.
7. All content meets the definition of significant work—creative, complex, and original.
8. The emphasis in cognitive development is on thinking, not covering predetermined content: Younger children learn to focus attention, seek relevant cues, distinguish same/different, recognize patterns, and expand vocabulary. As time passes and these essential aspects of cognition crystallize, they learn higher level thinking skills like using analogies, metaphors, and symbols, sustaining attention for long periods, transforming ideas across differing modes of expression, seeking transcendent meaning in specific ideas, and thinking about how they are thinking.
9. Literacy and numeracy skills, which are essential for successful functioning in our culture, are integrated in activities. The purpose is not to drill abc/123s (although we used some Montessori language and math materials regularly), but to improve these skills because hardly any problem can be solved without them.
10. Teachers' growth—their sense of cognitive engagement, intellectual challenge, and fun—and their collaboration with one another are as important as the children's.

Watch for these principles as we follow 3 years of birthday celebrations.

EVOLUTION OF BIRTHDAYS

In their first meeting of the 1994–1995 school year, the teachers predicted what the children might learn that year. They identified eight areas.

1. Children would certainly learn more about the school environment.
2. They would increase their skill using different materials.
3. The year would begin by talking about summer activities in order to better understand one another's interests.
4. Relationships would deepen in many ways.
5. Children obviously would do something with the turtle just given to the school.
6. They would continue to communicate with their friends at La Villetta school in Reggio Emilia, a relationship kindled by Amelia Gambetti, fostered by the gifts and letters that La Villetta children made for MELC children and Amelia presented on her arrival from Italy. They would exchange faxes, an interest sparked by the La Villetta children's exploration of how fax machines work.
7. Of course, they would pursue their interest in Coco.
8. Birthday celebrations would occur on specific dates. These, the teachers decided, were the broad themes for the year.

FIGURE 5.1. Tesha's portrait of Brandi

Brandi's fifth birthday on September 23 was the first. Tesha (5-1) drew her portrait. The teachers recorded Brandi's three girlfriends' descriptions.

Brandi likes to play with me and Cemetria and Tesha. She didn't be my friend, but she is now. She likes to play with all the fun things like the Legos® and she likes to go into the Studio and play with clay. Her brother loves to play with her. At lunch time she loves to sit beside me and Angela. Her hair is black, she likes to wear bows in her hair.

Kevin's fourth birthday was the second of the year on September 26. Otis drew his portrait and with two others developed his description.

Kevin brings pinecones to the turtle everyday. He thought they were pine*apples*. He likes the turtle, the turtle is his friend. He likes the game on the playground with all those different colors where you have to run and run. He likes the sand table, the Music Room, puzzles, and blocks. He always wants to play outside and ride bikes.

Portraits and writing varied greatly, and reflected two important values—friendship and attention to detail. Artists and writers had different styles. From most portraits you could identify the child easily. Comments were spontaneous since they emerged from discussion. Descriptions covered everything—favorite activities, best friends, physical features, clothing, disposition. It was a wonderful year of birthdays, but hadn't always been so.

Changing a System

Birthday celebrations had a history. Procedures from 1992–1993 were not working. Left to parents with little support from teachers, birthday parties differed greatly, some overly elaborate, others too simple, making families competitive. Children whose birthdays weren't celebrated at all felt bereft. Routines had to be revamped. In October 1993 Amelia presented inspiring slides of Reggio birthdays. It led to new procedures.

Revamping the Parent Teacher Committee. Initial changes were made through the Parent Teacher Committee (PTC). It had a history too. In the school's first years (1989–1992) there was little in the way of a program. In 1992–1993 the program was ineffective: Parents vied for titles like President or Vice President without defined jobs or structure, so did nothing. Change—like taking away someone's title—was risky. But not changing was riskier. Sonya and Wendy's memo captures the mood: "Making the change from officers to a cooperative group was a risk. . . . What a fabulous change it has been! A parent told us after our second PTC meeting, 'It's really working!'" The new PTC had five parents and two teachers. Its purpose: "to support the school and maintain a high level of exchange with one another, then to share information with all the parents" (W. Baldwin & S. Shoptaugh, personal communication, October 27, 1993).

Devising New Procedures. *October 13, 1993.* The PTC's first meeting lasted an hour, mostly devoted to birthdays. The Committee proposed these procedures:

- Each child will have a birthday celebration at school. If a birthday does not fall on a school day, we will celebrate it on another day.
- The PTC will ask each parent to provide a cake, punch, and utensils. If this is not possible, we can assist as needed.
- Children at school will make a present for the birthday girl/boy.
- Wendy and Sonya will send memos informing parents of birthday celebrations at school.
- The school will maintain a birthday calendar showing each child's birthday by photo, symbol, and name.
- By celebrating birthdays, we value each child and support friendships.

The PTC asked all parents for comments and reported at its next meeting: *Everyone* liked the new procedures.

The teachers were elated, greatly relieved that no more birthdays would be missed. It would make the extra work involved worth the effort. Sonya and Wendy informed the PTC that Jennifer was already making the birthday calendar to hang in the Dining Room. A parent suggested that birthday children draw on the calendar to mark their birthdays, an idea the teachers loved. New procedures were ready to use. Three considerations dominated the teachers' thinking: (1) systems they'd have to create to support the new procedures, (2) the celebrations themselves, and, most complicated, (3) how experiences could, gradually, build children's capacities to make gifts for one another and forge the relationships that make good friends.

Two Trials. *October 8, 1993.* The first test of new procedures began. Miss Wendy asked Galeesa's four best girlfriends to decide on her present. They suggested a bundle of balloons inside a sheet suspended from the ceiling. The children had experienced bundling and hanging surprises for new children who were phased in over 2 to 3 weeks in September. Galeesa's friends knew she loved balloons and thought that balloons floating all around her would please her.

October 12. The four worked with Jennifer to make messages to attach to the balloons. They worked secretly, barely concealing their excitement, everyone wondering what they were doing. Galeesa beamed when she realized the huge bundle was for her and squealed with delight as balloons engulfed her. It was the birthday she'd always remember.

Frank's sixth birthday was on the 24th. Two days before, Galeesa, Lorian, and Tiara made his present—a book with his friends' photos, beautifully wrapped in paper they painted just for him. It reflected their knowledge that Frank loved books and had many friends. He was so happy and immediately *read* the pictures, recalling the context of each: "That when we played with the cherry blossoms." "There Coco; he hiding so Donnell won't find him." He carried the book around proudly showing it to everyone.

Ages ago the ability to *read* other humans was essential for survival. In asking best friends to conceive one another's presents, the teachers tapped into what Gardner (1983) calls interpersonal intelligence—knowing what motivates and makes others tick. This essential skill rarely appears in curricula, but as every teacher knows, students' preoccupation with one another's emotions can thoroughly distract them.

Deciding How to Document. At the staff meeting following Frank's party the teachers considered how to document birthdays. Documentation was as integral to birthday celebrations as to every other activity. It required foresight and much discussion to plan documentation of events that had not yet occurred and processes that were so new. The teachers reasoned they would need to display:

- A month-by-month list, January through December, of children's birthdays. They'd call it the Birthday Calendar.
- A real calendar, one month per page. They'd choose one with beautiful photos and hang it alongside the Birthday Calendar where children would find their name and month, then determine the day from the real calendar.
- A panel with photos and conversations of children making presents.
- A panel with photos taken at birthday parties.

FIGURE 5.2.
Discovering
the Birthday
Calendar

The biggest question was how to document gifts. Obviously birthday children would take the actual gift home! They settled on an 8½" x 11" loose-leaf, titled The Birthday Book, in which to display good-sized photos as records of the work involved in producing each gift. It would testify to how well the children knew one another, and reflect the deepening friendships generated by birthday activities.

Jennifer organized what she needed to document birthdays—three full boards for panels; each child's miniature photo, 1½" square, and symbol, the same size; fadeless art paper; the dates of everyone's birthday; the real calendar. Two other panels blank for now—one for gift-making, the other for celebrations—would raise expectations.

The finished Birthday Calendar was beautiful, names of the months down the left column in 48 point Palatino Linotype on an array of luscious colors—January lime green, February steely blue, March soft mauve. Mounted on lift-up rectangles of the same color were photo and symbol of children with birthdays that month. Beneath the rectangle was the date. The layout was precise, eye-catching, and interactive. To its left hung the real calendar with photos of the interiors of famous Italian buildings, each month a new architectural wonder. Entering the Dining Room, the children immediately spotted the panels. A large group clustered around, excited to see photos and symbols, eager to find theirs. Children become aware of birthdays by age 3. The calendar provided year-long recognition of this important day.

Prepared Minds

The success of birthday celebrations lay in other activities that indirectly prepared the children: The MELC's emphasis on friendship fostered a desire to surprise their friends, and the emphasis on problem solving enabled them to realize their grandiose ideas for presents. The teachers forged intentional intersections of these themes.

Understanding Birthdays. October had the most birthdays—six! November had none. But birthdays became the focus of many other activities, for example, they were a regular part of the children's imitative play in the Housekeeping area where children set the table for birthday parties, made birthday cakes, or held celebrations. Birthdays were topics of conversation among small groups who discussed, among other things, what birthdays are. On January 12 a group made a special trip to the post office. Cemetria explained: "It was Amelia's birthday. That's her package." On March 24 Miss Wendy included birthdays as one of nine agenda items at a parent meeting. Birthdays were imitated, discussed, and celebrated regularly.

Birthdays and Friendship. The topic of friendship was nurtured intentionally. Taking attendance each morning teachers asked the children how many of their friends were there and how many absent. It helped the children learn who was who. Once they knew one another, the activity morphed to *predicting* how many were present, then seeing if they were right. In early fall the children had many conversations about new friends soon to start school, planned parties, and made presents for them.

Friendship and message-making were closely connected. All fall a huge amount of message-making occurred: writing to friends and family by dictating to teachers or using the invented spelling typical of preschoolers. They talked about how to respond to the 4-year-olds at La Villetta who sent gifts and messages via Amelia, and faxes. They discussed the meaning of messages and clamored for teachers to read the notes in their mailboxes to individuals, small groups of friends, or everyone at morning meeting. Writing and receiving messages from friends, family, or abroad became a daily activity. It was fun finding messages in your mailbox. Friendships flourished. When winter flu hit, everyone worried about their friends, considered what to do, and decided to mail postcards, letters, and messages. Their surprise Valentines were especially loving. Birthday cards were specialized messages. Because of the intentional cultivation of friendship, children eagerly anticipated receiving personal notes.

Drawing to Observe Detail. Simultaneously, teachers encouraged children to observe carefully. In one project early in November new children became acquainted with Coco, observed him, discussed his features, then drew him. In another project, small groups studied parts of the body. Two others drew teachers' portraits for the Greeting Room. In winter, they began a project seeking colors and shapes in school and out, and drew, painted, cut, and collaged them.

Observations spilled into projects: Phillip, age 5, drew well-shaped likenesses of himself, which he translated from 2-D pencil drawings into 3-D clay sculptures. In small groups of five or six, 20 children studied the shapes of their bodies in preparation for drawing each other's portraits. Three children visited and drew Consuela, the museum's goat. Renee and Quatesha drew portraits of themselves and their families. Six children drew portraits of Frank's father, Mr. Taylor, who visited in his mailman's uniform. On the playground, four children observed their movements as they climbed and slid, described what they did and how, then drew themselves climbing and sliding. Four others noted their different heights, measured themselves, then drew their impressions.

Every grade school task requires attention to detail, as do most activities—dialing phones, writing checks, driving someplace particular. In early grades learning to attend to detail is essential for success in the 3-Rs. Drawing real objects or living things helps children learn to focus on detail. The emphasis in Reggio schools and the MELC on drawing recognizes the precision it requires. The teachers fine-tuned their ability to entice children to draw, to make accurate renderings, to express ideas in drawings as facilely as in words.

Beginning to Make Portraits. The themes of friendship and detailed drawing first merged early in November 1993. Miss Wendy and Sonya each had a conversation with a different group of eight children about friendship. Then the children paired off to draw each other's portraits. Ten days later as part of the photography project in which they were studying parts of the body, Frank and Tiara closely examined their faces in a mirror, discussed what they saw, then drew their observations. The next day, Cemetria studied her own face then drew a self-portrait. The day after she took pictures of some classmates' mouths, continuing the study of faces. The combined emphasis in 1993–1994 on friendship, on observation of detail, shape, and color, on drawing from life, and on creating portraits paved the way for drawing each other's portraits as birthday gifts 2 years later.

BIRTHDAYS AS CURRICULUM

With procedures in place and children prepared, birthdays ran smoothly. Over time they evolved, the teachers playing them as a theme, the way jazz musicians riff on a melody.

1993–1994: Elaborate Presents

Birthday parties acquired a rhythm: The teachers consulted the Birthday Calendar and highlighted upcoming birthdays in the monthly parent memo on Important Events. They decided it was important to talk enthusiastically at morning meeting about an upcoming birthday in order to rouse the children's excitement, choose the right present-makers, and make the best gifts. As Jennifer said, "Birthdays were a big project this year."

Selecting Present-Makers. The teachers carefully considered who should make presents. Selection was never arbitrary, but made in consultation with numerous children who, because they stayed together for 3 years, knew one another well. The teachers also considered who would work with the children making presents and what support they might need—another teacher's assistance? Jennifer's expertise? particular materials? a specific work area? The teacher working on the present gathered the best friends. If the children thought others might be better, the group changed. But finally a group jelled and held a great secret meeting. Lively discussions followed about what the birthday friend would like and continued until they reached consensus.

Making the present itself was challenging. Then, presents had to be wrapped and birthday cards made. Other aspects of a celebration had to be considered—when to hold it, what moment the gift should be presented, by whom, what should be said. Knowing one another well, the children had lots to say about these matters. Children's involvement grew from genuine needs of situations, as did parent involvement. The teachers structured and ran the school so children's involvement drove the curriculum.

Making the Gifts. The birthday child was guest of honor. Gifts always hit the mark and were truly awesome. Alonzo, greatly admired for transforming a 3-D sculpture to a life-size drawing, was given a coloring book of his three favorite friends' self-portraits. Four girls made Cemetria a calendar, a picture for each month outlined in black ink and colorfully painted. Miss Wendy worked on Howard's gift with three children. They knew because of his great interest in how turtles move that Howard would play the turtle in a performance they were planning. The perfect gift, they concluded, would be

FIGURE 5.3.
Making
Ronald's
robot

a papier mache turtle. Glenn's present was puzzles that Charles and Howard drew, then painted and cut. Willie and Akil made DeMarcos a checkerboard. Latricia received a beautiful necklace, and Renee a mobile. Lorian's pocketbook was made from a box, textured with papier mache, painted her favorite rich pink, and finished with a wide ribbon for a strap.

Ronald received a robot, body and head made from boxes, arms and legs from cardboard tubes; it was large and well-proportioned with fully elaborated features. Otis received two drums made from thick cylinders, decorated with geometric figures, and topped with tightly stretched rubber that resounded loudly when hit. Three boys made a truck for Xavier from a cardboard box and many found objects—large, elaborate, and with features appealing to young boys. Ceola, who frequently wrote messages, received printed stationery. Her friends dipped objects from the Studio—corks, erasers, cardboard tubes—into tempera and printed the top of each paper. When dry, papers were tied with ribbon and wrapped in tissue. Angela, who loved to correspond, received a wooden cigar box outfitted with a wide assortment of materials from the Communication Center. Each gift was perfect for its intended recipient, one-of-a-kind, and executed with painstaking care. There was no typical gift or party; themes were original, gifts and cards handmade.

Assessing Effects. Many factors were considered and much effort went into planning celebrations. Should it be for a single child, or a group? Was a holiday being celebrated simultaneously? If so, it might be exciting to hold the party with lots of parents present. Did many birthdays fall together? If so, would those children enjoy celebrating together? Or, did a child need the sole focus on her? At year-end they held a *big* celebration for the five with summer birthdays.

The teachers sent parents 15 questions about birthdays. Asked what the children did with their presents, Alonzo's mother said his sat on his dresser. He talked about the present, but wouldn't let anyone touch it. Xavier's said his stayed on a shelf in the living room where everyone could see it. Latricia's mother said Latricia thought it was great that she could make a present for someone and share such a special day with classmates she loves so much.

1994–1995: Portraits in Picture and Word

After two early October birthday celebrations, the teachers spent a full meeting re-evaluating procedures. They discussed what they liked about the system, how to make birthdays more celebratory, what to change, and why. How should they document birthdays this year? How could they preserve last year's memories while making room for documentation of this year's? The prior year had gone well, so provided a good basis for improvement.

Changing Procedures. It was customary to invite all families to every birthday, and a big problem surfaced immediately. Last year's panel was still hanging, and new families were upset at not finding their child! The teachers were embarrassed, realizing it was disrespectful to have an outdated panel about something so important. Jennifer immediately began a new panel *in progress*: They would leave blank spaces for portraits and written descriptions of all 36 children and would mount small-sized copies during the celebration. By year-end, everyone would be represented on one big panel in chronologic order by birthday. Birthdays never became boring because the teachers continually made variations.

The first 2 birthdays were celebrated in September, the next on October 2, and two on October 11. The teachers finished their analyses in time for the sixth birthday of the year—Stefan's fourth birthday on October 16. Studying the celebration critically they saw need for several improvements. They should:

- remember to sit at the children's level;
- place tables and chairs so parents could be closer to their own child;
- generate more excitement, although how was not clear;
- focus attention on the birthday child by passing the portrait around for all to see and reading the description.
- play music after singing "Happy Birthday."

There were two more October birthdays. As Thomas said, "We have *lots* of birthdays in October!" Analyzing them the teachers concluded they had met their goal: Celebrations more fully respected the children, who loved the portraits and written descriptions.

October 28. The last October birthday was celebrated on the same day as Octoberfest, the fall tradition that mixed families, pumpkins, food, and frolic. The celebration began with Thomas's birthday party, followed by carving and decorating pumpkins. Parents signed up to bring everything needed. In critiquing the event, teachers noticed that the pumpkin activity brought parents and children together—both individual families and groups of families. Combining birthday and holiday made the birthday more festive. However, they had not planned adequately and needed to pay as much attention to detail outdoors as they did indoors. This analysis, like earlier ones, informed future birthdays. By November the procedure was well-established and teachers felt confident that celebrations would go well this year.

Making Portraits. Best friends analyzed the birthday child. One drew the portrait. The whole group described their friend, then the teacher read the description aloud and they edited until it was just right. The portrait and words, which became part of the birthday panel, revealed each child's many different interests, physical characteristics, and personality. The blank space on the panel—waiting for the next celebration—greatly heightened expectations.

December 13. E. C.'s description, fourth birthday:

> E. C. is brown and light-skinned. He got black eyes with black balls. He's got a round face like a ball. He's got black hair and he got his hair cut. E. C. likes to run all the time, he likes Power Rangers, playing games, and setting up lunch. He like the computers, he *loves* the computers. . . . He be playing it every day and he don't want to leave.

Ceola and Tamika (4-8) wrote about Latricia whose birthday was January 24.

> Latricia eyebrows black. She black. She wear her hair in corn rows. We friends, Ceola, Paula, and me [Tamika] and Latricia. We like to go in the house, in the block area, and in LEGO®; we always go together. We like to dress up, we play Halloween. She wears ballerina clothes. We dress up like girls, we dress like moms. She puts on high heels and puts the coat on.

The biggest change was not making a *thing*. One reason was to keep gift-making interesting, another to use portraits as a way to focus on relationships and self-identification. The new procedure heightened the emphasis on friendship and reinforced each child's uniqueness, thus joining two of the MELC's most important goals. Above all, it kept the teachers from becoming stale.

Learning Who We Are. *November 17.* Miss Wendy gathered six older children who had been in the school 2 or 3 years to discuss what a birthday is. The teachers wanted to learn what the children understood, what their expectations were, and how they liked birthday celebrations this year. The next birthday was not until December 13, so there was time to incorporate the children's reactions. To their surprise, they found some children did not yet know one another's names, much less birthday procedures.

The teachers were still acquainting—and reacquainting—children with the environment. To better acquaint them with one another, the teachers played games with photos and symbols, two different ways for children to recognize one another. In the MELC every family, on its first visit, chose a symbol from a huge collection. Some were realistic—vehicles, animals, common items; others were designs—shapes, snowflakes, crosses. Children kept the same symbol for 3 years. Symbols appeared everywhere—on cubbies, bathroom possessions and cots, folders of work, and wherever a system—like the 1993–1994 Birthday Calendar—required personal identification. Children who are not yet reading remember an image more readily than an abstract string of letters. The children loved symbols and quickly learned to recognize one another's. "Because symbols are a step toward understanding the significance of writing, they are important on the journey to literacy" (Lewin-Benham, 2006, p. 107).

A Curriculum Established. Eight children had February birthdays, and, after consulting the PTC, the teachers decided on one big celebration on Valentine's Day. Fourteen children prepared for it: Eight drew portraits and 13 wrote descriptions. Eighteen birthdays remained. By this time, teachers had the procedures down pat. Genet oversaw drawing the portraits, then recorded comments by small groups of best friends. There was one big party for May birthdays. Seven families prepared, three transforming the Dining Room with streamers, balloons, surprises, and matching tablecloth, napkins, and hats.

FIGURE 5.4.
Latricia
receives
her
portrait

The others bought a cake with names and birth dates of all seven children. The children were overwhelmed by their Dining Room's appearance. Summer birthdays were celebrated on the playground. Each child received her own description mounted on the back of her portrait, carefully wrapped by her friends. At year-end the teachers gave every child a book, *A Collection of Birthday Portraits*. The introduction said the children had learned that friends are both individuals and groups, that they knew they had best friends, but also realized there was a larger community and recognized commonalities among all their classmates.

MELC birthday celebrations and the emphasis on friendship stand in stark contrast to other schools I have visited, ones with identical demographics to the MELC. Huge charts are titled Fight-Free Days; they show the number of fights per month per grade, including the pre-Ks—and there are many. Fighting characterizes relationships among children when the value of friendship is not brought to the fore intentionally in frequent and genuine activities.

Next Years: Song and Dance

Everyone felt that birthday celebrations were running smoothly. But, to keep interest piqued, the teachers changed the present, to a song in 1995–1996 and to a dance in 1996–1997. Some were highly original, others were derived from songs and dances the children had learned. There were heavy negotiations: Some wanted rhyme, others to insert phrases from songs they heard on the radio, or routines from dances they saw on TV. It took hours of singing, talking, debating, humming, rewriting, and more singing to create a song, and equal time to choose the music and put together the steps of a dance. Some used instruments to accompany themselves. Whatever the children composed, the teachers wrote, and the children practiced, then performed. Parents were always informed and present at birthday celebrations. The teachers recorded the song or videotaped the dance as each child's gift.

A NEW TIME/SPACE PARADIGM

Typical preschool curricula run on lesson plans. Activities in Reggio classrooms run on a philosophy, a cornerstone of which is how to make use of time and space. The intersection of time and space defines the curriculum.

Time-Structured Preschool

Here is a typical preschool lesson plan, structured by time, based on the textbook *Total Learning* (Hendrick, 1994, pp. 82–84):

> 7:30–9:00 Tabletop activities including books about babies; play outside a while, weather permitting. Collect baby pictures.

Explanation: The theme-for-the-week is babies because one family has a new baby.

9:00–9:15 Bathroom transition.

9:15–9:45 Breakfast.

9:45–10:15 Story—*Curious George Goes to the Hospital*; song—"Rock A Bye Baby"; discuss what it was like when you were a baby; poem—"Five Little Monkeys" (later, outside, children will bounce on a mattress).

Explanation: Hospitals must be mentioned because one child has an operation scheduled.

10:15–11:45 Self-selected activity: Hospital and baby play (outside, weather permitting), blocks, make salad, make dough, play outside.

11:45–12:00 Bathroom transition.

12:00–12:30 Lunch.

12:30–12:45 Transition to nap.

1:00–2:30 Nap.

2:30–3:00 Transition.

2:30–3:15 Snack.

2:30–4:30 Self-selected activity outdoors with water play, baby buggies, and usual outdoor activities.

4:30–5:15 Story time, quiet play. Mother of African American twins shows their baby book to the group.

Hendrick (1994) lists mainly toileting, hand washing, and dismissal routines as transitions, with singing or discussion to "move transition along" (p. 83). Hendrick advises, "It is always possible to experiment with a variation for a week or two and then go back to the previous pattern if the change fails to solve the difficulty," and defines difficulties as congestion, or scuffling in the bathroom, or restlessness at group time. (p. 78). Notice the time demarcations, the predetermined discussion topic, and the lack of challenging activity. Such schedules constrain choices and eliminate spontaneity. The teacher chooses themes, books, questions, visitors. Other than the theme, nothing carries forward from day to day. The feeling conveyed is that teaching is a chore: "The major problem in scheduling that full-day centers must take into account is the problem of monotony and lack of variety in the curriculum that results from teacher fatigue and burnout" (p. 81).

Although most of us would agree that basing curriculum on the children's concerns and interests is the best way to motivate learning, the truth is that most curriculum ideas are chosen by teachers because they already have a box of learning materials available or . . . an activity book that offers lots of ideas on that subject. The reality of the daily teaching grind forces me to admit it may be necessary to rely on such embalmed resources from time to time. (p. 64)

Space-Structured Preschool

Contrast an MELC day, which might (or might not) look like Sonya's notes, structured by space and continuing activities:

December 9, 1993, 31 children present
Big Room, Morning Meeting:
—Linda shared holiday things she brought.
—Took attendance, discussed what the date is.

Explanation: Taking attendance was part of two projects, one on numbers, the other an overarching project on friendship that incorporated many other projects, like birthdays and messages, and was part of the school's bedrock.

—Read memo going home to parents.

Explanation: The memo to parents, read during morning meeting, contained minutes from the prior afternoon's PTC meeting. All memos were read to the children, discussed with them, and frequently decorated by them, an important way to foster ties between school and home.

—Anticipated Xavier's birthday.

Explanation: Anticipating Xavier's birthday was part of the teachers' intent to develop friendship by raising children's awareness of one another and celebrating important events.

Big Room:
—Children worked in block, train, house, & dress-up areas & drew at table.

Explanation: Blocks, trains, house, dress-up, and water hole were activities chosen by children; they probably began and ended that morning unless children wanted to save their constructions. All other activities were projects, carried over from prior days and continuing.

Lab:
—Tyresha, Ronald, Paul, Tesha, & Alex constructed their ideas about the environment using materials and shapes.

Explanation: An on-going project on shapes.

Communication Center:
—Frank, Tiara, Lorian, & Renee discussed the meaning of messages with Miss Wendy, then gathered and read notes from their mailboxes.

Explanation: Messages were the center, literally and figuratively, of the MELC (Chapter 6).

Water Hole:
—Group of eight explored water with Genet.

Explanation: Water play was an area requiring supervision.

Studio:
—Children made birthday cards.

Explanation: Part of the curriculum on birthdays.

Jennifer's daily diary for the same morning records that at their regular morning meeting before school began the teachers talked about where each teacher would be based on notes of yesterday's activities.

The reference to "holiday items Linda brought" reflected this November 29 letter to parents requesting help in reinforcing a classroom activity:

We want to encourage the children's investigation of this season. Will you help us support them by finding things at home that remind them of this holiday and bringing these items to school? For example:

ornaments	stickers	tinsel	bows
nut crackers	ribbon	cards	candy canes
stockings	stars	candles	angels

Please don't buy anything!! We only want small things the children can share from home without causing any difficulties. By bringing holiday objects, the children can make more connections about what is happening around them and thereby have a deeper understanding of their reality.

Explanation: Teachers tried to make families aware of what was going on at school and why, to engage them in activities, and to honor families' individual cultural traditions.

The first schedule exemplifies a typical free-play preschool with no evidence of small-group work toward a goal that excites and challenges children. In contrast, MELC activities were not preplanned, but grew from what was happening in school, taking place in the community, or occurring in the culture. Time takes on new meaning when every activity is connected to something else; it is not something to *fill* or *get through*. It is a resource like glue or paper, but more precious. Space also is more precious: If most of the children are on their own while the rest are involved in a project with a teacher, the options from which they are free to choose *must* be highly engaging.

Well-Designed Spaces

Vea Vecchi (2002) says typical early childhood environments are "reductive, babyish, and stereotyped" (p. 11). What visitors most readily grasp about Reggio schools is their expansiveness, sophistication, and originality, and children's copious work in diverse media. This is not accidental, but results from intensely considered, intentional decisions in which teachers constantly refine the space, much as the MELC teachers refined birthday procedures.

Design choices were evident throughout the MELC and impacted every aspect of the MELC's spaces—materials storage, Studio layout, containers, presentation of materials for activities. Every space was detailed so it appealed to children, was functional, and stimulated diverse outcomes. Planning and making birthday gifts increased children's understanding of how the school's different areas functioned, because they used resources from throughout the school for the gifts. Each gift represented significant work produced in the context of a highly intentional curriculum in which space was intricately planned and time entirely fluid. "To organize the space is to determine how the time will be used" (Lewin-Benham, 2006, p. 18). Preparing for parties made children keenly aware of time—both future, like calendars reflect, and present, like having gifts ready *today*!

INTENTIONAL CONTENT, INTENTIONAL TECHNIQUES

Research confirms our observation of the MELC children's growth. Their growth was consistent with the outcomes of research on Vygotskian-based practices, which found statistically significant gains in cognitive, language, and social development. The research provides

> Rigorous evidence that a curriculum model that departs from some of the conventional ways of conceptualizing early childhood education may be an effective option for improving learning and development . . . [and] the academic progress of disadvantaged children while also emphasizing play. (Barnett, Yarosz, Thomas, & Hornbeck, 2006, p. 26)

The conventional wisdom about early childhood practices is confusing: It advocates depth in content, but prescribes disjointed themes; it suggests teacher/child collaboration, but describes roles in which teachers mainly dominate or withdraw. What I have tried to show in this chapter is how the themes of this book connect: how specific features of the Reggio Approach foster significant work that is original, complex, and creative and how techniques—content and teaching—look in highly articulated practices. I have tried to show how content can have depth, and teaching can be based on collaboration. And I have tried to show how teachers scaffold children's interests with their own adult skills and approach everything by listening to children, asking questions, and orchestrating conversations, all the while requiring children to be self-regulated. The teacher who can simultaneously juggle these techniques will, in the well-known words of Margaret Mead, "raise the level of the dialogue." By this I mean deepening children's passion for big ideas through discussion and collaborating with them to realize complex ideas in concrete, tangible form. The process of making birthday gifts is one content area—with endless variations—in which teachers drew on children's big ideas and helped them articulate those ideas in elaborate and skilled constructions.

CHAPTER 6

Message-Making: Impetus for Parent Involvement and Literacy

Children are hungry to make friends and they learn to write in order to send messages. These are important documents, very carefully written.
—Loris Malaguzzi
(Q & A, Diana School, March 6, 1992)

THE COMMUNICATION CENTER, A VERY SMALL but vital area, was centrally located and in many ways the heart of the MELC. It was designed for the purpose of making and sending messages, and stimulated the children to communicate with everyone in their lives. Gradually from 1993–1994 to 1995–1996 it expanded to include many different ways to communicate, message-making remaining a strong focus. The children sent messages to their friends, families, teachers, Coco, the turtle, me, and children in other schools across the city and across the ocean. The Reggio feature central to this chapter is parent involvement; the teaching principle is emerging literacy.

Were you reading the documentation in early Fall 1994, you would learn about the children's communication—that their friendships with one another were deepening; individual children were learning about themselves through their friendships and were discovering the pleasure in sharing ideas and experiences. You would read that friendships budded from the conversations, drawings, and presents they made one another. And, you would learn about messages, the medium for extensive written communication, many prepared for their families.

Here I show how the teachers intentionally used messages to increase children's ability to communicate and draw families in, and how message-writing led to other communication projects, all supported—or contextualized—by the Communication Center. I describe how the design of the Communication Center supported its function, and how important message-making became for emerging literacy, the teaching principle of this chapter.

THE MESSAGE CENTER

Messages were made at the workbench in the Communication Center or sometimes at the typewriter, which stood on a nearby table. They were made for friends and sent and received in the 36 mailboxes that stood prominently nearby. The Communication Center provided a context for literacy and stimulated the children's emerging literacy skills.

A Context for Literacy

Message-writing began in 1992–1993 after the redesign of the MELC and the addition of the Communication Center. From the first the children were attracted to the Center. Its function was clear from its design. Anyone who works in an office might envy it: fully stocked with an enticing array of papers and writing implements, equipped with every conceivable tool to alter paper, organized so everything was readily accessible. Scissors, punches, embossers, varied erasers, and sharpeners were in one area. Inch/centimeter rulers, templates, and special-purpose rulers, like protractors, hung from adjacent hooks. Fasteners—brads, colored paper clips, gold paper clips, circular clips, tiny clips, rubber bands—were each in their own bin. Adhesives were lined up on the counter—an assortment of glues, tapes, and double-sided sticky tabs. A section of an adjacent wall 2-feet deep held markers—black lead pencils, fine-line ink pens, colored fine-line markers, and a great range of colored pencils. How materials were displayed varied as much as the materials themselves: Some containers hung on a grid system above the workbench; others stood on the bench itself. Some closed containers tilted open; others had lids, others flip-tops. All were transparent Plexiglas so items were always in sight, and there was easy access to items inside. Anyone who ever received a letter could deduce the Center's purpose, which was to share your thoughts and feelings with people for whom you cared, but without speaking.

Figure 6.1.
Communication
Center

FIGURE 6.2.
Looking
for
messages

We intended to spark children's interest in reading and writing by sending and receiving messages. Reading and writing skills are often so decontextualized that children have no sense of their purpose. Sending messages at the Communication Center provided a *purpose* for reading and writing long before children learned the skills.

Evolution of Message-Making

Work in the Communication Center evolved over 3 years—from simple gifts to full-blown messages of all kinds. Other activities filtered into the Center and gradually expanded its functions.

Learning to Send and Receive. Messages began as simple marks on paper, or a pretty piece of paper folded or wadded. That year the excitement of getting something into someone's mailbox and finding something in yours was the dominant attraction. The mailboxes were opaque with easy-to-lift doors. Not being able to see whether something was inside made the children expectant, like Ceola: "Maybe a surprise in here for my mommy." There was extra excitement when they found a gift—like jewelry, a carefully drawn picture, or an appealing piece of paper.

Initially the teachers wrote what the children said on the messages, helping them realize they could say something specific.

TYRESHA: "I wrote Tiara name and drew her a picture." They learned that messages could be sent to a particular person.

ALEX: "I mail a letter to Alonzo. I like Alonzo."

Learning to Send Thoughts. Small groups were touring the school with a teacher and discussing each area, one at a time, learning how each functioned. At the Communication Center rather than putting something in mailboxes they discussed how the Center functioned. For example, there was space for only four chairs so only four children could work there at one time. At morning meetings teachers frequently reinforced each area's functions and rules, as Miss Wendy did in May when she asked Angela to explain what she had done that morning.

ANGELA, displaying a sealed envelope: "I made this for Brandi."

MISS WENDY: "Can you tell us *what* you made?"

ANGELA: "It's a happy face."

MISS WENDY: "Why don't you put it in Brandi's mailbox?"

Such focus, day after day, impressed the function of the Communication Center on the children's minds. Over time the focus shifted from the act of sending to the content. Determining *what* to send was a more complex endeavor than the mere acts of deposit/seek/find. Adults take things for granted that are new to children. It made sense for the idea of send/receive—the *how* of communication—to become well-established before focusing on the *what*. Curricula sometimes push frantically ahead, leaving children's understanding behind. In the MELC there was tremendous repetition, which built understanding, yet did not bore the children because it involved activity that varied continuously.

Expanding the Content of Messages. The Communication Center came into its own as the children's expectations went beyond merely writing and reading messages. Those who had been in the MELC for 3 years and were now 5-year-olds realized the importance of messages in their friendships with one another. They recognized that the differences among messages revealed how special a friend was. An advantage in the same children's remaining together and with the same teachers for 3 years is that understanding expands to the transcendent meaning in an activity, in this case the sustaining nature of friendships. Cemetria knew exactly what kind of message her friend Tesha needed. Tesha had been dispossessed when a stranger moved into her bed; Tesha reported this in great distress, although the family never disclosed the circumstances and the preschooler couldn't fathom or was unable to express why. Cemetria understood Tesha's anguish: "I am putting Tesha picture in the mailbox. I made Tesha a bed. She is sleeping in a bed all by herself." The message, from a caring, perceptive friend, addressed Tesha's deepest concern.

Message-making is straightforward for an adult; not so for children. First something must stimulate a desire to communicate. Then that desire must be harnessed and translated into action. The action is complex—understanding what you want to say, choosing a medium in which to speak, rendering your thought in tangible form, transmitting it to a receiver. Modern communication is based on sophisticated models of the relationship between sender and receiver, first codified by Communication Professor Colon Cherry. He laid considerable groundwork in the field of Information Theory by recognizing that perception, a key element in communication, was not a passive process, but a variety of behaviors by which one orients oneself mentally in relation to the outside world, as part of the process of making sense of it (1957). Using an expanding range of media, the preschoolers were making their first foray into the world of communication. While they did not use terms like *perception, information exchange,* or *mental orientation,* they were engaged in all these processes.

Sending Messages Home

By early December 1994 the mailboxes were overflowing! Partly to make room so past messages would not impede delivery of future ones and partly to spark families' interest, on a Friday three teachers organized bags for children to take the messages home and share with their families. Teachers and children also wrote a memo asking families to create a message with their child to send to school. On Monday, there was bustling activity as the children sought out one another's mailboxes to deposit the messages. Some children wrote to one single friend, others to many. That Tuesday at morning meeting long conversations ensued as the teachers read all the messages. Cemetria remarked: "If you write me, I'll write you back!" She expressed what many children were coming to understand—the power of written communication to make something happen. A Montessori activity does just that. You hand a child a small slip of folded paper; inside is a message: Feed the fish. Or, Give me a kiss. Children have an "aha" moment when they realize silent abstract shapes cause big actions. The significance is that they learn the *function* of writing, that *their* writing can make someone do something or feel better.

Documenting Message-Making

One panel showed the flow of message-making, breaking the complex task into components: creating the message, sometimes making a gift as well, enclosing the message in a suitable envelope, finding the recipient's mailbox, then watching—sometimes surreptitiously, sometimes overtly—for the reaction. Otis described it: "I got Anthony name right here. I am putting it on his letter and put it in the mailbox so he can find it."

Another panel showed how messages take on their own life. Photos showed a recipient asking the sender to read the message. Children differ markedly in when and how easily they learn decoding skills. Some senders remembered precisely what they had said. A few actually read the words. Other times neither receiver nor sender could puzzle out the letters and had to ask a teacher. Sometimes a child shared a message with the full class at morning meeting. As it became clear that particular children were most engaged, message-making became a project for a regular group. Studying the panels, you could see that the Communication Center was truly the hub in a

FIGURE **6.3.**
Message-
covered
corner
walls

network packed with traffic in relationships. When they observed Valentine's Day, *the* message-sending holiday, *everyone* made cards for their friends. Traffic in messages branched, as networks do, into a rich array of projects.

Exploring Faxes

In mid-December 1994 a fax arrived from the La Villetta children. It was prior to the email era and faxing was state-of-the-art for *instant* communication. Mail from Italy would have taken weeks, postponing results for too long. With fax machines at both schools, Amelia had introduced this means of communication by asking her Italian children to send a fax to her Washington children on the day of her arrival. The fax was full of drawings, stories, responses to the MELC children's questions, and new questions for us. It provided an opportunity to learn about a new medium. We were particularly excited to read the Italian children's descriptions of activities similar to ours.

Their fax told how each day they counted and wrote down the number of children present; they described familiar games; both schools were making an advent calendar. We also noticed differences. The Italian children's references to their lunch routine prompted our children, not knowing about kitchens in schools, to ask, "What's a cook?"

The La Villetta children had explored the fax, developed theories of how it works, and translated their theories into elaborate drawings. The MELC children followed suit. Five children developed theories about how a fax machine works. Five different theories emerged, raising many questions. The children decided to ask Amelia and with the teachers' help developed a written list of questions. Amelia suggested asking the La Villetta children themselves. The children loved the idea and were excited about waiting at the phone to receive a fax at a predetermined time.

After Christmas, with interest in fax machines still high, Jennifer and Sonya read the children's theories back to them, then discussed how they could draw them. This was a challenge—the first time anyone at the MELC tried to represent a theory in pictures. The children listened to one another carefully, commented on one another's ideas, and provided suggestions if someone was stuck. Big challenges elicit children's serious attention. They know the difference between significant activity and time fillers. They understand what others in their culture value and pay close attention to it. As they began to draw, lively discussion continued, some asking questions, others answering, building on one another's responses. The result was more detailed drawings than ever before, with surprising articulation showing cables, buttons, and panels. The teachers replaced two earlier panels about messages with documentation about faxing.

Socially Constructing Knowledge

Drawings can be "a platform for discussion. . . . [They] help children develop a common referent and this in turn helps them reconstruct their misconceptions" (Forman, 1992, pp. 186–187). Reggio teachers engage children in frequent and sustained dialogue about their drawings. In these discussions children and teachers examine inconsistencies between words and pictures. Teachers may ask children to reinterpret drawings in three-dimensional models, another way to confront inconsistencies. For example, Alonzo, turning a large 3-D sculpture of a dinosaur into a drawing of the same proportion, had repeated problems rendering details like the shape and size of the tail. With Jennifer he observed his attempts and kept correcting his drawing until he got it right, showing "that a very young child will stick to an enormously challenging project . . . [which] was a big learning process for [the teacher]" (Lewin-Benham, 2006, p. 126).

Sometimes children correct their own misconception, sometimes others in the group do; sometimes the inconsistency stands, waiting for further experience or discussion. The dialogue among the group is the driving factor in this kind of critical thinking. Experiences like the children's theorizing about the fax machine helped the MELC teachers learn the technique of developing socially constructed knowledge.

COMMUNICATION EXPANDS

In 1994–1995 the children, now practiced in message-making, deepened their relationships by using the Communication Center to create books and write postcards. They investigated the post office to learn what actually happens to letters. Work at the Communication Center began to expand.

Beginning a New Relationship

There was a surprise in December 1994: Third graders from Georgetown Day School, meeting their school's commitment to community service, wrote and illustrated 58 books for the MELC, one made especially for each child, the others for the classroom library. The MELC children immediately wanted to know more about the authors who, it seemed, knew them well! A new relationship began. In their thank you letter, the children asked how the books were made. When the third graders' 60-hour community service commitment was satisfied, Jennifer remade the panel about the experience into a book.

The MELC children were eager to meet the Georgetown Day students who, unlike their La Villetta friends, were nearby. They had many ideas for surprises to make for the third graders. The exchange sparked the MELC children's interest in writing books about one another. The significance was that the children were enlarging their uses for writing. Some asked the teachers or their friends to write for them. Others wrote words themselves, spelling phonetically in irregularly shaped letters and randomly placing words as preschoolers do when they begin to write. The writing resulted from a network of activities—studying shapes, collecting alphabet letters at home, photographing objects resembling letters, using the Montessori sandpaper letters and movable alphabet—but occurred mainly as a natural outgrowth of message-making. Children begin to write spontaneously when they are in an environment where they see writing happening and comprehend its importance. At the MELC the children not only saw writing, but were involved in writing themselves.

Writing Postcards

The MELC was on several postcard lists—Amelia Gambetti and Giovanni Piazza, La Villetta's *atelierista*, sent postcards from Italy; I sent postcards whenever I traveled; the teachers sent postcards from their vacations. To provide a context, the teachers put all the postcards in transparent envelopes and hung them, visible and accessible, in the Communication Center. Pouring over them, as they did frequently, the children gained firsthand experience with another form of written communication. How, they wondered, did the postcards arrive at school?

The teachers addressed that question by adding postcard-writing as a new activity at the Communication Center. Now they could send postcards from school to home, a new way to involve families. Because the children had been mainly receivers of postcards, the teachers decided they should be senders also. Blank postcards for children to send one another over Christmas vacation went home in a bag. An accompanying memo explained that the postcards would enable the children to continue an activity they enjoyed and develop a new aspect of friendship—receiving and sending mail. Shortly after vacation, the children brought all the postcards they received to be read at morning meeting. Responses were enthusiastic. Each child recounted a memory of writing or receiving a card. Sending postcards was hot! The teachers added a stock of blank postcards so they could draw on one side. Word spread and soon everyone was sending postcards to their families or friends.

But the main impact was unanticipated: The experience ignited a huge curiosity—all over the school—about how postcards get from house to house. In one discussion four children wondered what happens to letters after you put them in a mail box. (Haven't we all!) In the block corner children made vehicles to transport messages. It stimulated a big project—how mail travels—and new experiences followed about complex systems that support a literate society.

Learning About Addresses

Early in February and unrelated to the communications activities, Miss Wendy was playing games to help children learn their addresses. It dawned on Alex that what they were learning had something to do with the postcards they received. It was one of those flashes in which the brain connects two heretofore disparate ideas: He grasped the relation between sending postcards and addressing them. His excitement released a flurry of activity, the children preparing postcards for Miss Wendy to address and mail. The teachers decided this was important, and Miss Wendy and the eight oldest children began writing or drawing postcards and addressing them to friends at their homes. The activity continued all month.

Also in February the children needed an address for another purpose—a thank you letter they wrote to a donor who had given the school a camera and tape recorder. They had long conversations.

> Miss Wendy, pointing to an address: "What does this tell us?"
> Alonzo: "When the mailman see this he knows where to take it."
> Quatesha: "I think they are just words that people read."
> Miss Wendy: "On the first line what would you find?"
> Quatesha: "Maybe MELC school or Renee's name."
> DeMarcos: "That's easy, like 904 2nd Street, NE, Washington, D.C., USA."
> Alonzo: "No, DeMarcos, Washington, D.C., go at the bottom 'cause that's where we live."
> Miss Wendy: "What does the number tell you?"
> Alonzo: "The numbers on the house so the mailman can give you and your neighbors ya'll letters."
> Miss Wendy: "What are addresses?"
> Tiara: "They are things that you call people on the phone."
> Quatesha: "No! Addresses are things that you put on your letters, like when I write to Renee."

The conversations show what different things the children knew. Conversation always tells teachers a great deal about what children know. Immediately after the conversation, they wrote postcards or letters to their moms. Quatesha echoed many of the children's feelings: "I like writing to my mom because she was gonna be surprise to get this card." They learned about addresses because they needed to use them, not because they were an arbitrary unit in a preset curriculum.

More lengthy discussions occurred—exactly where should you put the address? What are return addresses? zip codes? When do you use USA? What do stamps do? What do they cost? Tiara thought stamps cost 50 or maybe 500 thousand dollars. Alonzo thought about 500 dollars, DeMarcos about 30 seconds. All deduced correctly that letters cost more to mail than postcards because letters are bigger. Concepts about quantity and the cost of items rarely develop in preschool. Street, city, state, country hierarchies are also confusing to 4- and 5-year-olds.

The contexts in which writing occurred were expanding. Simultaneously, Miss Wendy was playing the sound game, using sandpaper letters, and dictating simple words for the children to spell with the movable alphabet, Montessori methods that teach children to connect letters and sounds, a skill essential for reading. Together the contextual and skill-building experiences provided strong support for literacy.

Visiting the Post Office

January 5. Twelve children walked to the post office with Sonya, Genet, and an intern. The immediate purpose was to mail a package to Amelia, the ultimate purpose to find out what happens there. The walk itself was exciting: through Union Station, across North Capitol Street, a heavily trafficked bus route and major thoroughfare jammed with postal vehicles coming and going. The post office, a historic structure close to the U.S. Capitol, was awesome—imposing façade, marble floors, fancy brass mailboxes, ornate windows with brass bars and a clerk behind each, serving long lines of people.

The children noticed everything and talked about the differences between these mailboxes and theirs at school. They used the weight scale, an oversized brass affair. A postal worker, seeing the children's excitement, invited them to the floor of the workroom where mail is collected, sorted, and sent, and gave *them* mail to sort! They themselves took Amelia's package to the bin where its journey to Italy would begin. As they left, greatly excited, they jostled their way to a pigeonholed table to collect forms—registered mail notices, certified letter labels, mailing receipts—the government's assurance that mail is handled with integrity.

By Friday it was clear to the teachers which six children were most interested in the mail system. Sonya gathered them to discuss how the forms they collected were used. She accorded them significant attention, eliciting the children's ideas and elaborating on the purpose of each. What could be more removed from preschoolers' experience than these forms? Sonya's serious discussion of papers that, in other practices might have been discarded thoughtlessly, is a hallmark of intentional teaching.

On Monday seven of the twelve children who had visited the post office drew pictures of the trip. Paula drew the walk with children holding hands.

Tesha drew a map of how to walk there. Otis drew himself and Alex as partners and the post office's exterior. Alex began a bus, but started over, adding the street outside with trees and snow. Angela drew two pictures: the post office and a letter with a stamp. Cemetria drew the mailboxes and package for Amelia. Tesha drew big and little mailboxes with the comment, "so they could get their mail." Anthony drew them sending mail and the mail lady. Five children drew the full process—writing, mailing, sorting, bagging, transporting. Full of the wonder of the experience, they talked incessantly as they drew, describing theories of how the post office works and mail travels. In small groups teachers and children discussed the similarities in their two modes of expression, verbal and graphic. Several children asked to visit the post office again. Their questions and observations were more pointed, their account at Friday's morning meeting more detailed.

The children began to realize that other school experiences were different aspects of communication. For example, when a postcard arrived in late January from Jennifer, the children carefully put it under transparent cover in the Communication Center to keep it safe. Adults treat postcards casually or discard them wantonly. For the MELC children, now avid postcard writers, they were significant—written by *someone*, just as they themselves wrote postcards; sent by someone they care about who also cares about them; mailed in a special building; traveling via a complex process that they were beginning to unravel.

The children had accumulated lots of information that connected school, home, community, and abroad through varied activities. Each involved different ways of generating, using, or deciphering written information.

IDEAS EXPAND

Other work found its way into the Communication Center. All year the children had been collecting letters of the alphabet. These would emerge in their message-making. Ongoing interest in the post office led to a visit from Frank's father, who was a mailman.

Using Letters of the Alphabet

Five children were engaged in an alphabet project, cutting and labeling magazine pictures with appropriate letters, one activity in the great emphasis on letters that year. At home children cut letters from newspapers, magazines, or mail, and brought them to school to use in various ways. The teachers added jars full of letters to the Communication Center. In discussing what they could do with them, the children decided to use them to make messages for their friends, a new activity in the Communication Center that continued steadily for 3 weeks. In December a group of children working with Genet thought up a new use for letters—they would use them to make words! They decided to make a different word beginning with each of the 26 letters of the alphabet. This sparked huge interest in sounding out words, finding the letters, then illustrating the word with a drawing. The teachers assembled the results into a picture dictionary. As we read in Chapter 4, the MELC children began school lacking essential language skills. Their spontaneously using letters to make words testifies to their emerging literacy skills.

Interviewing a Letter Carrier

March 4. In a conversation about their trip to the post office, Miss Wendy learned that Frank's father, Mr. Taylor, was a letter carrier. The children were very excited when she asked whether they would like him to visit. Quatesha suggested that they invite him by writing a letter, which they did that day.

March 18. Frank's father came, dressed in uniform and with his mail sack. Very formally, the seven children ushered him to the Dining Room and escorted him to a chair at the front of the room. They arranged themselves in a semicircle before him and began an interview, asking questions that had been forming in their minds through all their experiences with the mail process, questions they had discussed with Miss Wendy in preparation for this visit. Miss Wendy had those questions in hand but the children needed no prompting. Intently they questioned, and just as intently Mr. Taylor responded. They learned that he visited 350 houses daily, which he covered in 4 hours and 35 minutes, and that he had 30 minutes for lunch and a 10-minute break. De-Marcos asked how he knew where everyone lived, and if he used airplanes. Quatesha asked if he delivered puppies. Mr. Taylor explained that he does not, but the post office can deliver animals, and that he delivers frogs, crickets, and bugs to a high school on his route. Quatesha pursued: "What about cats?" and

Figure 6.4. Documentation of a big experience

Mr. Taylor replied, "Cats can be delivered to your house on a special truck." In answer to a question from DeMarcos, he did not think the post office delivered horses. When Quatesha asked if he ever had a backache or shoulder ache, he replied: "Yes, I have sprained ankles, backaches, you name it and I have it."

When DeMarcos asked if he had a mask to put over his face, Mr. Taylor said yes and apologized for not bringing it. DeMarcos also asked if he ever slipped on ice, Quatesha if he ever bumped his head with "that hat on." DeMarcos asked if he delivered mail to his own house. They all wanted to know if he had to stay with the mail all the time. He did. They were eager to learn everything. All the children tried on the hat and attempted to lift the sack. Frank beamed! Ten days later, after spring vacation, six children drew portraits of Mr. Taylor as a thank you for his visit and to document it.

MESSAGES EVERYWHERE, 1995–1996

Before the first day of school, the teachers put a message in each returning student's mailbox, and the children decided to make messages as surprises for new children soon to arrive. Message-making was off to an immediate start. Building on past years' experiences, the Communication Center had a life of its own.

Message-Making Evolves

The children made messages as surprises for their parents at the first parent meeting on September 29. Twenty-seven parents attended, 30 of the 36 families. The teachers attributed the turnout to several factors: This year word was out that there were not enough spaces and the school had a waiting list. The intense effort of the past school year to involve parents carried over. Parents now knew that this was a *school*, not merely child care.

As before, the teachers started the year by touring with small groups of children to discuss areas with particular constraints like the Lego®, block, and train areas; the house and dress-up areas; the lab and slide-viewing stand. This year, older children guided and narrated the tours. Renee, now 5 years old, asked the teachers: "When we first came here, did you have to teach *us* everything too? They don't know *anything*!" They spent almost 30 minutes explaining the Communication Center. The returning children told the new ones that only four could work there at once, explained the materials, then watched excitedly as the new children found their mailboxes and retrieved the messages. The typewriter stimulated a long discussion about its function and who uses typewriters. Older students explained the panel about communication with their friends in Italy, now an established practice.

October 28. The MELC hosted a party for children who were now first graders. The purpose was to maintain friendships and support families in their transition to public school. As a surprise the children made tissue paper flowers that they attached to a card with a message on one side. The teachers were still taking small groups on tours of the environment to deepen their understanding of each area and the resources in it.

Week of November 4. Teachers focused on the Communication Center again, discussing its contents, how to use them, and why. They also hung a panel about the typewriter.

Surrounded by Communication

The children's interest in working at the Communication Center never waned. The most social children used it with the understanding it would spur exchanges with friends. Others used it frequently to support a wide range of projects. They availed themselves of the Center's resources to make birthday and other greeting cards, draw pictures, and make gifts, thus expanding its uses. When they created weavings in the Studio, they used glue in the Communication Center to attach the weavings to cards, then used the writing implements to make messages, and found envelopes to enclose everything. The scale of productions at the Communication Center matched the space and materials—small and intricate, usually not more than 8" square, in contrast to the large-scale productions they made in the Studio or other larger areas.

This year children spontaneously brought messages they made or received to morning meeting every day. The conversations about friendship, an important impetus for message-making, became more complex: How do you *know* if someone is your friend? What you can *do* for a friend? How and why do friendships *develop*? They realized that people you've never seen—like the Italian children—can be your friends. When Galeesa said, "I like Cemetria because she makes me laugh a lot," she captured the spirit of friendship. The children drew their ideas about friendship, then told one another the stories in their drawings, explaining their concepts and opinions. Their oral language skills had expanded along with expanding uses of the Communication Center.

End of April. Many children made get-well messages for Timothy, who was in the hospital for an operation. In May a huge message-making project began as the children decided to hang messages from the large Cuckoo Bird sculpture they recently had made (Chapter 8). The sculpture reflected their eagerness to welcome new friends coming next fall. The messages they hung from it expressed their friendship.

June 9. A goodbye fax arrived from their La Villetta friends; it described their summer plans and where they would attend school next year. Galeesa asked if they had first grade like we do. She and the older children concluded that since they and their Italian friends were going to first grade, they would finally meet! On the last morning meeting of the year, they composed a letter to wish their Italian friends well on their continuing adventure and to say that we would miss them.

Many of the children graduating from the MELC had spent 3 years together, so there was lots of reminiscing—how they had changed, their memories of their first days at school, the difference between what they felt then and now. These reminiscences would be the final messages of the year—given to their families as graduation gifts from the school.

DETAILING A SPACE

The Communication Center occupied very little space. It contained three distinct areas: the workbench, the table with the typewriter, and the wall of mailboxes. All were *found* spaces—a jog in one wall, a blank space on another. When I say small, the workbench counter was about 2 feet deep and just long enough to accommodate four chairs. The furnishings were built-to-fit; had the mailboxes been any deeper, they would have extended into the doorway to the Big Room. We narrowed the moldings on door casings and removed baseboards to maximize every inch. It was fortune, not foresight, that the Communication Center was, literally, at the crossroads of the school's most heavily trafficked areas. I had chosen the spaces, not thinking of the hub function, but merely because the functions could fit in close proximity to one another.

Everything was aesthetic. The counters and grid system were white, the stock of materials colorful, a wide range of hues in beautiful tones. Under the grid and arrayed along the back of the table were small containers with interesting things to glue. The initial emphasis was on communicating, not making objects. Sequins, feathers, beads, and such were added later as the functions of the Communication Center expanded in response to the increasing complexity of the children's work.

The initial stock of items included photo-reduced copies of the children's symbols, black and white photos, and names. Now realizing the Center's potential to build reading and writing skills, the teachers added small jars with letters and numbers cut from magazines and words that children had requested from time to time in attractive fonts and different sizes, stored in 30 or more small jars. The teachers checked the Center daily to maintain order and restocked it regularly, varying papers and other expendable supplies to keep interest high. I had designed the space fully aware of the possibilities, but the actuality—for children and teachers—exceeded my imagination.

CONTEXTUAL LEARNING

The context for the Communication Center was a school in which the value of communication was showcased in many explicit ways. Memos, letters, or notices were sent home regularly to families, sometimes two or more daily, often three or four each week. Memos pertained to the substance of children's work rather than to administrative matters—information about what was happening in class, requests for help or materials, items about specific children. Children's decoration on the memos made families more attentive to them.

Documentation panels reflected the communication. Some panels contained examples of the different kinds of messages. Others had examples of children's messages to one another and photos of them making the messages, or portrayed the children's reactions to sending and receiving messages. Everyone—families and children—studied the panels. The reason may have been the slightly voyeuristic sense of reading someone else's mail; it was surely the pleasure any parent takes in seeing her child's work publicly displayed. Malaguzzi realized:

FIGURE 6.5. Parents could always be found studying the messages

Children ask us to pay close attention to their own personal histories, to how their families live. This is why we always try to have the family close to us. The educational achievements of those who have the family involved and those whose families are cut off are enormously different. (L. Malaguzzi, Question & Answer with a delegation at Diana School, Reggio Emilia, March 6, 1992)

The teachers learned to think about the potential for family involvement in every project. They asked the children for their suggestions about what their families needed to know, or how they could help them, and used their suggestions in letters they composed with the children. At the Communication Center the children embellished the letters with drawings or decorations. Reggio educators believe that families need to know about everything, why we need them, how we need them, that they are essential. In Amelia's words, "a school without parents is like a body without arms" (A. Gambetti, MELC Day presentation, June 14, 1993). "When families are sensitive and responsive to children's emotions, children are more likely to become socially competent and show better communication skills" (Weiss, Caspe, & Lopez, 2006, p. 2). Every message to the families was read to the children before it was sent home. Because children knew what the messages said and helped make them, they would insist: "Read this here!" Or, "Look! Alonzo drew that!" Families could not help but read the messages. The children would have it no other way!

SIGNIFICANT WORK

Malaguzzi thoroughly understood how communication between school and home, whether from the teachers or the children, built relationships among children, teachers, and parents.

> Teachers . . . must discover ways to communicate and document the children's evolving experiences at school. They must prepare a steady flow of quality information targeted to parents but appreciated also by children and teachers . . . [which], we believe, introduces parents to a quality of knowing that tangibly changes their expectations. They reexamine their assumptions about their parenting roles and their views about the experience their children are living and take a new and more inquisitive approach toward the whole school experience.
>
> [For children] . . . documentation . . . [makes them] more curious, interested, and confident. . . . They learn that their parents feel at home in the school, at ease with the teachers, and informed. . . .
>
> Finally, . . . parents and children [must] realize how much work teachers do together, . . . with what kindness they hide their worries, join children's play, and take responsibility. . . . They see a world where people truly help one another. (Edwards et al., 1993, pp. 63–64)

For many years I have tutored first and second graders in one of Memphis's inner-city schools. My children struggle mightily to express themselves. They lack experience shaping thoughts with words, and have a paucity of words with which to do so. While they master the mechanics of writing through repetition, they do not easily phrase expressions and some are challenged when asked to write any but the most meager thoughts. Their communities are virtually identical to the MELC children's—marked by poverty, high crime, many single-parent homes, some with four children under age 6.

The MELC children's message-making testifies to how powerfully children's correspondence draws families into a school. Message-making is evidence of what results from teaching practices that provide an intentional focus on friendship, immersion in verbal expression, and a context for literacy skills. If you compare the MELC children with those in laissez-faire or lockstep classrooms, the significance of the MELC children's achievements shines— and I shall look for cats in my mail, but not horses.

CHAPTER 7

Friendship with a Turtle: A Case History of Documentation

> Documentation . . . is visible listening, . . . the construction of traces that . . . testify to [the] children's learning paths and processes, but also make them possible because they are visible.
>
> —Carlina Rinaldi (2006, p. 68)

THE STORY OF THE TURTLE BEGAN IN school year 1994–1995. The turtle was given to us in September and remained in the children's lives in ensuing years, a story of lasting friendship. Here I show how it developed, how the Reggio practice of documentation figured in the story, and how the school's environment supported significant work that is creative, complex, and original. The relation between documentation and assessment is this chapter's teaching principle. Assessment through formal testing is inappropriate for children under age 6 (and even beyond). Authentic assessment techniques are better: teacher notes, recordings, photos or video, samples of completed work. This chapter explains how to use documentation to create authentic assessment of children's development.

THE STORY

No one had considered having a turtle. It simply arrived. But the school was flexible so when the teachers saw the children's excitement, they quickly accommodated.

The Turtle Arrives

A student in Options School, the junior high located in the MELC's building, brought a box turtle to the preschool. It wasn't huge, but was so much larger than the common green sliders sold in pet stores, it was impressive. The class was having morning meeting when it arrived, and the teachers set the turtle in the middle of the circle. The children greeted it with peals of laughter and a few cries of fear. The turtle turned, confused by the noise. The teachers caught this event because they had a camera at hand; they were almost always

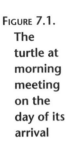

FIGURE 7.1. The turtle at morning meeting on the day of its arrival

ready with the camera. Were they not, they would have missed many moments in the school's life that were important to document.

A quick conversation between teachers and children determined that they should find a large, sturdy box. Turtle-in-the-box was carried to the Studio, which became its home. Every morning thereafter, different groups of children went to look at it. Days of observation ensued, a teacher joining their conversations. Watching the turtle withdraw into its shell spurred discussions about its feelings. In after-school meetings reviewing notes of the conversations, the teachers determined that the children's main concern was what the turtle would eat.

> STEFAN: "He gonna eat his food."
> LIZ: "He's eating the hamburger!"
> KEVIN: "And she eats apples!"
> MARY: "He's licking out his tongue and eating."
> WILLIE: "We tried to feed her grass."

The children knew the turtle must eat in order to live, and began to bring food—a carrot, a piece of celery, as time went on, an apple, orange, or bit of hamburger. Kevin brought pine cones for the turtle to play with; others brought grass and branches for it to hide under. Sometimes they ran straight to the Studio without removing their coats; other times they insisted their parents come. A strong friendship was developing between turtle and children.

The teachers asked one especially interested group of children whether they wanted to learn more about turtles and *where* they could learn. They instantly said, "The library!" The classroom had a good library—sizable space with comfortable seating and a large number of books, fiction and nonfiction. Whenever new interests emerged, the teachers borrowed public library books to supplement their collection. For days Miss Wendy and the children poured through books, Miss Wendy reading whatever piqued their interest, eventually everything in the library. Still wanting to know more, they made several trips to the public library. They learned a lot about turtles.

The teachers captured these first experiences on a large documentation panel: nine photos of the turtle's arrival and children watching it in its box; a map of the arboretum, a favorite field trip site, with five photos of children watching wildlife there; three photos of children watching slides of these experiences; two photos of the turtle eating; Willie's splendid drawing of a turtle; and a tentative pencil drawing by Kevin captioned "First Graphic Representation." The panel also had a transparent envelope with transcripts of the children's conversations about the turtle, recorded by the teachers and typed verbatim. The children's social development and linguistic and graphic capacity could be seen in the documentation.

Emphasis: Friendship

In the MELC as in life, beginnings and endings are rarely clear. Ideas from before emerge later. So, other activities, like butterflies and friendship, morphed into activities with the turtle. In September a group of children had made butterflies and suspended them on mobiles, which they wrapped as a surprise for new friends—children being phased in. As in every project, their work was informed by many searches through books about real butterflies.

Monday, September 20. Renee painted butterflies in watercolor; Tyresha and Brandi joined her on Tuesday. On Friday, looking critically at what they'd made, they decided they needed more butterflies. That day the whole class considered how to make the soon-to-arrive friends feel welcome, a subject they discussed frequently. Searching the school with Jennifer for how to hang the butterflies, they found two Japanese paper umbrellas. When the new friends arrived, all the planning culminated in introductions, exploring materials, and discovering surprises. The highlight was unwrapping the mobiles, so huge they'd required many sheets of tissue and two teachers to hang them. Excitement was palpable. Butterflies were, literally, in the air so, not surprisingly, found their way into the turtle project.

A Play: *The Turtle, the Butterfly, and the Moon*

Five children staged a show in the puppet theater, a space with its own context. Made of polished blond wood, it stood prominently in the Big Room with a large assortment of hand and finger puppets. The teachers used its wide façade for photos or drawings of projects underway. Currently it held photos of their turtle and magazine pictures of other turtles. As with everything displayed, they discussed the images extensively.

November 3. Miss Wendy worked with Jennifer on a new panel: "A Story on Our Puppet Theater." It would hang on the wall beside the theater. It contained a sizable photo of the façade with the turtle pictures and two large photos: In one Miss Wendy manipulated puppets, and in the other she wrote as the children talked. Between the photos were children's drawings and this text:

> Children noticed new pictures on the puppet theater. As we listened to the children tell stories about a turtle, we [teachers] used the turtle puppet to enact them. Then we invited [the children] to look at the pictures and tell a story with a sequence.

If these young children's focus seems unusual, remember that conversations were held throughout each day. During the prior year, the teachers had learned how to hold conversations: to take notes while children spoke, analyze notes to find children's real interests, ignore digressions, and keep the children focused.

> Before and after each step in a project, teachers used the children's own words and photographs to remind them what they'd asked, what they'd learned, how they'd reacted. This remembering spurred a project along. . . . It [had taken] months to become focused in conversation . . . but the teachers [had] persisted, consistently encouraging the children to contrast, question, and attend to detail. (Lewin-Benham, 2006, pp. 56–57)

On a panel to the theater's right in large letters and numbered 1 through 10 was the play the children produced: *The Turtle, the Butterfly, and the Moon.*

1. Once upon a time there was a little turtle and his friend the butterfly.
2. The little turtle wanted to swim.
3. Then he came toward the water and then he jumped in.
4. He is swimming in the water.
5. He is looking for his friend the butterfly. He can't find his friend.
6. Now he is swimming in tall grass with grasshoppers.
7. The turtle better watch out. The moon is coming out.
8. The water is shining because the moon did it.
9. His shell is changing colors because the light from the moon did it. Sometimes the shell comes off and he gets a new shell.
10. The turtle is gone now, maybe to find his friend the butterfly, or maybe to go home to take a bath and a nap.

The production reflects fantasy and reality. The parts about the moon are imaginative, anticipating a story by the children in which the moon makes stripes on the turtle's shell. The turtle's relationship with butterfly and grasshopper reflects many discussions about friendship; the ending about bath and nap reflects children's own daily activities projected, as children do, on animals or toys; the many facts reflect books they read and frequent observation of wildlife. The play also reflects the butterfly project, prior puppet theater productions, and, naturally, experiences with their turtle. Not tucked in a file but prominently displayed, the play shows how children listened to one another, building on the preceding person's lines. Sequencing individual ideas so a story makes sense is an essential literacy skill, there for all to assess in the documentation.

Turtle and Cat Meet

Soon after its arrival, the turtle had a surprise. Coco—drawn by the smell of hamburger or scents of turtle, grass, and branches, or simply by curiosity—jumped into the turtle's box. The turtle crawled way up the branch, drawing completely under its shell. Extremely upset, the children ran shouting to Jennifer: "Coco is getting ready to eat the turtle!" But as time passed, the children and turtle saw that Coco did not intend harm. Sometimes Coco would poke the turtle's shell, as if to play. Always he drank the water, but never ate the food. Gradually, turtle and cat became friends. Coco, it seemed, wanted to be near the turtle: He would edge closer, jump into the box, drink from the water bowl, lie there, and go to sleep. Sometimes the turtle ventured out from under the branch, other times not. But he no longer stayed under his shell when Coco came. Years later Miss Wendy commented: "Even the teachers had never seen anything like that friendship between cat and turtle. It was a learning experience for us."

The teachers captured Coco's foray in photos, and the children captured it in a series of six lifelike drawings by Cemetria and Angela: (1) edging closer, (2, 3, 4) jumping in, (5) in, (6) near the turtle. The teachers put the children's words into a book, *Coco and the Turtle: An Episode of Their Friendship*. It read:

> Page 3: That's Coco in front of the box trying to get the turtle because he wants to play with the turtle.
> Page 5: Coco is looking in the box at the turtle. His ears are poking up and he's in the Studio.
> Page 7: He looking in the box for the turtle. His head and his body in the box and he see the turtle.
> Page 9: Coco jumping in the turtle's box and he see the turtle. We see the back, the ear, the legs, and the tail. We don't see his head and his other ear.
> Page 11: Coco found the turtle and he was looking at the turtle. He's in the box. The rock and the turtle and the plate with water in the box.
> Page 13: Coco is already in the box and he hitting the turtle. He between the brick and the plate. He wanna play with the turtle.

The teachers documented the episode in three media—photos, words, and drawings—on a panel titled "A Turtle and a Cat." Along the bottom was the photo series. Above the photos were photo-reduced copies of Cemetria's and Angela's drawings, with other children's words telling each step in the story, and the 13-page book nearby. The documentation showed their growing facility at storytelling and collaboration. It also showed their incorrect use of many verb forms, a record to be compared with later examples.

As friendships grew among turtle, cat, and children, interest in turtles increased. So did trips to the arboretum where they saw turtles swimming in the pond, climbing up the bank, sunning on rocks, crawling under branches, jumping into the water if they heard noise, and playing with the ducks and fish. To learn more they also visited National Geographic Explorer's Hall and continued borrowing library books. The extensive documentation of experiences in the turtle project and many others enabled parents, visitors, and teachers themselves to assess the substance of the school's program and judge its adequacy.

Musical Interpretation

That winter an unusual experience began. Anne LeBaron, internationally acclaimed composer, began a 3-year residency at the school. Supported by Meet the Composer, she came weekly. The teachers had several discussions with the children about who Anne was and why she was there. On January 12 six children began working with her in the Music Room. In addition to observing the children, Anne studied the panels throughout the school to learn the children's interests and assess their social and cognitive skills. For 4 months they explored sound with Anne. Again and again they described how Coco jumped into the turtle's box, how afraid the turtle was initially, but how a friendship developed. With Anne's guidance they underscored their words with music, matching story sequence to musical sequence. The episode about cat and turtle became the basis for an original musical work and performance. It required many rehearsals. The performance was a dramatic, multimedia production: slides of the story shown with the children's music. The performance was a huge hit with parents.

Composer's and children's collaboration was portrayed on a huge panel titled "Musical Interpretations: Coco, the Turtle, and the Box and Other Episodes"; its subtitle was "A Dialogue Between Coco and the Turtle." Three large photos across the top, captioned "The Performers," "The Audience," and "The Entire Situation," respectively, showed the performance for parents on May 15. Explanatory text read: "These [photos] show actions taking place at the same time." The idea of simultaneity—things happening at once—had emerged as a theme of the project. Another photo and caption showed the children clustered in lively conversation around Anne, who held an electronic sound effects processing unit: "Children are finding appropriate sounds for the different voices of Coco and the Turtle. They are using a sound simulation computer." Also on the panel hung the children's myth captioned "How the Turtle Got Her Stripes: Children noticed the yellow stripes on the turtle's shell and made up a story about how they got there." Beside the story hung a musical score captioned "Turtle Tango: Using children's dialogues Anne LeBaron composed a song. The story and song will be used for a performance." Alongside a tape of their musical creation, four photos showed Anne and the children exploring sound in the Music Room.

The documentation enabled you to assess individual children's growth in vocabulary, sentence structure, and storytelling, and showed the increasing complexity of activities.

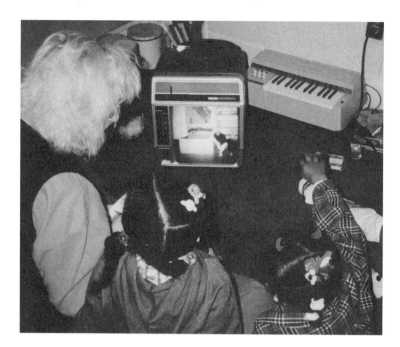

FIGURE 7.2. Composer Anne LeBaron working with the children on the musical composition

Performance is a valid but underutilized way to assess preschoolers' development. It requires social skills and a high degree of self-regulation. When children themselves create the production, it requires rich vocabulary, ideas fully developed in sentences that follow one another logically, sometimes drama or dance, and in this case music. Through documentation you can assess how children are integrating these behaviors. Looking back years later Anne said:

> Translating the children's delight and the ways they empathized with the cat and the turtle into a musical and visual performance served to enhance, validate, and solidify their experiences. I've often wondered how the multiple documentations of their interaction with the animals impacted their lives, then and now. (A. LeBaron, personal communication, September 2007)

Saying Goodbye

Everything changes. Seasons pass. Turtles grow restless. One day the children found the cardboard in a corner of the turtle's box clawed. They suspected Coco, but on observation were startled to see the turtle himself tearing a hole. They made a huge painting: turtle on hind legs in the corner of his box, front legs extended, clawing at the cardboard. The finished painting, over 3' high and almost as wide, hung on a prominent wall alongside documentation: photos of the multi-step process to make the painting, and children's conversations about the experience, more evidence with which to assess their increasingly long focus, attention to detail, and success at a complicated collaborative endeavor.

Innately empathetic, the children understood that if the turtle was clawing a hole, he must really want to get out, and concluded he was unhappy. Many conversations ensued about what to do. Among themselves the teachers agreed the time had come for the turtle to go. Vacation was coming; Coco spent breaks with Sonya, but no one wanted the turtle. Conversations, stimulated by the teachers, revealed that the children would accept the reality. They'd noticed how important it was to turtles to swim and climb in and out of water, something their turtle couldn't do. At the arboretum, they'd seen turtles in groups and commented that turtles had families, just like themselves, with mothers, fathers, sisters, and brothers. They'd realized each creature was with its own, just as they were. Wendy said, "Children always notice everything if they have time" (W. Baldwin, personal communication, January 24, 2007). In another conversation when the teachers suggested releasing the turtle at the arboretum, the children expressed concern that the turtle had been away for a long time, that maybe it *was* time for him to be with his family. They understood.

Figure 7.3.
The turtle was clawing a hole in its box

Figure 7.4.
Painting of the turtle trying to escape

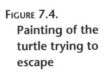

The day came to say goodbye to their friend. They put the turtle in its box in the car and sat next to it. One cried but the rest were happy, looking forward to finding a spot with other turtles in the water. Tamika ran straight to the pond: "There's his mommy!" "No," said Galeesa, "*there's* his mommy." There were cameras all over and security guards circling in small carts. One gave the children permission to release the turtle: "This is a good place because your turtle's at a pond where there are other turtles and fish and ducks. Your teacher said you come often, so you can visit and pick him up." When they let the turtle go, he made straight for the water, jumped in, and swam right under. Miss Wendy did not see him come up, but the children did. They also saw his daddy and sisters and brothers. They were sure that whenever they visited the arboretum they would find their friend.

Visiting the Turtle

Frequently the children asked to visit the turtle. About once a month they went to the arboretum, always straight to the pond. On the first trip the children brought clay presents—eating utensils, apples and oranges, and a hamburger that they arranged on the ground then threw carefully into the water. There were rules against leaving anything but the guard took Miss Wendy aside: He'd collect everything after they left.

On the next trip they brought beautifully decorated notes they had written to the turtle. Whenever they went, the children were sure they saw him. They jumped up and down excitedly, as close as possible to the water, so happy! Once three children stood at the water's edge discussing which turtle was theirs: "No! That's his *mommy*!" Or, "That's his *daddy*!" Or, "Ours was *much* bigger than that one!" Once they tiptoed up to the water and counted 14 turtles! Another time they left apples and popcorn. Once they left a letter.

Dear Turtle, We are making you presents. We miss you and hope you are going to have a nice summer and we miss you. We wish that we can come all the time to see you at the arboretum. Did you get the old party we made for you? Did you eat the apples? We love you. How are you and your mom and dad? Is the water cold now or hot now? We are very glad that you are there. We are happy for you. From MELC Children.

Documentation from throughout the year showed how their vocabulary expanded and grammar become regular, how much new content and many new concepts they'd learned.

Documenting the Visits

The year-end panel was titled: "We Saw the Turtle!" It had Kevin's drawings of a fish, six orange carp, and a duck, with the comment: "We saw the turtle and fish swimming together. Could this be the beginning of a friendship?" His lifelike drawings were beautiful and detailed; his comment posed a hypothesis. Another comment read: "We would like to think that the turtle

FIGURE 7.5.
The children knew: Coco was looking at the photos and drawings of himself and his old friend

wasn't alone and that she made new friends—fish and ducks." Empathy, an important measure of young children's social growth, was apparent throughout the documentation.

The following fall the teachers made a panel, "Celebrating the End of the Year," with a photo of last June's picnic. A second photo, titled "September 1995: A New School Year Begins," showed the children standing at the water's edge and pointing toward the pond. The panel provided continuity from one year to the next and an open record for all to see the children's development.

All told, documentation consisted of nine panels and one extra-large summary panel that included Coco's forays into the turtle's box. Opposite the summary panel was the black chair where Coco frequently sat. Watching the cat gaze steadily at the panel, the children understood: "Coco's looking at himself and his old friend." The following year they hung a panel dated June 2, 1995, titled: "At the End of the Year," and subtitled: "Saying hello and goodbye to our friend the turtle, a field trip to the Arboretum." It formed a bridge to the 1995–1996 school year, the friendship with the turtle now a focal point in the school's history.

An Unending Story

The story covers 2 years, but in fact continued into a third: The children so loved the story of Coco and the turtle, related on the summary panel, that the teachers left it hanging permanently. On top were photos of the turtle's first days. Under, much reduced in size, was the book about Coco and the turtle. Beneath were photos of them releasing the turtle in the pond. Next were photos of subsequent trips to the arboretum with this heading: "A big surprise and great excitement was waiting for us"; one photo showed Miss Wendy and the children pointing to *their* turtle. Another heading read: "A party for the turtle, the turtle's family, and us," accompanied by photos of picnics, and fish, ducks, and turtles swimming. A final caption read: "The arboretum and the pond are becoming very familiar to us. We went there and looked for the turtle and found her and her friends." At the bottom was this block of text—from the third school year after the turtle arrived—headed "September 1995: A New School Year Begins":

> Returning children toured new children . . . to share with them what they had done in previous years. Some of the new children were particularly captured by the project about turtle and cat. . . . Olivia said, "I want to see the turtle. . . . Take me to see that. I want to have my picture taken with the turtle."

Through documentation the story sparked interest long after the turtle was released and the story's protagonists had moved on to other schools.

Children's emotions drove the curriculum. Their empathy sprung from many observations—their turtle hungry, frightened, confined. Through the documentation you could see that the children appreciated the meaning of ponds, freedom, and caring for a friend. Identifying one turtle among many and telling a story to friends required higher level cognitive skills. Documentation captured it all. It showed how much the children loved what they'd done, how they expanded their memory, pondered the future, and transcended the single experience.

A SUPPORTIVE ENVIRONMENT

With its ample space and detailed design, the environment figures prominently in the turtle projects.

Ample Space, Minute Detail

One room/one class is the norm. The MELC had one huge room—the Big Room, two sizable rooms—Studio and Dining Room, and another smaller room—the Lab. In addition there were a Music Room, an entry, a Greeting Room, a hall for cubbies, Parent Room, Nap Room, Storeroom, and two spacious bathrooms. There was also considerable wall space in several long halls. Without lugging storage boxes or clearing space, teachers and children had ready access to slide-viewing stand, slide projector, overhead projector, and puppet theater.

If rich ideas emerged spontaneously, the teachers pursued them. Ample space and a well-provisioned environment remove barriers to spontaneity. Teachers know children expand their language facility by acting out stories with puppets. But if the puppet theater is stashed somewhere in a crowded closet and the puppet box is unlabeled behind a load of other boxes, a teacher

FIGURE 7.6. Floor plan of the Model Early Learning Center

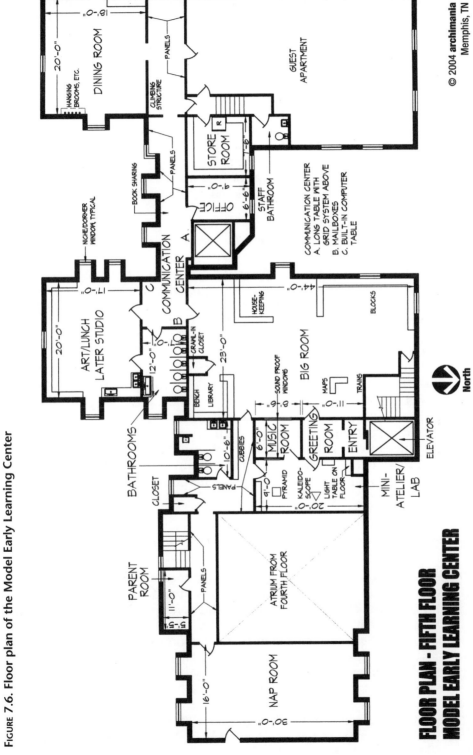

© 2004 archimania
Memphis, TN

FLOOR PLAN - FIFTH FLOOR
MODEL EARLY LEARNING CENTER

is unlikely to search during class time. Moreover, storage areas rarely have check-out systems, so teachers can plough through, never sure of finding what they're seeking. If later they remember to retrieve stage and puppets, it may be impossible to recreate the incidents that made them propitious earlier. While young children's interest can be extended over long periods, sustaining the flow of any given moment depends on many factors, one being a well-prepared environment. Tight space requires discipline: restrained design, clever storage systems, and absolutely no clutter.

The small Music Room between the Big Room and the Lab was visibly accessible because we had cut huge windows through opposite walls. We soundproofed the space so Music Room activities could be seen but not heard. The room was well-stocked with instruments hung on pegboard, arrayed on shelves, and arranged on the floor, always immediately accessible. When Anne LeBaron wanted to explore sound, she had readily available a well-designed space and ample collection.

The MELC believed that one of its purposes was advocating for larger spaces for early childhood programs. Occasionally you see a school with the generous, old-fashioned kindergarten room from the 1920s or 1930s that enables a program to breathe. Policymakers and building designers take note: 1,800–2,000 square feet is a nice size for a preschool classroom. Reggio classrooms are smaller, but each Reggio school has a large atelier, spacious piazza, and generous lunchroom augmenting three classrooms.

Spacious Walls

The MELC used no commercially produced-for-preschool posters or other wall items. Nor did it display all children's productions, partly because there were far too many, but mainly because documentation is not meant to exhibit, but to reflect. That is, its purpose is to review an experience in words and pictures; therefore, teachers choose the picture that most clearly depicts the experience. Were the walls covered with commercial materials or everyone's work, there would be no space for documentation, especially when a project like the turtle yielded nine large panels.

DOCUMENTATION

Documentation is the art of preserving experiences so you can relive them as a way to continue the activity, what Carlina Rinaldi (2006) refers to as "the creation and consolidation of concepts and conceptual maps" (p. 67). That is, if you watched the turtle clawing its box, and read about it in the documentation, it might lead to a conversation about the rights and feelings of animals, or to a discussion about what the clawing meant. A panel may begin with a photo of a single pivotal moment—children gathered around the turtle's box—and statement, such as Willie's: "We tried to feed her grass." Next day, teacher and small group look at the picture, read the text, and discuss it. The teacher notes the children's comments and questions and from them determines what the next steps in the project might be, usually discussing her notes with her colleagues. Documentation is not an append-age, but is integral to projects. It involves observing, listening, and record-ing, then analyzing and synthesizing—selecting information to display from what you have recorded so you can revisit the experience and listen again. Like photojournalism, documentation uses images and words to reflect key moments in noteworthy events. It provides the means for teachers' and chil-dren' continuously reflecting on what they've done. It focuses their atten-tion and aids their memory so they can consider thoughtfully what to do next. For adults it provides, literally, a picture of the continuum of children's development.

A Self-Reflexive Process

Documentation is self-reflexive: There is a relation between you and the photos of you. You watch or listen to yourself doing something *as* you are doing it. It is a powerful way to engage children and an intentional teaching technique that the adult knows could change the activity. The first panel about the turtle initially displayed just one photo with these remarks beneath:

TESHA: "We are talking about the turtle."
REBECCA: "And then you picked her up. Everyone was touching the turtle."
WILLIE: "The turtle was scared because you were all around."

The teachers hung it immediately after the experience. They had reviewed their notes of the children's dialogue carefully to pick succinct bits that cap-tured essential information *and* were most likely to extend children's interest. Immediately they brought the children to *revisit* the panel-in-the-making.

Children and teacher discussed the photo as the teacher read their words from the recent experience. Enough time had elapsed for the children to di-gest but not forget. Their attention was riveted because revisiting put them right back in the moment, spurring new thoughts about what to do next: "Let's see if the turtle likes *this* food." And "Maybe we can find out at the library." And from a teacher: "Would you like to watch turtles at the arbore-tum?" The children felt important because everyone could see their photos and read their words. "Documentation is particularly valuable to the chil-dren themselves . . . [as a way to see] the meaning that the teacher has drawn from their work" (Rinaldi, 2006, p. 72).

When the teacher brought them to the panel, asked them what they saw, and read what they'd said, we hear Tesha summarizing, essentially titling the scene, Rebecca elaborating, and Willie interpreting the turtle's feelings, all im-portant mental operations. As the children watch themselves, listen to what they said, and comment, the teachers see what excites them and hear ideas for what will motivate them to continue. Practice in recalling what you did focuses attention, builds memory, and provides experience in sequencing and relating stories—all essential skills.

When the children take the turtle's clawing its box as evidence that it is unhappy, there on the wall, on the panel depicting the turtle's release, is this comment: "A decision was made that the turtle had the right to be free." The statement is no surprise: The children have talked about creatures' feelings and how to treat them, and concluded that they have rights. Children are innately empathetic and, if encouraged through discussion, will come to fair decisions about how to treat living things. Documentation is the catalyst for such discussions. It is powerful because people of any age are attentive to replays of themselves in action and motivated when their comments about the replays are taken seriously.

A Reflective Process

Documentation is also reflective—a deliberate process that provides on-going, long-term records of children's progress. "Documentation . . . ensure[s] that the group and each individual child have the possibility to observe themselves from an external point of view while they are learning (both during and after the process)" (Rinaldi, 2006, p. 68). For example, the children's growing ability to write and draw is reflected in comparisons of early and later panels. Wavy, half-formed, illegible letters become recognizable words. Vague drawings become clear images. The many quotations reflect increasing language ability: Missing verbs, partial sentences, and other grammatical irregularities change over time as children amend their speech patterns—usually on their own, sometimes with overt adult correction—to correspond ever more closely to the language they hear around them. "The three-year-old is a grammatical genius. Experience interacts with wiring to give a three-year-old a particular language's grammar" (Pinker, 1994, pp. 280–281). In an era obsessed with test scores, schools could well use documentation as a means of assessment that reflects children's gradually increasing ability in using the spoken and written word.

How to Make Panels

When Amelia arrived in 1993 to begin her residency, she discussed the idea of each teacher's keeping a daily diary. Jennifer started hers that day. In it are references to 72 different panels created in the 1993–1994 school year, 112 additional references to making panels, 7 references to *re*making finished panels, and 98 references to other work in panel-making. Other work involves:

- physical construction, like building a hanging system, or removing something that could interfere with a new panel.
- discussion among the teachers about proposed panels—the purpose, everyone's ideas about what to put on it, who will construct it, and the actual making. In their discussions teachers learn who worked with the children on anything related to a panel. This enables them to decide who will work on the project if it continues.
- organizing whatever relates to the panel—images, objects, words, drawings, paintings, or other things made by children. In organizing, the teachers pull together and provide for the storage of related

items, considering what to archive, how to index, and where to store everything.

- selecting images that best tell the story—sorting developed prints and reviewing slides and negatives to find other promising images. Because so much was photographed daily, there were lots of images to sort and frequent trips to the photo store for film and developing (prior to digital technology). Selection of images is one of the most critical elements in making an effective panel.

- creating text by discussing everything children said relating to the panel's story. If the story requires clarification, teachers engage children in further dialogue after the fact. In other words, as you revisit a panel, the children may notice that you forgot to say something important; if so, you discuss with the children what they think is missing, remake the panel accordingly, then reread it with them. It is a form of collaborative editing.

- typesetting any text that will be on the panel—headings, subheadings, quotes. Jennifer's diary had 37 entries relating to text.

- locating the best wall space for a given panel. Some can hang anywhere but others require a particular area. "A Story on Our Puppet Theater" needed to hang beside the theater; panels about the school (philosophy, location), in the entry; facts and functions (staff, parent involvement), in the Greeting Room. The panel on the lunch setup system needed to hang in the Dining Room. Sometimes hanging a panel involved taking down or relocating other panels, or condensing several into one.

Condensing Documentation

The teachers summarized the turtle experiences at the end of 1993–1994 by making one large panel with the stories up to that time, using photo reductions and shorter statements to fit everything in. Jennifer remembers this panel as "a big learning experience" (J. Azzariti, personal communication, February 8, 2007). Because the subject—the turtle—was gone, they were entirely dependent on information they had collected months earlier, especially the children's images and words: "We three—myself, Sonya, and Wendy—did it with Amelia, trying to figure out how to put all the information together long after-the-fact; organization—the actual layout—was a huge issue" (J. Azzariti, personal communication, February 8, 2007).

Jennifer remembered that she wanted to do a mural about what the turtle found in the pond. The children told her what was there: "Rocks, mud, and fish." But she had an elaborate, preconceived image, so suggested that they imagine wearing goggles and diving under the water. Then, they came up with deep-sea diving images. Discussing the matter, Amelia exclaimed, "But Jen, it's a pond! Rocks and mud *are* on the bottom!" (J. Azzariti, personal communication, February 8, 2007). Jennifer was embarrassed; she had envisioned a grand scheme, insensitive to the reality! It was a *huge* lesson in how easily teachers can impose their ideas on children.

SIGNIFICANT WORK/ASSESSING DEVELOPMENT

Documentation was only one of several ways we assessed children's progress. Each child's large work was archived in portfolios about 3' x 3½', small work in legal-sized folders and closed 8½" x 11" envelopes. Computer files contained transcriptions of conversations. Jennifer's Magic List showed concisely and precisely what each child had experienced. The list ensured that no child slipped through the cracks: At a glance you could see if someone had not engaged in an experience. The teachers consulted the list regularly to decide which children to engage in which activities. The list provided concrete information that guided teachers in forming groups: Careful consideration of whom to include in a group ensured that children were with others whose competence would set an example. Sonya's and Jennifer's daily records noted instances of unusual accomplishments, like a child's first drawing or a breakthrough in using a material. In their diaries you have evidence of a child now taking his nap readily—increasing self-regulation; of friendships growing—social development; of an astute statement—cognitive growth.

Underpinning these practices were teachers' intimate knowledge of each child. When you teach an entire class at once, it is difficult to know who "gets" it; when you teach small groups, you can easily hear speech, see skills, and observe other aspects of development. Work in the MELC required increasing skill in the use of demanding techniques and involvement in projects that required complex thinking. The purpose was not to measure children against an arbitrary standard or compare them with one another, but to show each individual's progress. The work was both content-laden and conceptual so children's cognitive capacity was stretched. They expressed theories and collaborated to accomplish specific goals that crossed all disciplines—language, art, math, science, music, movement. Projects required wide-ranging skills—literacy, numeracy, dexterity with tools and instruments.

Years later Wendy recalled the turtle project.

This could not have happened in the schools where I worked before coming to the MELC. There, the curriculum was already planned, there was a schedule for everything, and time was not allowed for anything else to happen. There were no interests outside the curriculum. At the MELC we had the library in the classroom which kids were able to use whenever they wanted. In my prior schools, there was only a small number of books. At the MELC we had *so* many books and any topic you wanted. In all our projects we used both our classroom and the public library. Going to our library was the first thing we did; we brought the children's interest and went through books. (W. Baldwin, personal communication, January 24, 2007)

Wendy believed the Reggio Approach made a critical difference—listening to what children say and working with the core group that is interested. With the turtle, as in all projects:

We stood back and took notes and then as a group, in the evening, came up with questions to get the kids to ask more questions. The interest was already there, and we were there to support the interest; a project was not something we pushed on them. If we needed to go to the library or park, we did; if we needed pictures of turtles, we found them in books or magazines and had the children draw. The turtle lived in the Studio with Jen who saw the children's interest. We all talked about it—as a group we discussed everything going on—and decided we needed to follow this closely. (W. Baldwin, personal communication, January 24, 2007)

Wendy found the children's conversations amazing. Knowing nothing about turtles but just seeing one, they somehow knew it had to eat. Some had never seen a turtle, yet came up with ideas of what to give it to eat. Without being taught they understood that food is essential to living things. In many significant ways the children brought all this knowledge to their friendship with the turtle, which the teachers captured and portrayed in documentation that echoed in the minds and hearts of all who saw it.

CHAPTER 8

The Teacher's Role as Seen in Four Projects

Reggio educators prefer the word *research* to *method*; the former
emphasizes the concept of teacher as listener, not speaker.
—Carlina Rinaldi (1992)

THE EASTER DOVE, A BIRD MADE BY CHILDREN at La Villetta school, arrived in a *big* package! Giovanni Piazza, La Villetta's *atelierista*, brought it, marked fragile and checked as baggage. It was a gift, signifying the friendship that the La Villetta children felt for the MELC children. Giovanni presented many gifts, which the children opened one by one—long, thin markers to draw fine details like teeth or stems; watercolor paints in unusual colors; a shoebox diorama of La Villetta—flowers, birds, cars, turtles, trees fabricated by children; and a card expressing their friendship. The children also sent a recording of themselves singing favorite songs and a postcard of Reggio Emilia, which they all signed. The gifts were well-received. But when Giovanni presented the big package, its outer paper hand-painted, the children could hardly contain themselves. Then Easter Dove emerged.

In this chapter I describe projects called the Cuckoo Bird, Clouds, a Home, and the Nest. The projects were robust and evolved as the children's love for the Easter Dove grew. I use the projects to explain the teacher's role, one starkly different from that in typical preschools. The role, as it evolved in the Reggio Approach, is multi-faceted: Teachers are *researchers* who listen, observe, record, and hypothesize; *designers* who prepare an environment that fosters relationships among people and between people and materials; *orchestrators* who encourage relationships among time, space, materials, and people; *collaborators* who are children's accomplices and assistants in realizing their plans; *documenters* who take notes, photos, and other evidence to use as the basis for reflection; and *mediators* who intervene with intention, energy, and emotion. First I explain each of these aspects. Then I describe four projects to show which aspect of the role characterizes teachers' mindsets at particular moments, and follow with a deeper analysis of each of the role's aspects. (Caution: In practice, like the Reggio Approach itself, the role cannot be disaggregated. I do so only to explain the multi-faceted nature of this kind of teaching.) Finally, I analyze the MELC teachers' early questions, which reveal how hard it was to learn such a complex role.

A MULTI-FACETED TEACHING ROLE

According to researchers who "are developing new ways to measure how teachers interact with children" (Klein & Knitzer, 2007, p. 3), it matters *how* teachers teach. Among early educators the teacher's role is an important topic. The multi-faceted role of the Reggio teacher is essential to producing significant work. The various aspects are described here.

Researcher

As researchers, teachers listen for children's questions and ideas, observe their actions, and record what seems significant. Then, in after-school meetings they review their notes and hypothesize which questions and actions are rich enough to branch in diverse ways. Reading their notes to one another, teachers debate—heartily—exactly what the children meant. Once they home in and agree on a topic(s), they brainstorm, make a mind-map, or diagram how the topic(s) might branch. If the topic(s) seem rich *and* can translate into action, they review the children's words with them, closely observing the children's reactions as they—children and teachers—discuss together what the teachers have winnowed from their notes. There are no predetermined responses like the scripted dialogues in teacher guides. Rather, there is an exchange of ideas, debate, and negotiation among teachers and children. If conversation develops in some of the ways teachers brainstormed, there is a strong possibility a project will emerge, although, as in any research, the outcome is not certain. Who would have predicted a friendship between turtle and cat (Chapter 7)? or an interview of a letter carrier (Chapter 6)? or imaginative birthday gifts (Chapter 5)? It may take several days to home in on where to start because, when researchers are engaged with good ideas that genuinely interest them, their minds keep pondering. Projects like Turtle, Coco, and Messages evolved slowly after much conversation between teachers and children as well as among the teachers themselves. Cuckoo Bird projects gelled quickly.

Designer

The designer sets the stage, which means preparing the environment to support relationships among people and between people and materials. For example, the designer creates proximity between message-making bench and mailboxes (Chapter 6), and finds uses throughout the school for children's photos, symbols, and names (Chapter 5). She also provides tools to shape, fashion, or build literally anything, and makes materials readily available in the storeroom, Studio, and elsewhere. She augments materials by asking parents to send various items—whatever might be needed. She provides numerous good books, which can be supplemented from the public library. The thoughtfully designed spaces support small-group work. The environment, called a third teacher, is a silent partner, both stimulating and responding to emerging ideas. It is prepared to support children who are not engaged in projects, holding the majority's attention while a teacher concentrates on projects with small groups. In addition to setting the stage, teachers use the skills of designer as they collaborate with children, working side-by-side, bringing their knowledge of how to shape, fashion, and make things to bear on the solution to problems: How do we make a particular object? fasten two materials? display a finished product? The teacher-as-designer tends to all aesthetic considerations, as well as the design of documentation.

Orchestrator

Teachers are orchestrators when they gather children to begin doing something and instigate particular activities: Draw your ideas; transform your drawings into clay models. They ask leading questions: What do you want to know? How can we find out? Orchestration of a project begins with a discussion of why they have gathered, focusing, as we have seen, on the goal: "You said you wanted to make a robot. How do you think we can begin?" Often teachers ask children to clarify their ideas by drawing them, then discuss the drawings and have the children merge the best ideas into one collaborative drawing.

Teacher/orchestrators move projects along. They choose the group because one child has a wealth of theories, another skill at drawing, another facility with words, yet another talent for mediating. One is shy, another nurturing, another a natural leader. The teacher/orchestrator chooses children whose strengths enhance one another's. Instead of considering it cheating if children copy one another's solutions, orchestrators know that collaboration makes each individual stronger and the group more likely to succeed.

Collaborator

Collaboration is as much art as skill, teacher side-by-side with children, an observant, experienced participant whose minute-by-minute responses are extra-sensitive to the nuances of each child's particular strengths. Teacher/collaborator is a member of the team working on a project, but a member with something extra. If a project requires skill, the collaborator demonstrates; her finesse moves the task forward without stifling children's initiative. If it requires research, the collaborator slips into the designer role to adjust the environment accordingly—bringing more books, finding materials to test an idea. Reggio educators call this co-collaboration.

Documenter

Teacher/documenter means being in a situation and observing simultaneously. The documenter identifies pivotal moments—key questions, penetrating responses, on-target observations, skilled actions—which move projects forward. She captures such moments in words and photos, knowing she will mount them on a panel so that she and the children can reflect on what they are doing. Reflection is essential to thinking: Seeing photos and hearing words of what they've just done maintains children's focus, aids their memory, and stimulates further thought. Focusing, remembering, and pursuing a train of thought are essential brain functions and make significant work possible. Recall how the themes of friendship and creatures' rights in the turtle stories (Chapter 7) echoed in the school for years because of the documentation.

Mediator

Teacher/mediator is the central pillar in Reuven Feuerstein's theory of the Mediated Learning Experience. Mediators orient children to attend; they convey meaning in stimuli and guide children to connect this experience to prior and future experiences by intervening between stimuli and child with intention, meaning, and transcendence (Feuerstein et al., 2006). Mediators convey their intention through their attitude, which says: This is important! Attend! Be serious! Meaning involves focusing on a particular aspect of the stimulus: This wire is *heavy*; how will you cut it? This paper is *translucent*; what will the effect be? Transcendence means going beyond the immediate stimulus and connecting it to other relevant events: Do you remember when . . . ? What might happen if . . . ? This is similar to . . . because . . . . There are many other aspects of mediation (beyond this book's scope), but without intention, meaning, and transcendence, intervention is not mediation. Reggio teachers have honed the art of mediating.

Any one role is challenging. Teachers who are simultaneously researcher, designer, orchestrator, collaborator, documenter, and mediator have made the Reggio schools what they are. Watch each role in action during the story.

EPISODES IN THE STORY

From the arrival of the Easter Dove to the construction of the nest, projects followed one another seamlessly, their boundaries fluid. The projects began in April 1995 and continued through February 1996.

The Easter Dove Arrives

April 6. As he unwrapped the Easter Dove, Giovanni explained why the La Villetta children created it. They had heard stories about the MELC children—Coco, the U.S. Capitol Freedom statue, how they had polluted then purified water. They felt they knew the MELC children, so wrote to them. The MELC children answered and a friendship developed. When the La Villetta children learned that Giovanni would be visiting their friends, they decided to make something to show their feelings. The result was the enormous Easter Dove, almost 4' long by 3' high, its frame shaped from a long piece of aluminum, decorated with strips of paper and copper, and messages. Each message, painstakingly embellished with drawings, was folded carefully and hung on the frame. It made a huge impression. The MELC children immediately wanted to hear the messages; the dominant theme was friendship. They had to find a perfect place to hang it, after much discussion settling on the ceiling above the dress-up clothes in the Big Room. Daily they asked to hear the messages and in small groups visited the Easter Dove, recounting the messages to one another.

FIGURE 8.1.
Reading
messages
on the
Easter
Dove

The children's feelings for their La Villetta friends transferred to the Easter Dove. Perhaps it was how it arrived—traveling alone with the baggage. Perhaps it was the introduction—the double wrapping and drawn out expectations. Perhaps it was the love reflected in the messages. Perhaps it was, as children this age believe, that the Easter Dove became a real bird.

The Cuckoo Bird Is Created

The children had many discussions, provoked by the researcher/orchestrator: What could they do to make the Easter Dove happy? What would make Easter Dove love *them*? What must the Easter Dove be thinking, so far from the children who made him, in a strange place with nowhere to live? There he hung, children frequently clustered below discussing him. What was he feeling away from his mother? He must feel sad without a house. He must be lonely. He had no babies! The plight of the Easter Dove evoked the children's utmost empathy. They concluded they had to make her a baby, and a project was born.

Throughout the project the teachers' many roles were evident. Tesha, Thomas, and Kendra believed a baby would keep Easter Dove from feeling lonely. With Jennifer as collaborator they searched books to find the perfect bird; each imagined something different so selecting *one* was not easy. Finally they chose an African crane, which they named Cuckoo Bird. Among themselves the teachers discussed, as researchers do, many hypotheses for where the project might lead. They saw the potential for big experiences: an idea generated entirely by children and a difficult challenge. It was late April, almost the end of the school year; thinking about the next fall, the teachers had an idea. Miss Wendy, as orchestrator, proposed it: Would they like to make Cuckoo Bird with messages for new children who would come in September, just as they had received messages from the La Villetta children? Oh, yes!

The children decided that Cuckoo Bird had to look just like its mother, Easter Dove. What greater expression of love than to imitate? So, in collaboration with Jennifer, as teacher/designer, a huge amount of measuring took place to approximate the size. From prior projects, the children knew certain materials were better suited for specific purposes. They decided to use aluminum wire, chicken wire, and strips of white paper on which they glued the most beautiful things they could find: jewel-like plastic pieces. They knew how to weave, having done so with paper strips, feathers, fabric, leaves, and wire. They'd played with the effect of light through loose weavings. Now they wove the bejeweled strips of paper through the chicken wire. But a problem occurred with the beak: Try after try, they couldn't make it look like the Easter Dove's. Finally, the solution, finally, with teacher as designer/mediator, was to cut a paper triangle for a template.

April 25. Message-writing began; Sonya orchestrated thank you letters to their Italian friends and messages to their new friends—about themselves, their teachers, Coco, the school, and of course Easter Dove and Cuckoo Bird. Jennifer, designer/collaborator, attached the messages, then carefully stored Cuckoo Bird. School closed for the summer.

Second day of school, 1995–1996. Jennifer, as designer, wrapped and hung Cuckoo Bird in the Dining Room. It was a tantalizing package.

September 20. New children arrived. Excitement was palpable as they unwrapped Cuckoo Bird. There she was at last, huge, her feathers made from broom straws and sticking straight up toward the ceiling. It *did* look like its mother Easter Dove. Every message had to be read immediately. Bernice expressed everyone's thought: "Look! Cuckoo Bird flying!"

Clouds Are Made

From the moment it was unwrapped, Cuckoo Bird became real and the ceiling became the sky. Children talked about Cuckoo Bird at every meal. One day, looking overhead, Ben noticed there were no clouds. Others agreed: Cuckoo Bird needed clouds.

October 2. Jennifer, as orchestrator, gathered the children to talk about clouds, and another project began. First they discussed clouds. In many trips outside, teacher and children, all researchers, peered at the sky, studying clouds, then augmented firsthand observations by pouring over books until cloud's shapes and colors became familiar. As designers, they explored cloud's texture by feeling everything around them. Finally it was time to make them. But from what? Jennifer mediated more long discussions. The children had many ideas: cotton, clear materials, mesh. Different clouds emerged, the first made from small clear plastic boxes joined with transparent glue.

October 12. The children made more clouds by cutting and bending shapes from aluminum screening, and tying them to a length of dowel by long threads sewed on by the teacher/designers. Miss Wendy helped Jennifer hang the mobile-like group, nine in all, each about 8" wide. Cloud-making became a favorite activity. By early November Cuckoo Bird flew through a fine collection of clouds.

A Home Is Built

While making clouds, the children frequently worried that Cuckoo Bird had no home. When teacher/orchestrators asked what a home would look like, the children described a bird feeder. Many conversations followed.

October 19. Miss Wendy and four children undertook research—a field trip to the Nature Company to examine birdhouses. They brought brochures to Jennifer and sketched how their bird feeder should look. Still new at projects, the teachers interpreted bird feeder literally.

For several days the children drew, then, carefully carrying their drawings, went with Sonya to Mark Thevenot, one of the museum's exhibit builders. Sonya orchestrated a long discussion. Mark asked what they had in mind and, using their drawings, the children explained. It was left to Mark to meld their drawings into one, choose the wood, and do most of the construction. Under his patient hands Thomas and Howard hammered some nails. The result was

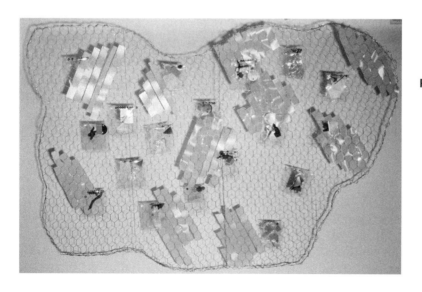

Figure 8.2.
Other
clouds
were
made of
wire laced
with shiny
materials

FIGURE 8.3.
The children explained their drawings to Mark

a first-rate bird feeder. The children glued on finishes—small pieces of ceramic tile and shiny metal. By the end of October it was finished, and also hung in the Dining Room. To the children it served three functions—"for Cuckoo Bird's food, water, and a place to rest while flying in the clouds."

A Nest Is Constructed

But Easter Dove did not have a nest! It disturbed the children's sense of fairness. Paula, Mary, and Thomas asked if they could make one. All November and after Thanksgiving too, the three talked about little else. On December 11 they went to the public library with Miss Wendy, this project's orchestrator, to find pictures of nests. At the playground and arboretum they peered through leafless branches for ideas. Research continued until Christmas.

Individual Drawings. Jennifer was orchestrator. First, each child designed a nest on paper using black markers. Then they described their drawings. With three possibilities for how the nest could look, Jennifer mediated a discussion about the final design. It yielded this list:

"Big for the Easter Dove can sit and eat her food."
"Soft so the babies can sleep and the mommy can lay her eggs in there."
"Circular so the eggs won't fall out."
"High up in a tree so no one will steal her babies."

"Pretty 'cause the mommy want to look at it."
"Tall sides because she won't fall out."
"With a bottom so she don't get hurt."

The qualities they listed reflected their research and their concern for the bird.

Collaborative Drawing. Orchestrating the procedure, Jennifer suggested the children collaborate by using the strongest features of each drawing to make one single design. First, Jennifer read back their comments about the qualities they wanted. Using their own ideas, the children decided which parts of the initial drawings met their criteria.

MARY: "Mine is the biggest one."
THOMAS: "I drew tall sides."
PAULA: "I put sticks all over the place and the Easter Dove won't fall through."

Together they drew a final design, which became the reference for each one's clay model. Jennifer said this was one of her favorites—where her understanding of projects "really clicked" (J. Azzariti, personal communication, February 8, 2007).

Clay Models. *January 22.* Jennifer, still orchestrating, asked each child to make a clay model. Paula molded hers by piling up coils. Thomas laid coils in rows to form the shape. Mary hollowed out a hunk of clay. Then Jennifer asked them to draw their models. Jennifer observed that they drew the way they had modeled—in lines, coils, or a mound. She documented their work by drawing their building process. She couldn't follow all three at once, so chose the two who were struggling as the more interesting. The documentation became a guide to construct the nest.

The Nest. The initial question was what to build the nest from. Terrill, Mary, and Paula were among the oldest children, having been in the MELC for 3 years, so, in Jennifer's words, "had lots of things in their pockets" (J. Azzariti, personal communication, February 8, 2007). They determined they needed paper, sticks, corrugated cardboard, paper twists, grass, flowers, feathers, and fabric. When Jennifer, designer/collaborator, asked, "What can we make the nest from?" they responded, "Wire," and found hardware cloth, which is easy to bend and holds its shape well. The children were concerned: Hardware cloth is hard! After much discussion, they decided to collect lots of soft things to cover the wire. But another problem surfaced: The small holes were difficult to weave materials through. Their solution, after extensive discussion, was to bundle materials—shredded paper, brown crinkled paper, pine needles, cotton—which they then attached easily with wire. To surprise the children when they arrived one morning, the teachers, thinking as designers, hung large empty branches from the ceiling. What they meant as a provocation to heighten excitement became a structure to hold the finished nest.

FIGURE 8.4.
They used wire to bundle the materials and attach them to the nest

The children's discussions as they built show their collaboration, focus, and understanding of cause and effect.

PAULA: "I cut the wire."
MARY: "So the Easter Dove have a place."
THOMAS: "'Cause we need to make it strong."
PAULA: "First we folded wire up."
MARY: "So nothing could fall out."
PAULA: "So the Easter Dove won't fall out."
MARY: "And the eggs."
THOMAS: "It was hard because we couldn't push it back."
MARY: "First we pull it through then we put it together."
PAULA: "We tried to make it into a bow. We hold it and put a bunch inside."
MARY: "We put the flowers in there, then we could twist it up and push it around."
THOMAS: "You could poke it around the holes."

The nest was amazing—large, sculptural, and original enough to hang in an art gallery. Years after, audiences seeing slides gasp: "Did the *children* really do that?" People don't expect such a complex construction by such young children. The birds remained in their places, Easter Dove, her nest alongside, and her baby, Cuckoo Bird, flying through the clouds, her house nearby, for the rest of the MELC's existence.

THE TEACHER'S ROLES IN ACTION

Projects don't just happen; they are carefully orchestrated. Each aspect of the teacher's role comes into play. Here I describe the teacher's complex role in action as she researches, designs, orchestrates, collaborates, documents, and mediates.

Researching

Researching itself involves discrete activities—an inquisitive mind that undertakes scientific investigations, the making of hypotheses, and, perhaps above all, the propensity to listen closely, observe carefully, and alter a hypothesis based on what you hear and see.

Inquiring Minds. The science underlying the Reggio Approach is human development. Reggio teachers inform their work through study of eminent persons who are pioneers or on the cutting edge in understanding diverse aspects of human development. Avid readers, they digest and discuss writings in philosophy and psychology. They are deeply conversant with ideas of John Dewey, Jean Piaget, Karl Popper, Nelson Goodman, Paolo Freire, Jerome Bruner, Seymour Papert, Howard Gardner, David Hawkins, Lev Vygotsky, and many others, including such Italian epistemologists as Bruno Munari, whose contributions range from design to human development, and Gianni Rodari, a children's author, but also a philosopher. They are equally knowledgeable of the Greeks and Enlightenment philosophers like Locke, Hume, Kant, and Rousseau. They have thoroughly plowed these and many others' work for ideas that they translate into practice by posing questions for themselves. American teacher education is, for the most part, curiously devoid of the philosophical questioning that occupies our European counterparts. This void in our training is a clue to why some Reggio-inspired schools lack the depth of their antecedents: We copy the form without knowing the substance.

Hypothesizing. Researchers hypothesize, making tentative assumptions to test their observations. For example, Reggio teachers hypothesized that innate differences exist between males and females. They tested this by equipping a room with a wooden horse-on-a-stick, small bed and dolls, make-believe food, and other props, then observing 2-year-olds play, first four girls, then four boys. They documented the toddlers' interaction with one another and the props. Differences were significant. Boys jumped on the bed and ran from prop to prop, testing each: Could it be ridden? Would it hit? Was it edible? Girls immediately fed the dolls and put them to bed, caretaking and nurturing.

Hypotheses underlie every project: If 2-year-olds find a huge, hollow cardboard column in the middle of the piazza, they will investigate it in varied ways. Let's try to see what happens! If we simultaneously provide 2-year-olds with ample supplies of paper and water, they will spontaneously mix them. Let's try it! If 5-year-olds hold a live dove, their drawings of birds will be more lifelike. Let's see if that's so! Stimulated by on-going study of philosophers and scientists and buoyed by their own inquisitiveness, their questions have no end: What do we predict will happen if. . . . Once they have formed a hypothesis, teachers test it by setting up situations or, as in the Easter Dove projects, taking advantage of experiences, then listening, observing, and recording what happens.

Listening. This is the essence of teacher/researcher. Frances Hawkins, wife of physicist/philosopher/educator David Hawkins and longtime preschool teacher, recounted an experience as head of the Los Alamos preschool. One teacher noted that only the children at Frances's table ate. Another asked, "Frances, why do children listen when *you* speak?" She wasn't sure, so had her teachers, one at a time, observe. Long discussions informed Frances's answer.

> I expect them [children] to listen, ask appropriate questions, then include another child or two in my listening. It is not magic, but requires . . . courtesy, savvy about age levels, and genuine intellectual curiosity about the dynamics of young children. . . . The ear and mind become tuned because the adult is not giving half-baked attention. (F. Hawkins, personal communication, May 8, 1985)

A teacher/researcher listens with full attention, eyes alert and always on the speaker, body concentrated, mind poised for thoughtful response, and with her own "intellectual curiosity in situ" (F. Hawkins, personal communication, May 8, 1985). This is *active* listening, the foundation for research. Feuerstein calls it mediation with *intention*.

Designing

Designing has several aspects—preparing the environment, choosing particular materials, and the consciousness that how the environment is prepared and what materials are available will determine how the children spend their time.

Preparing an Environment. Design influences relationships. Taliesin, Frank Lloyd Wright's home, workplace, and school, is magnificently sited to capture desert vistas, colored to reflect its surroundings at different hours or seasons, and rigorously detailed. But Wright made no provision for window shades, flagrantly neglecting the relationship between building and occupants! In contrast, Reggio educators design spaces to foster relationships. They position windows, doors, and mirrors to stimulate interaction. Vistas from room to room are calculated, in Carlina's words, like looking "through an aquarium" (C. Rinaldi, lecture to delegation, Reggio Emilia, March 2, 1992). Babies broaden their perspective by observing toddlers just older than themselves. Piazzas are in the center of schools, reflecting their importance as the center of Italian town life where markets are set up; residents stroll, meet, and gossip; political groups emote; and children play. Furniture, room separators, and nooks stimulate children to interact, for example, playing peek-a-boo around fabric strips that curtain off a comfy nook. These first games, encouraged by the design, are forerunners of increasingly complex games older children make up. By 3 children are in spaces designed as "classroom-laboratory-library-atelier" (Hawkins, 1983, p. 79).

Influencing the Use of Time. But there is a deeper meaning: Reggio educators believe that classroom design determines how children use their time. For example, low benches move so easily that children can arrange them end-to-end as boat, train, serpent, or other symbolic forms; corner-to-corner to facilitate conversation; in rectangles to contain space. How children arrange the forms determines what they will do in the space. Here research and design intersect as teachers study how children make choices. I am reminded of the Eskimo carvings that, when held in different orientations, reveal different animals or different poses of the same animal. Anthropologist Edmund Carpenter (1973, p.145) calls this "simultaneous perception of multiple meanings within one form." The point is: Everything in a Reggio school is designed for multiple potential; the design both offers possibilities and forges the intersection of space, time, and relationships. Examples throughout this book show the impact of such design.

Collaborating

As collaborators Reggio teachers understand that each member of a group provides his or her own perspective, that collaborative endeavor evokes each group member's particular skills, and that outcomes are stronger when forged from differences. Each person, from babyhood, is unique. Combining various dispositions, abilities, and experiences gives others a range of approaches to copy, adapt, or reject. Doing so hones each one's ability against others' strengths.

British anthropologist Peter Reynolds hypothesizes that as humans evolved, collaboration drove tool-making and language. He bases his theory on many years of study of Australian Aborigines. They were not

> "jacks-of-all-trades with crude stone tools" . . . [but depended on] "task specialization, symbolic coordination, social cooperation, role complementarity, collective goals, logical sequencing of operations, and assembly of separately manufactured parts." (cited in Wilson, 1998, p. 171)

"Reynolds believes the *character* of the group interaction was the critical stimulus to the emergence of human language and intelligence" (p. 170, emphasis in original). He and other scientists are correlating the neurological links between *small-group collaboration* and the cognitive processes involved in hand skills, gesture-making, tool use, and language. This resonates strongly with what we observe in Reggio classrooms and the MELC: teachers using collaborative process as the means to help children develop hand skills and thinking skills.

Orchestrating

The orchestrator/teacher *plays* the environment and children as the orchestra conductor *plays* the sounds of instruments and musicians' dynamic interpretations. For example, in the Reggio project "To Make a Portrait of a Lion," Amelia, the teacher, orchestrated the children's affair with stone sculptures of lions. Experience followed experience—first climbing all over, then sketching the lions, seeing slides of the experience, painting lions, playing with shadow screen images of the lions, interacting with a life-size lion puppet, drawing, mural-making, sculpting. Or, the teachers orchestrated the children's fascination with Coco through talk, ink, markers, clay, and video. The teacher does not write a script any more than an orchestra leader writes the music; rather, they both interpret behaviors.

Documenting

Teacher as documenter is a new and unique role. Carlina Rinaldi (2006) says, "Documentation is a new concept of didactics . . . more similar to the science of communication than to the traditional pedagogical disciplines" (p. 69). Documentation makes the listening process visible. The panels don't contain pretty pictures of children, but freeze-frame seminal moments in the life of a project. They are visible traces of the evolution of a project that enable teachers and children to watch themselves thinking, sometimes struggling with new ideas, sometimes having an "aha" moment. The role also is discussed above and in Chapter 6. I merely mention it here.

Mediating

According to Feuerstein, the mediator's intentionality orients the child to attend to and connect this experience to prior experiences. He says that mediators must be energetic and emotional (Feuerstein et al., 2006), traits you see in Reggio teachers who begin many lessons by commanding: "Alors! Attenzione!" They speak with conviction that alerts the child, with demeanor that says, "I expect you to be fully present," with attitude and posture that say, "Something exciting is about to happen," with emotion that says, "I respect your ideas and care about what you have to say." Their intention influences children to be attentive, engaged, and expectant. The other two conditions Feuerstein says are essential for intervention to be considered mediation are *meaning* and *transcendence*. Throughout this book we see the teachers discussing meaning: Recall Wendy in Chapter 2 teaching the meaning of words; Jennifer repeatedly instructing on the nature of particular materials; Sonya frequently orchestrating discussions about the meaning of friendship. And we see them stretching the children to transcend experiences by transforming drawings into models, making analogies, and extending projects in new directions.

Teacher/mediators believe in every child's capacity to learn. Feuerstein believes that with effective mediation anyone can learn regardless of condition, age of onset, or severity. Gardner (1983) says: "What recent research has shown, virtually uncontrovertibly, is that whatever differences may initially appear, early intervention and consistent training can play a decisive role in determining the individual's ultimate level of performance" (p. 316). Reggio educators are intuitive mediators; MELC teachers were learning to be.

Every Easter Dove project began with teachers' discussing some aspect with the children—their feelings toward the Dove, ideas about materials, concepts of nests—and listening. Children's responses and adults' collaboration guided the next steps. The nest resulted from teachers' hearing strong protests: Cuckoo Bird has a nest, so must Easter Dove! The researcher understood the importance of first informing the children about nests; the designer enlarged the collection of books, and the orchestrator instigated field trips. The designer/orchestrator elicited ideas about nests' features and which materials to use. The orchestrator launched the children on the draw/model/build process, as the collaborator/mediator participated/scaffolded, and the documenter recorded.

LEARNING A NEW ROLE

The MELC teachers were beginning to analyze their process. In their own words they:

- looked for children's *questions*;
- read children's *products*—words, drawings, objects—literally and metaphorically;
- considered what *problems* might occur next in a project;
- *hypothesized* what issues or ideas would re-emerge;
- looked for *things of interest to themselves* as well as children;
- made *choices*.

Let's watch how the teachers wrestled with those problems.

Finding Questions

Children's questions in the Easter Dove projects were easily determined because children stated their desires directly, and the teachers, as researcher/listeners, heard: "Easter Dove is lonely and needs a baby." "There should be clouds for Cuckoo Bird." "Cuckoo Bird needs someplace to get food and water." "If Cuckoo Bird has a nest, Easter Dove should too." Teacher/researchers grab clear statements and questions and use them, not to provide answers, but to help children develop understanding. David Perkins (1995) maintains that intelligence means

> coming to know your way around different situations (experiential intelligence) . . . and . . . around decision making, problem solving, learning with understanding, and other important kinds of thinking . . . strategies, habits, concepts, beliefs, values, and more. (p. 236)

Basing activity on children's questions contrasts with direct instruction in which preplanned lessons meet specific objectives by providing bits of information to cover in a predetermined amount of time: Learn the sound "u" in "hug," 5 minutes; count plastic bears, 10 minutes. Instead, questions are designed to probe transcendent ideas: What is friendship? Why do we communicate? How can we express love? Understanding develops gradually as children have varied experiences. They grapple with their questions by fashioning something tangible or representing their idea concretely, in a drawing or model, which can be analyzed, discussed, and refashioned. Yet, merely desiring to use children's questions to address transcendent themes does not make it obvious what the content of projects should be, or how to start, continue, and conclude projects. Lesson plans have clear boundaries, but teachers cannot predetermine projects' evolution. Content is not always clear, as examples in Chapter 2 show, and some projects, like those above, require many months to come to fruition or branch to spawn new projects.

Reading Products

Determining what to produce, guiding production, and interpreting it, especially metaphorically, is not as easy as seeing children's desire to make an ambulance or pollute water, two things that keenly interested the MELC children and led to projects: Children's interest in the TV show *911* translated literally into producing a 3-D ambulance; the obvious response to questions about pollution was to conduct experiments. But how to respond to their interest in seasons, colors, and Coco required intense consideration. A breakthrough for Jennifer came when children expressed their understanding of how leaves fall by making a zig-zag-shaped sculpture, metaphorically representing the path of a falling leaf. The experience taught her "that when one thing stands for another, it need not be a literal representation" (Lewin-Benham, 2006, p. 114).

As the Easter Dove projects began, the teachers were not yet thinking metaphorically, so took the children's idea for a bird feeder literally. Clouds were more abstract than the bird feeder, but less representational than the nest. We see teachers' growth in the nest, a more original, yet still clearly recognizable, representation. Literal and metaphorical productions are appropriate at different times. Learning this takes experience.

Pursuing an Idea

Thinking literally about making a feeder look like a feeder presented the problem of turning children's drawings into something realistic. Not very imaginative, the project nonetheless provided experience with woodworking and built a relationship with a carpenter. In making the nest, the teachers drew the children out more about how it should look and held lengthy discussions, and something more imaginative resulted.

Sheppy at age 3½ asked me to make a helicopter. Using eraser, thumb tack, and paper, I made something that looked nothing like a helicopter, but

Sheppy loved it and immediately flew it around. Young children are unconcerned if what they produce doesn't look like what they say they are making. They invest whatever they make with the qualities of what they are thinking about, regardless of whether idea and reality match, accommodating the object to their idea. The teachers had to learn to accept this disjunction. Eight-year-olds try to represent reality closely. Younger children simply explore; the more problems challenge them to explore, the more they learn. Among many things they learn are production techniques and refined hand movements; moreover, they acquire a disposition to enjoy challenges.

Hypothesizing

Reggio teachers brainstorm projects to determine what *might* emerge. Easter Dove might have produced this brainstorm:

- ideas *predictably related* to birds—nests and eggs, or materials like feathers and straw;
- ideas *tangentially related*—worms, earth, and birdbaths;
- *pictorial references*—images in books and magazines;
- *avian references*—robins, sparrows, or canaries;
- *auditory associations*—chirps and cackles;
- *fantastical ideas*—birds that talk or transport people;
- *spacial references*—parks, forests, or backyards;
- *literary references*—Eskimo raven tales, Aesop's "The Crow and the Pitcher," Andersen's "The Ugly Duckling."

After brainstorming, teachers match their thoughts and children's words, seeking connections. The more matches, the better a project they can anticipate.

New to hypothesizing, the MELC teachers focused more narrowly: What might happen tomorrow that builds on today's work? After making wire clouds, would children want to use other materials? Would they want to make the baby birds they so frequently mentioned? Given the complexity of the role they were learning, their narrower thinking pales before the mere fact that they persevered. As their understanding of the role deepened, their ideas of what might happen next broadened; recall the evolution of seasons projects (Chapter 3), Coco projects (Chapter 4), birthday celebrations (Chapter 5), and the cluster of Easter Dove projects.

Realizing Teachers' Interests

In Reggio practices, teachers' continuing growth is as important as children's. The MELC teachers were especially challenged by children who were stymied—who never drew, had low self-esteem, or had problems at home. Capturing these children's interest was one way the teachers stayed challenged. For example, Alonzo never drew, but transformed a 3-D sculpture to a to-scale paper rendering. It challenged Jennifer to collaborate without being too directive. Birthdays challenged Sonya to juggle composing groups, producing varied gifts, coordinating with parents, and collaborating with other teachers. The city challenged Wendy to use library, arboretum, hospital, vet, or U.S. Capitol to stretch children. As she said, "We watched them grow" (W. Baldwin, personal communication, January 24, 2007). Holding conversations challenged Genet. Initially, she had no idea how but, once over that hurdle, welcomed any opportunity to engage the children in discussion. Teachers need challenge just as children do.

Making Choices

Choice is the essence of teaching. Yet, knowing what to choose is perplexing. How do you select the most pregnant idea, leading question or phrase, best mix of children, most suitable materials? Easter Dove projects consolidated prior experience and stretched teachers' understanding of how to weave different children in and out of long-lasting projects, sustain a project's momentum, and wait for ideas to gestate. Such choices are foreign to teaching in which the objective is to raise test scores, but are part of schools that form around philosophers and sages, of progressive education and best practices.

To teach young children is to perform without a rehearsal. Development is so rapid, relationships are so intense, each day is so different. The complex roles of a Reggio teacher require minute-by-minute responsiveness that often means quickly switching gears—now lead, now follow; intervene, demur; demonstrate, observe; tell, ask. These dramatic choices involve being on your toes every minute. Anyone trying Reggio-inspired work will make their own choices, not follow others' lesson plans.

FORGOTTEN SPACE

Ceilings figure most prominently in Easter Dove constructions. Ceilings often are forgotten, mainly out-of-sight, generally unused. The birds and clouds, ephemeral and intricate, added immeasurably to the rooms' visual intrigue, drawing children's attention upward. One doesn't expect to see sculpture hanging from school ceilings, much less sizable pieces by young children.

> Designing the space of an infant-toddler or preschool . . . requires . . . pedagogy, psychology, architecture, sociology, and anthropology . . . [which] generate[s] a kind of research that is open to the contributions of . . . music, choreography, design, performance, and fashion. . . . This guarantee[s] that the space . . . itself [will be] a research project and therefore capable, day by day, of taking stock of its own outcomes, the effectiveness of its language, and its capacity for *dialogue with the process of becoming* which is the basis of true education. (Rinaldi, 2002, p. 8, emphasis added)

The MELC teachers and children were undergoing different processes of *becoming*—the teachers with a role that required designing provocative spaces, the children with skill in expressing themselves. Many relationships fostered their growth: children across the ocean, Italian teachers, a museum carpenter, bird-like constructions, resources in their city, materials in their school, and of course one another, the adults in their lives, and the environment.

The large-scale Easter Dove projects stretched the teachers' ability to use the environment as a catalyst to help children notice detail and appreciate beauty. Children recognized the drama of the constructions and noticed visitors' reactions—stunned, awed, impressed. The sculptures markedly altered the space, affecting the entire environment, literally and figuratively opening new vistas.

COMPLEX, ORIGINAL, CREATIVE WORK

Howard Gardner (1993) explains that artists' works—painters, dancers, poets, designers—are not complete without audience and critics. At the MELC, educators, psychologists, museum professionals, funders, and other visitors functioned as audience and critic. Most could not believe the children had been rampantly out-of-control in the school's first years or were from financially impoverished backgrounds. Visitors saw their self-confidence, articulateness, and complex productions, and assumed they were from economically advantaged homes or had parents who aggressively sought opportunities for their children, or were preselected for intelligence. But we accepted children first-come, first-served once the D.C. Public Schools certified that they met federal poverty guidelines. We had the city's least financially secure, most underexposed children, all subject to inner-city perils. The competence our visitors noted resulted from the children's innate abilities and mediation by teachers committed to a new role and to the belief that young children can undertake significant work.

CHAPTER 9

Building
a Bridge

We are not born to be teachers. Teaching "is created through the work."
—Loris Malaguzzi (Question & Answer with a Delegation
at Diana School, Reggio Emilia, March 6, 1992)

THIS CHAPTER PORTRAYS A CHALLENGE TO two preschool children to build a *big* bridge in clay. It shows how Malaguzzi used challenges to inspire excellence, and how Amelia faced a cultural clash in offering the challenge to American children. It expresses my concerns, as Director, about accepting the challenge in a public spotlight, including media, the university/research world, international visitors, and other VIPs. It portrays a young teacher facing the challenge, and two children struggling to meet it. The theme—professional support for teachers—is part of Reggio's bedrock and important in early education. Some details are portrayed on an unpublished video of the project; others were related by Amelia Gambetti and MELC staff at programs run by the MELC for visiting educators.

THE PROTAGONISTS

April 1995. Day One—making sure the children had some familiarity with bridges and had used clay. Day Two—building the bridge. Protagonists: Jennifer, Renee, and DeMarcos. Instigators: Loris Malaguzzi, Amelia Gambetti, and Giovanni Piazza. Supporter: Ann Lewin. I explain their mindsets first.

Malaguzzi

Malaguzzi exhorted Amelia to give the teachers and children in the MELC a big challenge. The Italian word he used was *provocazione*; the literal translation is *provoke*, in which Americans hear pejorative connotations: exciting anger, enraging, irritating, or causing fights. For Italians the sense is evocative—calling forth, stimulating, arousing, or causing appetite. It conveys an air of expectation, exploration, wonder, involvement. The provocation with which Malaguzzi challenged two Reggio preschools and the MELC—build a large bridge in clay—challenges everyone working with young children to consider what it means to support teachers.

Malaguzzi had a long affair with America. He studied our philosophers of education—Dewey, Bruner, Hawkins, Papert, Gardner. He knew their writings well, quoted them often, and reveled in exchanging ideas when they visited Reggio. As a youth, western movies influenced Malaguzzi—Charlie Chaplin, John Gilbert, Mary Pickford, cowboys with eternal allure: "I loved the prairies of the far west. They go forever without a borderline, a sheriff, no hierarchies, no regulations" (L. Malaguzzi, lecture, March 6, 1992).

Malaguzzi himself was a master impresario: designer with a sense of the spectacular; orchestrator who conducted elaborate productions; collaborator who saw in children's smallest acts the drama of human development. He believed the human quest for mastery was the source of young children's energy—the excitement of a challenge, search for novelty, joy of discovery, ecstasy of an "aha!" He not only recognized but had a genius for evoking "ahas." In December 1993 Malaguzzi gave Amelia a provocation for the MELC: Undertake the challenging project of building a *big* bridge in clay.

Amelia

Following a mandatory policy, Amelia retired after teaching in the Reggio schools for 20 years. Full of zest to continue her work, she chose preschool education in the United States as her next forum.

> I wanted to share my experience. I was scared, outside my culture, curious about the huge number of questions U.S. delegations asked. I had retired, but still wanted to be challenged. (A. Gambetti, talk to visiting teachers on an MELC Day, June 20, 1994)

Thus, in the 1993–1994 school year Amelia was in Washington, D.C., as the MELC's Master Consulting Teacher. I had persuaded her to help us adapt Reggio practices. In December Amelia returned to Italy for the Christmas holiday. Malaguzzi, eager to learn about her experiences, met with her many times, delving into her descriptions, probing to find what attracted Amelia to the U.S. school, expectant about the transfer of the Reggio Approach to America. He peppered her with questions.

Amelia recalled the meetings: "I felt as if I had three Ph.D. exams. He wanted to know everything." After listening intently, Malaguzzi challenged Amelia: "You have created a context in Washington, D.C., with human beings who want to flourish. Let's see if there are analogies to our experiences." He suggested she carry out a project as a provocation for the MELC students.

Malaguzzi first suggested that Amelia try a project with fountains. Remembering the project "Amusement Park for Birds" at La Villetta School, Amelia was aghast: "That would be too difficult!" The project had lasted 2 years. The children's ideas had antecedents in earlier projects so they had intimate knowledge of the field where the park would be. Documentation of earlier experiences hung on La Villetta's walls.

Memories abounded, one of children, teachers, and families collaborating to restore the field after winter storms. Another was a giant fresco covering a wall in their piazza, depicting the field from an ant's perspective. Once the park project began, children undertook a huge study, many discussions, months of prototypes, pilot tests, measuring, and physics problems. The combined pleas of children, parents, and teachers convinced the town's water division to install water pipes for the constructions. Ultimately, children, teachers, parents, and townsfolk collaborated on building an imaginative park for birds. That was the context Amelia remembered as she responded that the MELC could not possibly do a project with fountains.

"So, your children do not know fountains?" Malaguzzi broke in on her thoughts.

"Yes, but . . . "

"There are no fountains in Washington?"

"Of course, but . . . "

"Your children have never seen these fountains? Birds then! Surely, your children know something about birds!"

Again, Amelia thought about the La Villetta children; they knew the creatures in their park well, all the relationships—cats with birds, birds with squirrels, and their own with all the animals. They endowed the animals with ideas tantamount to their own, and thus knew what to do to please birds. This long history led them to incorporate two bird observatories in the park. There the children used binoculars to watch birds and devices to call them; provided food to sustain birds, and decorations to entice them. Amelia thought of these deep relationships. She knew the children's next project was on flight, that at this moment they were constructing an enormous working model of a bird's wing.

"No, it's too much, too long!"

"No birds? A rainbow then!" Malaguzzi insisted.

Amelia thought of "Arcobalena" (rainbow), a project led by Vea Vecchi, *atelierista* at Diana School, the Reggio preschool where Malaguzzi and Vea created the role of *atelierista,* engaging in extensive dialogue that extended over many years. Three boys, ages 5 and 6, had conducted a lengthy series of experiments discovering how to make rainbows using a mirror, tub of water, flashlight, and ultimately the sun's rays.

Reading Amelia's thoughts, Malaguzzi interrupted: "You should feel guilty! You refuse analogies, you refuse challenges. Do you have bridges in Washington? Children *must* have an image of bridges. American bridges are so huge!"

> VEA, who had been listening: "Let's ask two of our schools and the MELC to do the same project. Don't say no, Amelia!"
>
> MALAGUZZI: "You don't respect your children! Observe them. See if two children can work together to build a bridge in clay. Make it a *big* bridge. Please, make sure before you begin that they know about bridges."

Less than a week later, January 31, 1994, Malaguzzi had a fatal heart attack. In February 1994 Amelia returned to the MELC. Perhaps because it was his last provocation and she was still in shock at his death, perhaps because children at two Reggio schools were already building bridges, perhaps because it made sense, Amelia accepted the challenge. She would find children to build a big bridge in clay. She observed the block area to see whether any children knew about bridges and the Studio to see whether they knew about clay. Some did. Malaguzzi's last provocation would be effected. The MELC children would be challenged to solve problems and work out strategies together. She understood what a huge effort this would require of children, teachers, and school.

Analyzing what supports teachers, we see Malaguzzi, a dynamic leader, and two exceptional teachers candidly expressing ideas, doubts, controversies. Malaguzzi epitomizes the role of leader as instigator, initiator, challenger who inspires, cajoles, and insists. Leadership is essential to support teachers.

Giovanni

Giovanni and Amelia had worked together for 20 years collaborating on many projects. Their teamwork was impeccable, their styles complementary— Giovanni contemplative, Amelia forceful. Both were gifted in using the structure of projects to help children express their ideas and stretch their capabilities. Giovanni would videotape the Bridge project. Video is effective in helping teachers reflect on their performance.

Ann

A lot was at risk in the Bridge project. By April 1994 word was out that the MELC was adapting the Reggio Approach. Teachers, administrators, and the press were flocking in ever-greater numbers to Reggio. There Reggio educators talked about their Washington school that validated the Reggio Approach, proving their practices would work elsewhere. We knew what happened in Bridge would be widely reported. But we did not know how our children would respond, whether they would accept the challenge.

We had a flood of concerns: Could DeMarcos and Renee transfer what they knew about building with blocks to building in clay, transposing from one medium to another? Would boy and girl collaborate or use conflicting strategies? Would they persist? Would they solve the problem? How would Jennifer respond? What effect would videotaping have? How would the Washington and Reggio projects look side-by-side? The Reggio children were capable of such sophisticated work. Would ours look inferior?

Jennifer

Two pros were watching. Jennifer was scared.

> Most of our children have no prior experience with glue, paint, clay, weaving, drawing, markers, pencils. Their first response is often, "I can't." It is a big challenge to get them to feel comfortable using materials. Many first projects are simply exercises with new materials—short projects, maybe an hour, a morning, a week.
>
> I didn't know what to expect from DeMarcos and Renee. We chose them because we knew, from their past clay work, that both liked working with it. During an exploration with six children, DeMarcos spontaneously made three small bridges, like a snake of clay, each end attached

to its own slab on either side. Amazingly they stood. Before the Bridge project, DeMarcos and Renee had explored clay only three times. But both were generally available to try new challenges. DeMarcos loves the Studio and is always eager to do anything involving it. If I invite Renee, who is skilled at using materials, she always replies, "Sure." (J. Azzariti, lecture to visiting educators, September 29, 1995)

Supporting teachers means putting them in situations that are novel and complex. They, as all humans, require challenge, which sometimes means walking a high wire with no net!

DeMarcos and Renee

DeMarcos, age 6, and Renee, age 5 years, 10 months, had barely worked with clay, but their block-building showed they knew something about bridges. They also had memories about bridges. Both mentioned drawbridges as the project began. DeMarcos had a theory about why drawbridges open. During the project when they were stymied, Renee knew: "We can make the bridge like it's open!" So much was at stake: the children's self-confidence, the teacher's sense of competence, the Reggio educators' assessment of whether their approach would transfer, the MELC's reputation.

THE STORY

April 12, 1994, 9:38 AM. Jennifer brought the children to the Studio. The video recorder was on, Giovanni taping, Amelia observing. Jennifer recalled:

I was so nervous. I had never done anything like this, and two experts were studying every move. I believed that I couldn't interrupt to ask questions, to get their suggestions or comments, that I was completely alone. I knew the expectations for this project. The same project had already begun in two Reggio schools and they were counting on us. (J. Azzariti, lecture to visiting educators, September 29, 1995)

Explaining the Challenge

JENNIFER, to Renee: "The other day in the Studio I saw some wonderful things you made—the car, the house for the dinosaur, that tree. Remember the tree?"

JENNIFER, to DeMarcos: "And DeMarcos, *you* did something, the bridge! Remember? You actually made three bridges. Did you *see* a bridge somewhere?"

DEMARCOS: "I see a bridge that opened; that's why I made it."

JENNIFER: "A bridge that opened? Wow, incredible! Why did it open?"

DEMARCOS: "For the big boats."

JENNIFER, to Renee: "Have you ever seen a bridge like that?" Renee comments on a drawbridge she has seen.

Jennifer continues introducing the project: "I had an idea. Since you two are *so* good with the clay and are such *capable* builders, I thought today we could *try* to build a *big* bridge."

Indicating a large sheet of blue paper on the table: "I have this blue paper right here." It covers most of a 4' x 2½' table, leaving a little exposed at each end. "This," pointing, "could be the river, like the Potomac."

DeMarcos: "Like the *water* . . ."
Jennifer: "Yes, this could be the water. Okay?"
DeMarcos: ". . . and be floating."
Jennifer: "Exactly. So we need a bridge. But," placing her hand on the uncovered table on DeMarcos's side, "it has to have one side here . . ."
DeMarcos, excited, talking at the same time: "It has to be *big*."
Jennifer: ". . . and one side here." Gesturing from one side of the table and placing a hand on the other side: "It has to go *over* the river."
DeMarcos: "It has to go down in the water."
Jennifer: "Exactly. Do you think you could try that?" DeMarcos and Renee nod eagerly.

Introducing the Materials

Jennifer, walking to a nearby table with clay and other supplies: "What's this?"
The children right beside her: "Clay!"
Jennifer: "Yes! Do you like the new clay?"
DeMarcos: "Mmmmmm!"

Jennifer is supported by the well-prepared environment, Amelia's tutelage, Giovanni's documentation, my enthusiasm, and her growing understanding of how to choose children for projects.

On the table are several hunks of clay and a huge rectangular block, 25 pounds and 15" high, cut into halves; a wire utensil to slice clay off a block; many wooden cylinders of varied diameter and height, some over 1" thick, others thinner than a pencil, some 16" tall, others barely 4"; wood slats, about ¼" thin and in varying dimensions, some as large as 6" by 12"; and two jars of slip, a paint brush in each.

Jennifer, stirring the slip: "Have you used *this* before? It's clay with water. What does it do?"
DeMarcos and Renee: "It's glue to make it stick to your piece."
Jennifer: "Yes. And there are some pieces of wood if you need them and wires to cut your clay. We're going to start with clay. If you need something else, you can come back."
Renee, delighted: "Yeeee!"
Jennifer: "I want you to work together and figure out how you're going to make this bridge. So, start whenever you're ready, but you might want to talk about what you're going to do."

As the children look at the supply table, Jennifer reminds them: "It's going to be a *big* bridge."

The Children Start

DeMarcos brings one of the huge clay halves and a jar of slip. Renee brings clay and some pieces of wood.

DeMarcos, looking at the huge amount of clay: "We probably can make *two* bridges."

Jennifer, who, as an artist, has an innate sense for how to constrain problems: "No, we're only going to make one, but it's going to be a *big one* so it will take a lot."

The artist's perspective can reorient other teachers' entire approach. Having an artist as collaborator is a novel way to support teachers.

All you hear is the sound of fists pounding clay and slabs hitting the table as the children begin to turn their hunks into thick pancakes, flipping them from side to side. Jennifer watches, taking notes on their comments and sequence of activity. The reflective nature of the practice—allowing time to observe and record—guides her.

Renee, after a long silence: "DeMarcos, you forgot to use the glue."

DeMarcos: "But I didn't need the glue."

Renee, revealing how carefully she had listened: "Didn't she say, 'don't forget the glue'?" DeMarcos begins to brush slip onto his pancake.

Renee, also starting to brush slip onto her pancake: "Why you doin' that?" More time passes.

Jennifer, unsure how to move the project forward: "Now that you put the glue on, what are you going to do?"

DeMarcos, starting toward the wooden cylinders Renee brought to the table: "I'm goin' to use a stick . . . "

Before he can get to them, Renee reaches for the two largest cylinders and hands one to DeMarcos: "The sticks hard. You can't even break 'em, DeMarcos."

DeMarcos, pushing the cylinder into his clay pancake so that it stands upright, and answering: "Yes, you could, if you . . . " He makes a sweeping gesture, accidentally hits the stick, and topples it.

Renee, painting slip on her pancake with one hand and holding the stick in the other: "I'm *holdin'* mine, DeMarcos."

A Plan

DeMarcos, pushing his cylinder in again, picks up a small hunk of clay and pats it flat. His determined actions reveal he has a plan: "We can stick our clay together, and we'll make the bridge." He starts painting the top of his cylinder with slip: "This is where I'm going to stick the bridge at, Renee."

Renee, staring at DeMarcos's upright cylinder and imitating what he has done: "*I'm* doing the same thing." DeMarcos continues painting slip on his cylinder, removing it from the clay, carefully painting slip up and down its sides.

Jennifer, still unsure, addresses DeMarcos, hesitating: "Uh, could you tell me what . . . " DeMarcos stops painting slip and sticks one end of the cylinder into his thick clay pancake.

Jennifer, her artist's sense taking over, points to the jar of slip and addresses DeMarcos. She mediates firmly: "This probably won't help the wood stick to the clay. Why don't you use more clay?" Now sure of herself and *very* directive: "*Try to stick it on with more clay* because *this*," pointing to the slip again, "won't hold wood." DeMarcos tears a small hunk of clay off the block, pounds it onto a pancake, then presses the small dab onto the top of the cylinder. Renee copies.

Excited, DeMarcos carries his construction from his side of the table to Renee's, places it on the table close to hers, and cries, "Wooah, *Daddy*!" thinking that, with a bit of clay spanning from his cylinder to Renee's, the bridge will be done!

"Uh . . . DeMarcos . . . ," questions Jennifer, "why are you putting yours on that side of the table?" Renee is balancing one of the flat rectangular wooden slats on the tops of her cylinder and DeMarcos's to span the few inches between them. DeMarcos presses the wooden slab down and holds out his hands, as if to say, "Voila!" Renee crows with glee. They believe the bridge is done!

Jennifer, mediating, stands up: "That's a good idea, but it needs to be longer"; gesturing: "it has to go *over*, from *that* side of the table to *this* side."

DeMarcos, removing the flat piece, disbelieving: "*Longer?*"

Jennifer: "We have to figure out . . . from *that* side of the table," pointing to DeMarcos's side, "to *that*," pointing to Renee's.

DeMarcos: "How we gonna do *that*?"

Jennifer, thinking as a designer: "That's what you need to talk about. It needs to be longer. Do you need help, or can you *carefully* carry yours back to your side of the table? You can figure out another way." DeMarcos removes the slab of wood, carries his construction back to his side, and leaves.

The Children Start Over

Jennifer, as collaborator, removing pieces of wood and hunks of clay from the blue paper: "Can I move these off so you can see where you're going? Let's make this," pointing to the water, "clear." She rearranges things so the water is free of supplies: "Okay! Now!"

Renee, gesturing across the span of blue paper: "Now, DeMarcos, how we gonna make the bridge cross over all the way . . . ?"

DeMarcos, from across the room: "*You* gonna do it. *You* think of it. *I* ain't thinkin' of it."

Any teacher can relate to the situation: A challenge beyond a child's capacity triggers resistance. Do you acknowledge that the project may be too challenging, or persevere? Perseverance requires a supportive climate, one with time and an attitude accepting of trial and error, untested theories, and unworkable hypotheses. Supporting teachers means allowing them to fail.

DeMarcos returns. Both children go to the supply table to get more clay. DeMarcos brings the other half of the block *and* another huge hunk. Renee takes a huge piece to her side and begins to push clay around the base of the thick cylinder. She has an idea. DeMarcos keeps trying to get the wood steadied on top, while Renee works on the base.

Later Jennifer said:

> I had no idea how much or when to intervene. I was especially nervous at the children's picking up the wood. I didn't know if there were rules, if they were supposed to use only clay. Fortunately, Giovanni and Amelia gave me an encouraging look, so I knew that using wood was alright.

The experts responded at a critical moment.

An Approach Emerges

JENNIFER, as designer, picks up on what Renee is doing and, pointing to the base, suggests: "Use more clay. Put clay *next to* the pole because DeMarcos is adding things to the top." Showing Renee how: "This needs to be stronger down here. Smoosh it with your fingers."

RENEE, steadily pushing several wads of clay onto the base, pressing them in and up the sides of the pillar until, finally, it is reasonably steady: "There!" DeMarcos also begins to add clay to the base.

RENEE: "DeMarcos, it doesn't need it . . . it's strong enough!"

DEMARCOS, wiggling the cylinder: "It don't feel like it's strong."

JENNIFER: "It will wiggle a little, but Renee has done a good job." DeMarcos takes a small, thick slab of clay and pushes it down on top of the cylinder.

JENNIFER, mediating, firmly correcting his technique: "Don't push so *hard*. Be gentle."

Renee goes to DeMarcos's side of the table and works on his pillar, pounding pieces of clay, then pushing and smoothing them around the base to steady it until it's sturdy like hers.

DeMarcos, still at Renee's cylinder, takes a second small thick slab of clay and, using slip, presses it onto the first. The two pieces form about an 8" extension from the top of Renee's pillar toward DeMarcos's side. But the heavy span topples off.

Renee has watched, and now goes to the supply table, neatly slices a *thin* slab of clay from a huge hunk, puts slip on top of DeMarcos's pillar, and deftly attaches her clay slab. Then she attaches a second thin slab, this time propping the end with a slat of wood that she steadies in the "water." It balances! She smoothes more slip on the clay span and adds a third thin clay slab to lengthen the span. Realizing her approach will work, she crows delightedly: "Two!"

Jennifer recalled:

I thought they'd use the wood to support the clay until it dried; I still was unsure, thinking it might be cheating to use wood as pillars for the bridge! (J. Azzariti, lecture to visiting educators, September 1995)

Competing

DEMARCOS, still trying to attach his thick slab, which keeps falling off, taunting: "You about to get beat, Renee!" DeMarcos has added a huge, bulging donut of clay to the middle of the thick wooden cylinder.

JENNIFER, leaning toward DeMarcos: "It would be stronger if you put it," referring to the donut, "on the *bottom.*"

RENEE, taunting DeMarcos, sing-song: "Look-a wha-at you-oo did!"

DEMARCOS, embarrassed: "Everybody's lookin' at me!"

RENEE, laughing, still taunting: "Everybody's lookin' a-at DeMarcos!" DeMarcos's ungainly clay donut balances for a moment . . . "DeMarcos, *what* are you doin'!" . . . but falls again!

RENEE, laughing uproariously: "Yours is fallin'! It's so *funny!*"

JENNIFER, intervening firmly: "Renee, maybe you can *help* DeMarcos make that part stand up. Do you think you can *help* him?" Repeating: "Can you *help* him?"

RENEE: "Uh, maybe," but keeps working on her side.

JENNIFER, insisting: "*I* think so. Why don't you see if you can help DeMarcos *right here,*" pointing to the lump on top, "because it keeps falling and he needs some help."

The MELC teachers have a good sense of when to intervene, insist, and redirect with no wishy-washiness. They are intentional.

Collaborating

Renee goes to DeMarcos's side, removes the huge donut, and pounds it into a large flat slab: "It won't keep on fallin' if that thing's not heavy." De-Marcos watches her intently. With one hand Renee holds the thick slab of clay on top of DeMarcos's pillar while with the other she reaches for a slat of wood. She places the slat against the thick cylinder, tips it toward her side, and pushes it into the clay base. Then she supports the clay slab with one hand while she pinches it with the other to make it grip the thin top edge of the slat. She accomplished this in one continuous, dextrous movement. "Whew! We're building a bridge, all the way over here," pointing to her side of the table. "Look! Yours is straight and mine is over there."

Maintaining Focus

10:30. Over 50 minutes have passed. Time supports teachers who are engaged in big challenges. Renee works and DeMarcos moves off to the side. The children converse, unrelated to the bridge. Renee, prattling on, works as DeMarcos replies, watching but not taking part. Jennifer, firmly bringing DeMarcos back on task: "DeMarcos, what if you try to work on *that* side," pointing to the other end of the table. DeMarcos takes a huge hunk of clay to the other end and begins to break off pieces, adding them to the supports Renee put in place. Renee, back on her original side, tests the large pillar: "It's not steady."

DeMarcos takes a bathroom break, returning at 10:36.

Jennifer sits behind Renee's pillar: "Can I make this a little stronger here?" In the role of collaborator, she molds the clay around the base, expert fingers shaping and steadying the structure so it will stand firm. Complex roles provide teachers with many ways to intervene.

10:40. Renee, enthusiastically looking at the two spans on each side, and recalling the drawbridge: "We can make the bridge like it's open!"

10:42. Jennifer on DeMarcos's side, her hand on the wood he added to copy Renee: "We need something to help this stand up." Jennifer and DeMarcos together work clay around the base of the wooden slat.

FIGURE 9.1. Renee added a fifth support

A Structure Emerges

10:44. On Renee's side there are four supports, on DeMarcos's two. A large distance remains, but a structure is clearly emerging. Renee looks across: "Whew! A bridge! We're gonna get it!"

Jennifer is collaborating with DeMarcos, steadying a thin cylinder while DeMarcos flattens clay to make his third support. Jennifer, as DeMarcos gets ready to add a slab: "What size . . . ?" Then: "We're getting there, we're almost touching." To Renee, who is pounding clay for her side of the road: "Don't bang too hard!"

Renee's road starts flat, parallel to the table top, takes an abrupt angle upward to meet the first cylinder, then up slightly to the next, and even higher to meet the fourth, which is too thin. She finds a short, squat cylinder and balances a thin slat on top! It tilts her next slab of clay way up, but it holds: "Wow! My bridge! It's gonna be touching."

DeMarcos's third cylinder supports the clay. "Bingo!" he shouts. Both children have the technique. Renee adds a slab of clay and tries her fifth support but it is too short and the road angles steeply *down* to meet it. She removes the clay and balances the fifth cylinder on the short squat one! *Two* cylinders now balance on the same support! "Bingo!" she exclaims.

Both children pause to examine what they've done, singing: "It's gonna touch it, it's gonna touch it!"

DeMarcos, his fourth support holding well: "It's gittin' closer, closer!" Their excitement mounts, the structures on each side clearly beginning to close the distance. DeMarcos chooses a thick squat cylinder for his fifth support.

A Constraint

JENNIFER, not content with the emerging solution because more and more wood fills the "water": "We have to leave room for the boats." Her artist's sense constrains the problem, adding complexity. It is another example of how the artist's perspective shapes problems.

RENEE, moving DeMarcos's thick, squat cylinder away: "We need room for the boats."

DEMARCOS: "We *can't* leave no room for the boat!"

JENNIFER: "We *must* leave room for a boat."

DEMARCOS, sticking out his tongue and raising his eyebrows at the thought of removing the stabilizing wood! He adds another slab: "Renee, I'm gettin' closer!"

RENEE, letting out a whoop, squeals: "Closer!" Jennifer moves to a better vantage point. DeMarcos moves to the midpoint on the long side. Renee is opposite him on the other side.

DEMARCOS: "Oh, Renee, we're getting there!"

JENNIFER, from her new perspective, seeing just a small gap remaining: "Wow!"

DEMARCOS, observing the space in the water between the two spans: "Why is it so big?"

RENEE, rubbing the space in the water: "'Cause this is the room for the boat."

End in Sight

> DeMarcos: "We just have to make . . ." running his finger back and forth in the water from one span to the other, singing, ". . . da daa, da daa, da daa." Less than 6" remain between the spans. Renee, meanwhile, has pounded a piece of clay, longer than needed, to bridge the remaining 6", and is putting slip on the road.
>
> Jennifer, pointing to where his just-finished section joins the previous one: "Make sure you squish together here." DeMarcos firmly presses his last two slabs together, squishing as Jennifer suggested. Renee presses the last clay span onto her side. The children are so close together their hands almost touch. Renee holds the unattached end of the last span in her left hand while she reaches with her right hand and puts slip on the end of DeMarcos's last slab, the one that will join the road.
>
> DeMarcos, wide-eyed, watching: "Renee, you're gettin' it. Do it, Renee, do it, do it!" As DeMarcos shouts encouragement, Renee lifts her last, long slab directly over the end of DeMarcos's. It overlaps by a couple of inches. She lowers hers onto his, holding them together gingerly.
>
> DeMarcos: "Renee, you got it!"
>
> DeMarcos and Jennifer: "You got it!"
>
> Jennifer, pointing to where the roads join: "Just squush it together right here."
>
> DeMarcos's hands quickly help Renee press her slab firmly to his. "Uuh!" he grunts, with the pressure, their four hands touching as they join the last section of road.
>
> *10:49.* DeMarcos, shouting: "We got it!"
>
> Jennifer: "Fantastic!"

The bridge stretches almost 3 feet across the table. Gleeful whoops from DeMarcos! "Now," says Renee triumphantly, "I have to make a boat." Ebullient, she jumps up, joyfully flinging two arms and a leg!

Figure 9.2.
"We got it!"

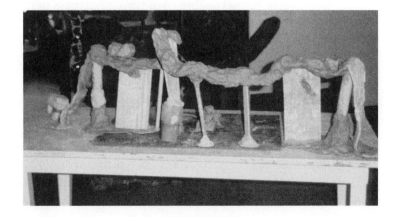

SUPPORTING TEACHERS

The most frequent questions from MELC visitors were how to train and renew teachers. The brief answer is that Reggio teachers work in a system with built-in teacher support. It takes many forms: two teachers per class, many nonteaching support staff, administrators, cooks and other helpers, late-afternoon staff, a puppeteer, *atelieristi*, and *pedagogisti*. Teachers are expected to learn continuously. Selection is rigorous, five or six culled annually from hundreds of applicants. The community highly respects its teachers. Above all, teachers share an underlying philosophy to which everyone subscribes. Shared beliefs and collaborative teaching, coupled with the many other supports, create a climate in which teachers are not *trained*, but learn on-the-job. As Malaguzzi (1993) said, "We have no alternatives but in-service training" (p. 66).

Shared Beliefs

Because everyone, including the community-at-large, shares the same philosophy, a culture has evolved, as around any belief system. Classrooms vary in particulars, projects, and documentation, but *not* in what teachers believe about children or how they interact with them. Sociocultural theory is well understood by all: that we—teachers as well children—are formed through our interaction with our environment and the things in it, but especially through relationships with people. To be *created through the work* means through interaction with children, families, other teachers, and others in the school system and in the community. This is the essence of the Reggio Approach to teacher education. They share a philosophy partly because they have the same roots and are products of the same culture, partly because everyone, for over 30 years, was influenced by Malaguzzi, whose charismatic leadership, unique energy, and perspective developed and drove the schools. Malaguzzi believed that every person is "capable of creating [and] that *each* person contains many people and is lots of pieces of history" (Question & Answer with a Delegation at Diana School, Reggio Emilia, March 6, 1992). This acknowledges each individual's complexities and potential to contribute. In their interactions, Reggio teachers draw on each one's "history" and richness: They listen, no matter who is talking, according each time to express herself. The group members respect individuals' ideas, whether or not they agree. Respect gives new teachers courage to draw on their experiences, trust themselves, have ideas, and act on them. The expectation that new teachers will learn on-the-job supports their development.

Collegial Relationships

After the intense selection process, new teachers, as young as 19, begin teaching alongside teachers with as many as 15 years experience. From Day One they team teach with a pro, an immediately accessible role model there constantly, in effect a personal trainer, a colleague also *created through the work*.

These two teach together daily for many years, working with the same children and families, sharing every experience, discussing hundreds of ideas, arguing over different interpretations, influencing each other. The experienced teacher is role model, discussant, debater, and coach for the novice. Minute-by-minute, directly and indirectly, the experienced teacher shapes the skills that the new teacher acquires, creating the teacher whom the novice becomes. For her part, the new teacher provides a fresh viewpoint, her ideas constantly renewing and challenging the mature teacher's perspective. Her questions provoke the experienced teacher to explain, reflect, and examine her teaching through new eyes.

The practice resembles a master/apprentice relationship, with this exception: From the start the experienced teacher gives the new teacher's ideas full accord, considering them as important as her own. From the start the two share insights, plans, observations, concerns, differences. They have equal voice in parent/teacher meetings. New teachers are not relegated to function as classroom aides, but are fully contributing partners. The experienced teacher expresses no sarcasm or cynicism, issues no orders or to-do lists. Everything is by consensus. Mutual trust grows and they become a seamlessly functioning team.

It was years before Malaguzzi decided that every classroom should have two teachers. Belief, not work load or adult/child ratio, drove the decision, the belief that the *multiple perspectives of two adults* would enable the teachers to be better observers and more responsive to children. The commitment required huge budget increases and stormy political action. Malaguzzi himself lead the fight.

Supportive Environment

In Reggio classes, I witnessed teachers' frequent discussions and debates, perceived their candor, heard disagreements, felt affection. I saw their respect for the *pedagogista*, noticed the *atelierista*'s frequent presence in the classroom, sometimes talking with one or both teachers, sometimes with a child or group, occasionally explaining something to me. The flow was natural, easy, supportive. Later I realized how much feedback took place in those interchanges, how informative they were for a teacher questioning what she was doing. The people resources—peer teacher, other teachers in the school, *atelierista*, *pedagogista*—erase fear and engender trust.

The system is rational. Hours are reasonable, vacations generous, pay good. Parents are deeply involved and genuinely helpful—making classroom equipment, lobbying for funds, hosting visitors, building playgrounds, arranging outings, participating energetically in parent meetings. Parents' roles are well-defined: not to make decisions about content or teaching techniques, but to collaborate with teachers, to better understand how to facilitate children's growth, and to bring the community along in support of the schools. Finally, *teachers*, not administrators, school boards, or parents, make pedagogical decisions and control the educational environment with autonomy and resources few American teachers know.

Observation/Feedback

In two long sessions the MELC teachers reviewed the Bridge project with Amelia and Giovanni, receiving immediate feedback from experts. Reggio teachers receive such feedback constantly; it hones their performance, amply rewarding their effort. Carlina explains observation using the word's Latin roots, *ob*—toward something; *servare*—to keep or conserve: I put myself before something in order to preserve it, a reciprocal process between the teacher and what she observes (Rinaldi, 1992). It implies a relationship between the observed and observer. A teacher initially may not understand what is happening. But as a project evolves she meets a problem over again, perhaps from a different angle, discusses it, hears colleagues' comments, and gradually comes to understand.

In the Bridge project we see Jennifer entering what Malaguzzi called the "risk zone, unexplored, unfamiliar situations" (Question & Answer with a Delegation at Diana School, Reggio Emilia, March 6, 1992). Each time Jennifer intervenes, she becomes surer. The presence of experts, the pressure of being observed, the anticipation of feedback, the magnitude of the challenge, its risk, the novelty and complexity—all are calculated to build a teacher.

WHETHER BELIEFS AND CULTURE SUPPORT PRACTICES

No American Reggio-inspired school of which I know has a Malaguzzi. Some are in communities that have little awareness of the school's beliefs. Others have parents who consider children's progress in the 3-Rs the only important evidence of their growth. Few grasp how belief in children's power or sociocultural theory looks in practice. Schools lack both the experienced teachers as minute-by-minute role models and the coaches and other supportive educators available in the Reggio system. Adults have known mainly environments where teachers talk and students listen, or where teachers fail to teach, mistakenly thinking children learn best through discovery on their own. In America time pressures of home/work/family compete with demands of Reggio-type teaching. These differences are the reality of our culture.

Many early childhood teachers are unprepared for intentional teaching and don't know how to challenge children. Nothing in their experience prepared them for the multi-faceted role described in Chapter 8. I have worked with beginning Reggio-inspired teachers, sincere and hardworking. Their materials were a mish-mash, for example, cartoon-like plastic animals with abstracted wooden ones, a few realistic plastic insects and arachnids that dwarfed the dinosaurs. We eliminated the cartoons and sorted the collection by scientific classification—arachnid, mammal, prehistoric reptile/bird. The teachers tried it with the children and reported that they stopped running around and played, classifying the animals, for a long time. The Reggio Approach is not passive; collaboration requires teachers' direct involvement in engaging children in activities that are challenging enough to redirect energy from running about to intellectual pursuit. The Reggio Approach requires teachers to mediate by intervening in the relationship between child and stimulus. The art of teaching means knowing when to intervene, what to say or do, and when to withdraw, knowing minute-by-minute how to play each of the teacher's roles described in Chapter 8.

Creating Reggio-inspired practices requires support for teachers and a culture of enlightened leadership, penetrating scholarship, extraordinary dedication, and long hours. It requires financial support not usually available in America, and release from the constraints of the teach/test mentality currently driving policy. As long as these requirements run counter to the political will, Reggio-inspired schools will remain outside the mainstream, boutique instances with little effect on typical practices, and disconnected from low-income families.

The MELC, with all its advantages, could not survive the political climate that was evolving during its existence. Hopefully, the superhuman efforts of those trying to run Reggio-inspired schools will prevail wherever they are. These pioneers, hopefully, will be inspired by these stories about the challenges and triumphs of MELC teachers, children, and families. Hopefully, the stories will help bridge the cultural gap.

CHAPTER 10

Shaping
Preschools

When I used to read fairy tales, I fancied that kind of thing never
happened, and now here I am in the middle of one!
　　　　　　　　　　　　　　　　　　　—Lewis Carroll (1941, p. 47)

I N THIS CHAPTER I SHOW HOW THE RESEARCH and examples described
in this book provide guidance for policy on best practices in early education. I briefly discuss five aspects of early education—teacher quality,
assessment, special education, program/population match, and family involvement. Then I suggest ways to flesh out existing standards so they better
convey to educators, parents, and policymakers the texture of best practices. I
conclude with some ideas for change.

ASPECTS OF EARLY EDUCATION

In addressing the five above-listed aspects I am neither comprehensive nor
objective. My statements in no way resemble a literature review; others' descriptions of educators' and psychologists' research are covered exhaustively
in numerous journals and books. My discussion is personal, subjective, and
circumscribed, based on 4 decades of experience in early education working
mostly with economically disadvantaged families, first as social case worker,
then as so-called change agent to bring new thinking into public education
mainly in schools whose students met federal poverty guidelines, and now as
author/lecturer/consultant/tutor in diverse settings.

Teacher Quality

It is a given: A method or curriculum is only as good as the teacher using
it. Nothing is *teacher-proof*. A curriculum is a tool; what it yields depends on
who wields it. Moreover, research has established that a person, especially
if committed, sensitive, and intentional, is essential to transmit culture across
generations. Education—whether formal or informal, written or oral, practiced by the clan or in state-run schools—is the bedrock of culture. Research
has proved conclusively that in formal systems of education in the United
States "teacher quality is a key element in a successful program" (Policy

Research Institute, 2006, p. 2). "Caregivers with more formal education provide higher quality care" (NICHD, 2002). Discussion over. Except for questions of how to educate teachers.

Teacher Education. Teaching consists of the minute-by-minute teacher/student interactions when a teacher is actively present with her students and attuned to this connection with intention, meaning, and transcendence (Chapter 8). High-quality teachers are never on autopilot, but are continually reflective, even when silent—recall Jennifer continually questioning herself about when to intervene in Bridge (Chapter 9). Great teaching at any level—preschool through postgrad—is the highest art form; its goal the hardest to achieve: to shape emotion and intellect so that, evermore, students will behave/think to broaden their minds and deepen their understanding.

Teachers are educated in three ways—imprints of their own parenting/schooling; courses, training, and instruction; and on-the-job experience. Imprinting and on-the-job experience have the most dramatic (or traumatic) influence; instruction (other than fieldwork) almost always lacks the emotional impact of real experience. Consider: A teacher is in charge of a chaotic classroom. Does she search her memory for what the textbook or professor said about restoring order? Does she react like a disciplinarian parent, bellowing some version of "sit down and shut up"? Or does she rely on the words of the mentor teacher she observed? Father or mentor is more likely to influence a teacher's response. Moreover, once she finds a technique that works, she is likely to make it her immediate—and eventually instinctive—response.

It is expecting a lot for training to replace teachers' immediate, instinctive responses. All teaching is influenced by

> pattern-driven cognition, ego defense, and the cognitive load bottleneck . . . [as well as] many people['s] strongly valu[ing] quick intuitive thinking over more extended reflective thinking, . . . [and] technical knowledge gaps. (Perkins, 1995, pp. 169–170)

Perkins also observes that

> pattern-driven thinking often subverts the work of reflective intelligence in situations of novelty, unusual complexity, or risk. (pp. 276–277)

Teaching *is* a process of taking risk and confronting novel, complex situations. If Perkins is correct that one's patterns subvert one's likelihood to take risks, and if we accept the fact that to teach means to take risks, then teachers perforce will be unlikely to be reflective; yet, best practices require constant reflection. This problem can be tackled by being aware of it and taking steps—like being teacher/researchers (Chapter 8)—to address it.

Teacher Educators. The teachers of teachers are at the top of a pyramid in which students form the bottom. But the top often appears too thinly populated because of a shortage of well-trained, experienced, insightful trainers. Teacher educators are gatekeepers—deciding who gets credentialed. If someone weak heads the department, how can students make their concerns known? Similarly, how can colleagues criticize one another when they might need support for their next promotion or journal submission?

Content that doesn't excite teachers, and trainers who don't engage their minds passionately, won't convey ideas that make it into classrooms at any grade level. If teachers are to absorb content, their educators must be experts and content must be substantive: geology (children love finding rocks, but do they know how to use scratch tests and streak plates to identify them?); poetry (children's poetry is superb, but so are T. S. Eliot's "Jellical Cats," a rap, Langston Hughes's "Dreams," an analogy, and Robert Browning's "Pied Piper"); topology (Klein bottles, certain loops and knots, and Mobius strips—which children themselves can make—are mathematical shapes that fascinate children). Subject matter is irrelevant as long as it provides substance to feed children's boundless curiosity. Birthday parties might seem mundane but they stretched children's capacities (Chapter 5) because teachers helped them construct their own fantastic ideas for presents, which simultaneously strengthened their mastery of materials and processes, and their relationships with their friends.

Increasing emphasis on accountability has shifted the content of teacher education: Teachers-to-be are taught to prove that lesson content covers specific objectives, to provide evidence of coverage, and to make lesson plans that conform to teacher guides. The emphasis has shifted, literally, from content to form. Instead, preparation for teachers must be substantive and mind-stretching, challenging them to delve into content, stimulating them to form new concepts. To improve the content of teacher education we must stop teaching how to use preplanned lessons and start teaching meaty content and big concepts!

Assessment

Early development is rapid, irregular, and dependent on the alchemy among children's own natures, their environments, and the mediation (Chapter 8) they receive. No assessment can account for these variables. Some issues impacting assessment are a teacher's own knowledge about assessment options, a teacher's purpose, and meaningful use of ratings.

Choosing Assessments. Caution: Teachers must define why they are using assessment and be wary of tests purporting to give a complete picture of children's accomplishments. What test could have demonstrated what Zeze learned when he accidentally mixed colors (Chapter 2), or tracked the children's growth in holding conversations on big topics like what makes snow (Chapter 3), or probed children's understanding of how faxes work (Chapter 6)? Teachers who don't know much about testing can ask experts to explain what particular tests do and what results mean. Reliability, validity, and statistical significance are given great weight by administrators and some policymakers; test scores are what matter to politicians. If the purpose is to convince someone of a program's worth, choose an assessment with clearly stated criteria, one proven to be valid and reliable. Otherwise, naysayers will discredit the achievement.

Caution: Young children are unpredictable. Therefore, their own teachers, at times *the teachers* deem best, should assess children as they undertake their regular activities. Children should be assessed over long time periods; some aspects of development leap forward quickly, while others emerge slowly. As examples throughout this book testify, documentation is an assessment technique that showcases children's evolving capacities.

Purpose. Why assess? Assessments can reveal that children who are not progressing might need assistance outside a school's province—speech pathologist, eye exam, better diet, more sleep, less TV. When young children are entrusted to out-of-family caregivers, all aspects of development become the joint responsibility of home and school. Assessment helps teachers determine what they are not doing so they understand where they need to change or get help. Recall Jennifer's confusion over the role of Studio and Studio teacher, and the teachers' not knowing how to use their notes (Chapter 2). They themselves identified these as problems and concluded that they needed help.

Approach. Assessment shows children at particular moments in time. "The younger the child, the more difficult to obtain reliable assessment data. . . . It is particularly difficult to assess children's cognitive abilities accurately before age six" (National Education Goals Panel, 1998, cited in Epstein, Schweinhart, DeBruin-Parecki, & Robin, 2004, p. 4). An alternative is "systematic observation of children's activities in their day-to-day settings" (p. 6). This is called informal, naturalistic, or authentic assessment, and techniques include photos, video, records of verbatim statements (grammar unchanged), and work product, all collected over time and archived. When you see September's and May's documents side-by-side, change—or lack of change—is obvious. Documentation (Chapter 7) provides a way for children to reflect at each key step on what they've done, and for adults to see the continuum in their development.

Ratings. Ratings by teachers and parents mark change over time. As with tests, rating scales developed and approved by experts carry more weight with supervisors and funders. The Maryland state rating is an example of a scale with benign terms like proficient, in process, and needs development (Bruner & Copeman, 2003, p. 11). If teachers use their own notes that document children's specific behavior as examples of what is proficient or what needs development, it authenticates ratings. Teachers' notes add substance and are key to helping parents understand where their child is: Tiffany says 9 is less than 7; it shows she needs work on the concepts of more/less, larger/smaller. Alonzo sounds out words, but doesn't know their meaning; we need to expand his vocabulary. Darlene missed the point of the fable "The Pitcher and the Crow"; she knows a *picture* is in a frame, but does not know a *pitcher* holds liquid, and pronounces both words the same. Annotation helps teachers see which skills they themselves need to emphasize. Jennifer's Magic List (Chapter 7) showed the teachers what they were *not* doing. Explicit information raises everyone's understanding of exactly where to focus. Note: young children need to be compared with themselves, not their classmates.

Special Education

Special education covers a broad range of children—those who are acting out, learning disabled, hyperactive, autistic, slow learners, to name a few (Narrol & Giblon, 2001). Generally, special educators use excellent techniques. Special ed classrooms are often the best equipped and designed, and teachers are trained in the use of eclectic materials and approaches that would serve all children well. Unfortunately, special ed classes may be used to remove children with behavioral problems from regular classes, along with low performers whose test scores lower the average.

Feuerstein's Research. Feuerstein's work with Down syndrome children created a revolution in their treatment, and he and his colleagues have made major breakthroughs with every other condition, including children given up as hopeless because of severe manifestations of learning disabilities, brain damage, or autism, as well as gifted underachievers. Numerous research studies verify the efficacy of Feuerstein's theories and materials (Presseisen & Kozulin, 1994).

In 2004 Feuerstein published classroom materials for preschoolers that apply decades of work with older students to 3- to 5-year-olds. I urge readers to become familiar with his theories and materials. Early, consistent, and effective mediation (defined in Chapter 8) could prevent many special ed placements, as Feuerstein states.

> Many children who suffer from learning disabilities, ranging from attention deficits to other incapacities to focus and select stimuli, are children who have not been provided with mediated learning experience sufficient for their needs to establish cognitive functions. . . . With insufficient or absent . . . [mediation] they are more likely to respond in episodic and impulsive ways. (Feuerstein & Feuerstein, 2004, pp. 9–10)

MELC's Experience. Approximately 17% of D.C. Public School students, the population from which MELC children were drawn, are in special education (Parents United, 2003). The MELC accepted all children sent to us (except one). They were a random sample, over 150 in the school's 8-year life. Each received a lot of mediation (Chapter 8) different in kind or frequency from any other child. All progressed and sooner or later (over the 3 years they spent in the school) did the significant work—original, complex, and creative—described throughout this book. They learned to be self-regulated (Chapter 4), to savor friendships (Chapters 5 and 6), to communicate with increasing skill in spoken and written language (Chapter 6), to show empathy and respect the rights of other creatures (Chapters 4, 7, and 8), and to express themselves skillfully in diverse modes—musical composition (Chapters 5 and 7), poetry (Chapter 3), scale renderings (Chapter 3), and map-making (Chapter 6), for example. We recommended no children for special ed, nor felt any might be placed there, just the opposite. Our results are limited by small sample size and lack of funds to track students so we do not know how they progressed in grade school. I could hypothesize that, commensurate with their public school system's statistics, 17% would have become special ed students, but I doubt that even one did. I will always wonder.

Feuerstein's theory of the importance of mediation supports our limited experience. Inclusion works, provided that: (1) instruction takes place one-on-one or in small groups; (2) firm ground rules ensure that all children become self-regulated; (3) mediation is immediate if behavioral corrections are warranted; and (4) frequent one-on-one or small-group mediation occurs many times daily for both affective and intellectual cognitive functions. Further discussion is beyond this book's scope except to say that it is essential to understand why a child is labeled "special ed," and to provide high teacher/student ratios and specialized teacher preparation.

Program/Population Match

Demographers project that the U.S. Caucasian population will be the minority by 2050 as diversity increases. Attire, forms of address, and countless customs and behaviors are culture-specific; gestures, hugs, or words common here are contemptible there. Some education practices are ineffective with diverse persons; others reflect ignorance of different cultures. For example, Israel has received waves of immigrants who are trauma victims; in the early 1980s Ethiopian Jews suffering from famine emigrated there. Israel's resettlement program involves instruction in the Hebrew language. But resettlement centers failed to teach the Ethiopians to read. On examination, Feuerstein realized that their culture had no tradition of literacy, but was strongly oral. When taught orally, they demonstrated immense intellectual capacity. As another example, immigrants in America without green cards are wary of providing names and addresses, or of being visible. Some express this fear by neither returning school forms nor attending parent meetings. Schools can support undocumented families by issuing explicit statements in the families' languages that the school has *no* interest in knowing a family's immigration status and no dealings with INS.

Families can be teachers' allies in learning what is culturally appropriate and acceptable. Teachers' modest, genuine requests for families' help can be effective in engaging families *if* enough time is invested to establish trust. The MELC built trust not by focusing on cultural differences, but by building a school culture on commonalities—seasonal changes (Chapter 3); birthday parties (Chapter 5); messages (Chapter 6); family photos and the school's need for materials (Chapter 1). The initial focus was *what we all shared*. Once trust was built on common ground, it was easy to ask families to share traditions and culture-specific customs.

Family Involvement

Preschools without family involvement may as well be orphanages. Family/school interchange about children's school and home lives should be a given. At the MELC a staff of middle-class teachers learned to engage a school of economically disadvantaged families. One key was to make the school's activities visible with a huge flow of written information to the home, all discussed with the children before it was sent. Another was to ask parents to help solve specific problems, like the need for additional materials and the necessity for revising birthday and holiday procedures. Ultimately all families participated in virtually all activities.

Family Choices. An ideal of American public education is to provide enough homogenization to guarantee that people of disparate cultures unite in a spirit of freedom of expression. Public schools where hijabs are worn, languages other than English are primary, or religious customs are observed fall outside the mainstream and often engender controversy in their communities. When the *Zeitgeist* is permeated with separatism, it requires juggling to establish a balance between honoring families' different cultures while building common ground. Educators may find their programs buffeted by separatist sentiments not of their making. Particular problems can arise when families' and school's languages differ. Some schools offer English language classes for parents and children together. Others use interpreters for meetings and parent conferences, and translators for written matter as ways to honor language differences.

Respecting Families. Once the MELC built parents' trust, we incorporated many of their preferences into school practices. Trust developed partly because we made what we did transparent, telling families about our problems as well as successes. Remember how we admitted failure and reworked procedures to make birthday celebrations succeed (Chapter 5)? We made constant efforts to ensure that parents saw their children's many accomplishments on the walls in documentation, in sculpture throughout the school, in writings that went home, in the children's individual folios, in slide shows, and in frequent meetings at which teachers described children's activities. Nothing respects families more than schools' ensuring that children thrive and develop competence and skills.

If simultaneously families are engaged in discourse about *their* concerns, they will play meaningful roles in the school. "Renee's mother said, 'I must have asked 500 questions . . . I was new at the motherhood game, but I'm doing it. Whatever I asked, you all took care of it'" (Lewin-Benham, 2006, p. 138). "Rickie's grandmother said, 'This is not a place where you just drop your child off. You can see what children are involved in, through the pictures around, and . . . children enjoying themselves in what they are doing'" (p. 138). As families and school gradually bonded, the MELC became a *learning community.*

STANDARDS

The push for standards responds to the burgeoning need for early care, resulting from well-educated women's working en masse and welfare policies that require single moms to work. Concurrently, rapidly accumulating research proves the importance of the early years in establishing the physical, social/emotional, dispositional, and cognitive platform on which later well-being rests. Current standards specify what development should take place before children enter kindergarten or first grade. In this section I refer to standards found in: (1) the Position Statement on Curriculum, Assessment, and Program Evaluation of the National Association for the Education of Young Children (NAEYC); (2) the National School Readiness Indicators 17 State Initiative/State Early Childhood Policy Technical Assistance Network developed by KIDS COUNT; and (3) various papers from Rutgers University's National Institute for Early Education Research. Respectively, these organizations represent: (1) the largest membership organization, regarded as the *voice* of early education; (2) hundreds of providers, advocates, elected officials, and representatives of state and local agencies in early childhood health and education; and (3) university-based independent, nonpartisan researchers. The three organizations' standards are nonspecific and virtually identical. Here I summarize the standards and use examples from this book as suggestions to flesh them out.

Standard 1: Physical Well-Being and Motor Development

In a sports-oriented nation, the standards are silent on preschoolers' physical well-being except to mention running, skipping, galloping, balancing, and climbing. I recommend:

1. Allowing children to move whenever, however, and for however long they choose, provided their movement does not violate others' rights to pursue their activities. Recall the MELC's rules about movement (Chapter 1).
2. Including *in every classroom* physical apparatus that children use when they choose, so those who can't wait for recess can be vigorously active. Recall the MELC's climbing/tumbling apparatus (Chapter 1), which enabled children to climb, crawl, and jump without disrupting others. In Reggio, every classroom has climbing and jumping apparatus that children use as readily as they use pencils or blocks, with no disruption whatsoever to others.
3. Providing every school with well-equipped outdoor space designed, and possibly built, collaboratively by families. The public school where I tutor has pre-K and K classes but, until this year, no playground or outdoor equipment. Moreover, outdoor recess has been all but eliminated because of the pressure to spend more time on drilling abc/123's.
4. Engaging regularly in moving-to-music.
5. Playing movement games frequently.
6. Providing analytical experiences about movement. Recall the children's forming wire sculptures of themselves skating; running through leaves, dancing around cherry trees, then drawing images of leaves as they fell; drawing one another sliding and climbing on the playground; making a bird prop to "fly" before larger-than-life slides of the Capitol grounds in springtime (Chapter 3); studying Coco's movements and making a video (Chapter 4); interpreting their own movements in drawings (Chapter 5).

The standard is also silent on small-motor development, by which I mean the ability to manipulate with increasing skill anything requiring the pincer movement (thumb, index, and third fingers). Examples of pincer movement development appear throughout the book and are too many to enumerate. It was essential to many MELC experiences. I recommend providing the following for children to use whenever and for however long they want, and intentionally encouraging their use:

1. Colored and black-lead #2 pencils, fine-line markers, scissors, glue bottles, and the like;
2. Small-scale manipulative materials in sufficient quantity to ensure simultaneous access by most of a class; examples include Legos®, pegs-in-holes, mosaics, table-top blocks, and attribute blocks.

The standard further calls for health and safety issues that are beyond this book's scope.

Policy Implication. Fund improved teacher education, better facilities, and more supplies and equipment.

Standard 2: Social/Emotional Development

The standards use somewhat different words but the same ideas: Children should respect others' rights, not be too shy or withdrawn or too overbearing or aggressive, willingly give support, communicate their wants and needs, and treat others as they want to be treated.

The MELC's emphasis, related throughout this book, on discussion and conversation with the full class, with small groups, or one-on-one helped children develop self-regulated, socially acceptable behavior (Chapter 4). They cooperated in large and small groups, participated actively in school endeavors, and followed directions—indicators of social/emotional competence. Moreover, they were courteous and empathetic, and valued one another's friendship. These behaviors resulted from intentional teaching strategies like using firm commands to bring aggressive behavior into line (Chapter 1); regularly involving children in rule-setting and conversations about rights and responsibilities (Chapters 4 and 6); grouping children so their different dispositions would influence one another. Great thought went into choosing children for groups. A small group and teacher working together established a culture of collaboration; the huge emphasis on friendship developed children's disposition to treat others as they want to be treated (Chapter 7). The extremely wide range of materials and modes of expression described throughout the book were calculated to ensure that every child could find her voice, thereby developing increasing cognitive skill and experiencing success.

Codifying these practices into standards, I recommend:

1. Having two adults per class for all grades below fourth.
2. Conducting most activities in groups ranging in size from one-on-one to no more than six.

3. Consistently following the four rules: Use your quiet voice and walking feet; keep hands to yourself; put things away.
4. Engaging children in frequent discussion about one another's rights.

Policy Implication: Fund two teachers per class and improve teacher education programs.

Standard 3: Approaches to Learning

This refers to dispositions, to name several: concentrating, being leaders or followers, being cooperative, inquiring, empathetic, or responsible. Standards say children should show "enthusiasm, curiosity, and persistence in completing tasks" (Bruner, Floyd, & Copeman, 2005, p. 5). KIDS COUNT (2005) adds "creativity, independence, [and] cooperativeness" (p. 69).

Harvard Project Zero researchers David Perkins and Shari Tishman (2006) say that current school practice is focused on attempts to capitalize

> on [children's] initial abilities, to equip learners with skills, knowledge, and understanding, in the expectation that these will be readily and appropriately deployed. [The] dispositional perspective argues that this is profoundly untrue. In many real-world situations, underdeveloped or contrary dispositions constrain both initial learning and later performance at least as much as limits of capability. (p. 3)

Considering whether dispositions can be taught, they conclude that dispositions transmit by "osmosis" from the culture teachers establish in the classroom (p. 30). So again we find that teachers, their beliefs and intentions, and how they mediate are critical influencing factors (Chapters 1 and 2). Early educators recognize the importance of dispositional factors. But standards are silent on how to get from lists of desirable dispositions to ways to develop them.

Disposition means one's innate characteristics and natural tendencies. Consider the role of disposition in the Bridge project (Chapter 9). Jennifer selected Renee and DeMarcos because they were *open* to new experiences, her only ace in hand in trying to position the risky project to succeed. Notice how leadership shifts between Renee and DeMarcos: First she copies him, later he copies her. Notice their different attitude toward persistence: DeMarcos walks off; Renee continues. Notice Jennifer's attention, focus, persistence, firmness, and, mainly, silence. It would be interesting to try the project under the direction of a less intentional teacher or one who believes young children should not confront big challenges. Many such teachers visited the MELC; whenever we presented the Bridge project, they vehemently argued it was beyond preschoolers' capacity.

Did Renee and DeMarcos acquire a disposition to be persistent? I don't know. Had Jennifer chosen children not open to new experiences, would they have persisted? I think so; Jennifer would have scaffolded and strongly encouraged them. In other projects the teachers consciously chose children *unlikely* to succeed, like Terrell, who, when asked to draw, became "obstinate, . . . [was] completely stuck, [and] refused to try" (Lewin-Benham, 2006,

p. 97). The teachers did everything necessary to support these children, to prove they could master something they'd shied away from. Every project in this book can be analyzed for what it reveals about children's dispositions and how the project's goals, the influence of the small group, and the teachers' beliefs (Chapters 1 and 2) figured in the outcome. Should we challenge preschoolers more as a way to influence disposition? Absolutely! Bring on the bridges.

Policy Implication: Fund two teachers per class, more materials, and improved teacher education.

Standard 4: Emerging Literacy

First I present the standards as written, then start over, suggesting different standards. Finally I propose a culture of literacy.

As Written. Standards according to KIDS COUNT (2005):

From the Executive Summary:

1. Size of vocabulary
2. Recognizing letters
3. Understanding letter and sound relationships

From p. 66:

4. Print awareness
5. Early writing

Rewritten. I offer this list:

1. Active listening (full class, small groups, and one-on-one) with total attention paid to the speaker in frequent daily conversations that are intentional, meaningful, and transcendent (going beyond the immediate stimulus and connecting it to other relevant events).
2. Transcripts of conversations (from teachers' notes) prominently displayed, along with photos showing the context, reread and discussed often with children (Chapter 6).
3. Phonics and dictated spelling taught.
4. Writing used as the route to reading (Chapter 6).

Numbers 1 and 2 create a culture of conversation. Humans speak long before they write or read. The route to writing and reading lies with speaking. Yet economically disadvantaged children (Chapter 3), children with stressed-out, distracted parents, or too much TV have little active listening or extended discourse at home. In order to read and write, you must use language and love it. Holding frequent, intentional, and meaningful conversation with children from infancy on would be better preparation for reading and writing than drilling the sounds of letters. Drilling isolated "aaa's," "buh's," and "cuh's" conveys no meaning whatsoever. Yet, *the essence of literacy is to make meaning.*

Numbers 3 and 4 lead to reading and writing. Using drill/kill tactics to teach preschoolers phonics is wrong. The Montessori "sound game" with sandpaper letters, followed by the movable alphabet, are joyful small-group or one-on-one ways to begin phonics education. Briefly, children listen for sounds in familiar words (ssss—ki*ss*, *s*nake, *s*oon; mmmmm—*mommy*, ham*m*er, *m*itten), then trace a large sandpaper letter as they say the sound. The input is simultaneously visual, auditory, and kinesthetic. Weeks or months later many children will connect sound and shape spontaneously. Then, the teacher dictates—emphasizing each sound (*no vowel sound attached to consonants*)—and children *spell* with 3" movable letters (sat: ssss-aaa-t, pop: p-ah-p, gum: g-uh-m). This consistent method helps children learn to read by writing (with cut-out cardboard letters). They literally discover reading, realizing words are visible speech!

A Culture of Literacy. Do you recall that, spontaneously, the children came up with the idea of using letters to make words (Chapter 6)? Or, when they were trying to understand pollution, they came up with the idea of using the dictionary to figure something out, and when the dictionary offered nothing, suggested looking in library books. This is called *contextualized curriculum.* Most MELC experiences involved a strong literacy context. Recall in all chapters children's constant conversing, using books, *reading* documentation, making their own ideas visible.

When literacy experiences are joyful and exciting, children are disposed to love language: Do we want to see pictures of turtles (Chapter 7), or butterflies (Chapter 3), or cats (Chapter 4)? Then let's look at books! Do we want to learn *more*? Let's get more books. Where are more books? At the library. Let's go! Ask the two questions: What do you want to know? and How can we find out? And be prepared to listen, actively. I have never met 3-year-olds who did not want to know—*everything*! But the desire dies early if they spend their time being drilled. They might learn to associate sound and symbol before the age of 6, but at what price?

Policy Implication: Fund in-classroom libraries, field trips to public libraries, and Montessori language materials with training in how to use them.

Standard 5: Cognition

"Cognition encompasses language and literacy, math, scientific thinking, the arts, music, and knowledge acquisition, creative expression, reasoning and problem solving" (KIDS COUNT, 2005, p. 68).

The standards list specific skills such as:

- Observe.
- Note similarities and differences.
- Solve problems.
- Ask questions.

For math (Executive Summary) the standards add:

- Count.
- Spatial relations.
- Patterns.

Cognition is a big topic: Much of what the brain does is cognition, including emotion and self-regulation (D'Amasio, 1994). The standards are anemic and as such leave children at risk for developing learning problems. Problems can manifest in affective and emotional cognition, in the more intellectual areas of cognition, and generally in both, since affect and cognition are integrally bound. Here I first briefly discuss building cognition, then describe Feuerstein's cognition-building preschool program, Feuerstein Instrumental Enrichment–BASIC.

Building Cognition. Cognitive capacity is built in a "progression from understanding the content of experience to the formation of concepts. This leads to the acquisition of mental operations, which is the adaptive manipulation of concepts" (Feuerstein & Feuerstein, 2004, p. 19). For example, a 6-year-old has this task: Match 3-D shapes—squares, circles, triangles—to 2-D outlines of the exact size. The child matches correctly and knows the names for circle, square, and so on, but when asked what she's been playing with, cannot apply the word *shapes*. Thus, she understands the content but not the concept. Concepts are a higher level of cognition than content. Without the capacity to form concepts, children have difficulty performing mental operations that take place at still higher cognitive levels. Anemic standards leave low-functioning children—whether their problems are environmental or organic—in the lurch, and set the bar too low for high-functioning children.

Preschool Curriculum in Cognition. Feuerstein has identified a comprehensive range of areas that preschoolers should master first in order to form a solid content basis on which to develop concepts. It includes, for example, comparison, orientation in space, and identifying emotions. Responses are judged by whether they are logical, emotional, sufficiently intense, and so forth. The goal is to enable children to

> develop the mental operations which will help them compare, contrast, specify, and make their content knowledge less undifferentiated and more functional . . . [using] contents needed to operate on the world. Without these tools—perceptual, attentional, linguistic, etc.—the child will not be able to handle incoming stimuli. (Feuerstein & Feuerstein, 2004, pp. 8–9)

Feuerstein maintains that preschoolers' affective and emotional cognition can be addressed through thoughtful presentation of basic content related to daily living, and such basic cognitive behaviors as attending to stimuli, focusing, imitating, question and answering, seeking relationships, predicting, making analogies, and many other increasingly higher levels of cognition (Feuerstein & Feuerstein, 2004). It is beyond the scope of this book to lay out more detail. I urge readers to study the Feuerstein Instrumental Enrichment BASIC Program and recommend its use in preschools. It is based on well-researched, long-used theories and robust series of applications, and builds cognition in a comprehensive, systematic manner while integrating the affective/emotional and intellectual aspects of intelligence.

Policy Implication: Fund teacher training and materials for FIE–BASIC.

CHALLENGES TO POLICYMAKERS

Every standard has policy implications, virtually all requiring funds. Funding, in turn, requires legislative action. But preschools sit far from policymaking, which takes place in offices with good equipment and support staff. Policymakers who rarely leave the office don't know the realities of life in a preschool, and politicians who *kiss the baby* rarely connect the dots between thriving babies and adequate resources for their health, welfare, and education. A full account of the state of America's children is on the Web site of the Children's Defense Fund, which runs a tireless crusade urging politicians to pass humane legislation. A great disjunction exists between espoused American values and actions. Closing the gap requires better pay along the entire spectrum of child caregivers, from custodian to CEO. It requires funds to revamp teacher education and funds to build and equip centers that are aesthetically uplifting. No policymaker would work in an office with child-care-type aesthetics.

Policies need to be flexible so teachers' creativity and professionalism are enhanced, and their need for continued growth met; restrictive policies kill joy, and without joy no one can provide adequately for children's well-being. Flexibility is costly. If politicians want to benchmark America's child care standards, they should contrast some of the world's better child care centers—China's children's palaces, Italy's or Scandinavian countries' children's centers—with America's prototypic preschools. If politicians understood the impact of early experience, they might move abroad to ensure their own children's excellent early education.

Educators have failed to educate policymakers on the full costs of ensuring that children's early out-of-home experiences are excellent. It is a travesty for us, the as-yet richest country in the world, to allow so many young children to be in centers devoid of laughter and light, where their images of life are provided mainly by video, and their outdoor experiences are dominated by asphalt and plastic. We are already reaping the results in inner-city problems. The publication *Tough Choices or Tough Times* (National Center on Education and the Economy, 2007) makes clear that our economic survival is at stake when we fail to ensure children experience best practices in the most vital, fertile period of their development. In this sense education *is* politics. It matters whom we elect, how we inform them, what we charge them to do, because the policies they legislate will determine not only our children's future, but the future of America.

LOOKING AHEAD

It is the best and worst of times. There is gloom, but also hope that early child-hood practices will improve.

Gloom

All standards have this fallacy—the alarming paucity of high-quality care-givers and teachers willing to work for the low salaries offered in early educa-tion. The differences between inner-city providers and high-society centers are enormous, yet price, corporate management, or university affiliation offers no guarantee that best practices are in effect. Some reputedly best centers have programs that are insipid and reductionist. Children from well-to-do homes will do well if their home environment supplements what preschools do not provide. But compared to what schools in Reggio Emilia have shown about children's capacities, too many American preschools pale.

The concern, as public schools move into early education, is that their form of education is inappropriate for preschoolers: sit still/face forward/be quiet; one-size-fits-all; teach 'em/test 'em. No standards or assessments will ensure that young children get what they need in publicly run programs that are textbook bound and benchmark everything on test results. Nor do regulations ensure quality. They might provide a floor, but will not chal-lenge anyone to reach for the heights. We have woven a web of regulation that intends to prevent harm to children, but is largely unenforceable. Drive through vast tracts of any city and observe their child care centers if you re-ally think standards/assessments/regulations can touch most economically disadvantaged children's preschool experience; the low level of facility and caregiver is alarming. Or, sit in a public school kindergarten and watch 5-year-olds required to be motionless and silent—except when they give the teacher the right answer—for most of the day; it is unnatural, joyless, and mind-deadening.

Webs of accountability threaten to entangle the occasional social entrepre-neur who actually might do something of quality for preschoolers. Account-ability ensures that new layers of *accountants* will have jobs, as will the bevy of professionals who study raw data and write reports—all at larger salaries than those of the caregivers they monitor. We have a nation of wordsmiths on children's behalf. We need a nation of warriors.

On October 29, 2007, two warriors—A C Wharton, Mayor of Shelby County, Tennessee, and Harold Ford, Jr., former five-term U.S. Congress-man from Tennessee, raised their voices in a long article, "Fixing Broken Dreams," in Memphis' daily newspaper. They opened with this quote from the Urban Child Institute in Memphis: "Undereducated children have no fu-ture," and made an impassioned plea, especially for economically deprived parents, that we demand parent-centered education. They urged community leaders "to have the fortitude and open-mindedness to consider new ideas" (Wharton & Ford, 2007, pp. V1 and V3). Then they suggested offering incen-tives—money—to ensure parent involvement. What a bizarre idea—to pay parents to get involved in order to realize what the authors themselves state as every parent's aspiration: "that their child will obtain a college degree" (pp. V1 and V3). Are we so befuddled in our systems of education that we must pay parents rather than pay for excellent education? The MELC parents were motivated to become involved once they realized we truly valued their participation and when their children's accomplishments became obvious. Parents will come if there is something worthwhile to see.

Hope

Problems. What has worked throughout most of evolution to educate the young is wanting today, not because the process of human development has changed, but child-rearing patterns have changed dramatically (clan to single parent) and mastering the job skills for high tech societies is so much more complex than learning agrarian or industrial skills. We are all aware of the problems that plague early education, but they can be addressed.

Solutions. Humans are adaptive and will muster the will to devise effective strategies if they are inspired to do so. Most inspiring are masterful teachers whose performance is totally in sync with their children. Such teachers are at a new forefront for human endeavor. They are at the nexus where today's patterns of child rearing and the process of human development meet. They are pioneers, the brave new souls in whose hands it rests to carry forward the culture. Policymakers, are you listening? Teachers are our most precious resource. Let's pay enough to attract, educate, and keep the best and brightest.

Blue Sky: Educating Teachers

Training involves two aspects of teaching: the techniques of communicating with students and the content to be communicated.

Ideas for Techniques

- Video the micro-actions of the *world's* (not just America's) greatest teachers—their minute-by-minute interactions—across wide-ranging behaviors like observing, listening, conveying information, teaching specific skills, conversing, taking notes, asking questions, disciplining. Then study, analyze, and mimic them.
- Make model schools where teachers-to-be or teachers-in-retraining can observe excellence in action and engage in discussion to ensure they understand its characteristics.
- Have masters, like *pedagogista* and *atelierista*, who work side-by-side in classes demonstrating, guiding, and coaching. They do not evaluate; they work as colleagues.
- Videotape ourselves in action, critique the video with masters, and immediately practice the critiqued behavior, videotape, critique, and teach it again, and so forth, until we get it!

- Teach in teams of expert/novice so an excellent model is readily available.
- Make sure experts can cross-teach, which means having different areas of expertise. Like the Reggio combination of artist/early childhood expert, there are many possible experts—woodworker, linguist, poet, cognitive psychologist, nutritionist, gymnast, mathematician, theater director.

Ideas for Content

- Deepen teacher education with year-long courses in subjects like philosophy, classic literature, geology, topology, music theory, marine life, soil conservation, animal husbandry—the list is endless. The goal: Instill specific knowledge in at least two different fields— electives chosen because they excite the teacher-to-be. The reason? Everything in the universe is appropriate to introduce, but most likely to excite preschoolers are ideas about which teachers feel passion. Let's awaken preschool teachers' passion for knowledge.
- Teach the use of tools: hammer, drill, saw, protractor, compass, transit, balance—real tools used to design, measure, cut, shape, mend, and join. Every tool has a long history—why it was needed, how it was invented, where it originated, when it was first used, how it evolved, who was responsible, what it has produced. Tools' origins are the stories of human history, geography, communication, and technology. Preschool teachers need to know these stories, convey them, and be competent tool users.
- Teach design to break the stranglehold of highly saturated primary and secondary colors and the tyranny of manufactured classroom decorations. Design includes classroom layout, furniture and materials selection, and graphic techniques for documentation. It applies to the minutest detail in the classroom, the items in every basket, the images on any wall, the colors, the layouts.
- Ensure teachers know how to teach phonics, number content and concepts, and attributes. Montessori materials are concrete and thorough.
- Teach teachers about how ecosystems behave so they broaden the classroom fishbowl or gerbil cage into microcosms reflecting the interrelatedness of animal, vegetable, and mineral kingdoms.
- Have teachers learn about human development—species and individual—and how it is influenced by evolution, culture, community, and mediation.
- Teach the latest research on the brain—its evolution and its development from the prenatal period forward, not chapters in textbooks but lectures by neurologists who, literally, have their hands on human brains.
- Ensure would-be teachers know how to listen; that means trainers must listen to *them*.

Parents can be children's strongest advocates. Their collective will to do right by children can unite them, and united they can cause political action. It is time for such action for early education. Excellent teachers and exemplary practices, wherever they exist, offer the blueprint. The history of the United States—individuals banding together to make change—provides the model. The potential in each baby's brain depends on it. The future of the planet demands it.

Glossary

Atelier, Studio: A room, like an artist uses, for production. It contains many kinds of well-organized materials like paints, clay, wire, and found objects, and has good light and ample wall and shelf space to store work in progress and display finished work, and tools.

Atelierista, Studio Teacher: A teacher who is an artist or craftsperson and skilled in using a wide variety of materials. Her perspective adds a different dimension to other teachers' interpretations of children's work.

Authentic Assessment: Means of keeping track of children's progress by collecting work samples, quotations, and photographs over months or years as evidence of their development. Includes teachers' regular notes on children's activities and behavior.

Azzariti, Jennifer: Studio teacher at the Model Early Learning Center and the first *atelierista* in the United States.

Belief: The acceptance of something as true that is so deep-seated that, whether or not a person can articulate the belief, it forms the basis for emotional and cognitive behavior.

Children's Defense Fund: A research and advocacy organization on behalf of economically disadvantaged children.

Collaboration: The process in which children work with one another in small groups, teachers work together to study children's interests, and teachers work alongside children on projects.

Collaborator: An aspect of a teacher's role in which she works side-by-side with children as an observant, experienced participant whose every response is extra-sensitive to each child's particular strengths and to the group's interactions. Collaborators act as children's accomplices and assistants in realizing their plans.

Concept: A name for a class of ideas, for example: *color* for red, green, turquoise, purple; *shape* for circle, diamond, rectangle; *number* for quantities and the symbols that represent them. Concepts enable the mind to organize information, and people to communicate meaning efficiently.

Content: Specific knowledge. It may be the ability to apply the word *red* to instances of that color, or to apply correct names to shapes, or very complex information that only specialists use.

Context: Surrounding conditions—text surrounding a word, materials nearby to work with, the aura of a place or era.

Culture: The collective beliefs and behaviors of a group as small as a family or as large as a nation. In sociocultural theory and the Reggio Approach, a classroom's culture is established collaboratively by teachers, children, and families.

Designer: An aspect of a teacher's role in which she prepares an environment so that it fosters relationships among people and between people and materials.

Diana School: The Reggio school for 3- to 6-year-olds where Vea Vecchi was *atelierista* and with Loris Malaguzzi helped shape this role.

Disposition: One's innate tendencies that include traits like perseverance; leadership; being withdrawn, outgoing, or empathetic; having the capacity for enjoyment.

Documentation: The large panels that tell the story of projects in photojournalistic manner. They reveal how children are thinking, provide a window into the school's life, and are a means of assessing children's progress.

Documenter: An aspect of a teacher's role in which she simultaneously participates and observes to identify a project's pivotal moments. She captures these in notes or photos to use on panels as the basis for reflection.

Elaboration: The essential major learning and thinking processes that are the core of cognition and turn stimuli into distinctive, organized knowledge.

Emergent Curriculum: An exchange of ideas, debate, and negotiation among teachers and children that leads to the initiation of a project and determines how a project will continue or branch. It also may be called negotiated curriculum.

Emerging Literacy: Beginning stages of the skills required to write and read, like realizing that words are made up of sounds, associating sounds with symbols, early attempts to write and sound out words, and increasing ability to grasp the meaning of speech and text.

Environment-as-a-Third-Teacher: The practice of preparing a classroom environment as a silent partner so teachers trust it will keep children occupied on their own as meaningfully as if they were involved with a teacher.

Feuerstein, Reuven: World-renowned psychologist who proposed theories of human development and cognition, pioneered a new paradigm for assessment based on a dynamic relation between teaching and testing, and created robust classroom practices in which teachers mediate—or intervene—in children's experiences to build or improve their cognitive structure.

Focused Conversation: Extended discourse with a full class, with a small group of children, or one-on-one in which the teacher has a goal such as expanding children's memory, lengthening their focus, enlarging their content knowledge, or helping them form concepts.

Gambetti, Amelia: Retired Reggio teacher who works in various countries as a lecturer or consults with schools making serious efforts to adapt the Reggio Approach.

Gardner, Howard: World-renowned psychologist who proposed the theory of multiple intelligences, was co-founder of Harvard's Project Zero, and is a powerful spokesperson for progressive ideas in education from infancy on.

Hundred Languages: The poetic phrase that Reggio educators use to convey the idea that children have the capacity to learn diverse means of expression in a range of modalities such as linguistic, mathematical, or musical.

Intentional Teaching: The practice of intervening in children's activities with purpose, meaning, and the aim of focusing on specific content or achieving a particular goal, often determined with the children.

Intervention: Coming between a child and a stimulus to scaffold; conveys no negative sense of interference or interruption.

La Villetta School: The Reggio school for 3- to 6-year-olds where Amelia Gambetti was a teacher and Giovanni Piazza the *atelierista*.

Listening: The active process through which teachers take notes or photographs, or collect other evidence of children's activity in order to learn what deeply interests them and what they understand.

Malaguzzi, Loris: The educator/philosopher who devoted his life to developing the Reggio Approach. He had penetrating insight about children, a gift for choosing and inspiring greatness in teachers, and an unusual sense of drama in provoking experiences to excite children's interest.

Materials: The wealth of items—a majority recycled, teacher made, or collected from nature—that are stored in the classroom and *atelier*, and are readily available for children to use in projects or other activities.

Mediator: An aspect of a teacher's role in which she intervenes between stimuli and child with intention, meaning, transcendence, energy, and emotion.

Mini-*Atelier*: The small studio that is part of every Reggio classroom and provides a place to make things and to store and display many materials.

Model Early Learning Center/MELC: A preschool for 36 Head Start-eligible children in Washington, D.C., one of the first Reggio-inspired schools in the United States, and the only one ever accredited by the Municipal Preschools of Reggio Emilia. The MELC existed from 1989 to mid-1997.

Modes, Modalities: The virtually infinite number of ways in which humans express themselves using combinations of different sensory and motor systems.

Municipal Preschools of Reggio Emilia: The many city-supported preschools—infant/toddler centers, preschools, and their administration, and political and community involvement. Generally considered to be the best in the world.

National Association for the Education of Young Children [NAEYC]: A huge membership organization which proposes standards for classroom practice and teacher education, provides information through conferences and publications, and accredits preschools.

North American Reggio Emilia Alliance [NAREA]: A membership organization to support knowledge about and the spread of the Reggio Approach in North America.

Numeracy: The ability to understand the concept of quantity, number symbols, how to manipulate the symbols and quantities, and how to use them in abstract and real-world applications.

Orchestrator: An aspect of a teacher's role in which she gathers particular children to begin an activity, asks leading questions, and moves projects along.

Pedagogista: In the Reggio system, an experienced teacher or psychologist who works with a small group of schools to add another perspective on all aspects of a school. American schools have no comparable position.

Piaget, Jean: Father of the field of developmental psychology and among the first to work with children, not animals, as the basis for understanding human development; proponent of stages of development as the primary driver of human growth.

Piazza, Giovanni: The long-time *atelierista* at La Villetta School in Reggio Emilia.

Practices: The teaching techniques and curriculum, or content, a teacher uses, which are determined by her beliefs or mandated by the state.

Project: Work done by small groups of children, typically four to six, with a teacher. It is usually stimulated by something a teacher hears in children's conversation that she believes has potential to develop into significant work. Projects may last hours, days, weeks, or months.

Provocation, Provoke: The words Reggio educators use to refer to stimulating or eliciting children's interest; there is no negative connotation as in the English word *provocative*.

188

Reggio Approach: The name commonly given to the philosophy and practices that developed in the city of Reggio Emilia, Italy, and today are inspiring early educators throughout the world.

Reggio Children: The organization run by the Municipal Preschools of Reggio Emilia to respond to worldwide requests for information about or assistance in using the Reggio Approach.

Reggio Emilia: The small Italian city, population about 140,000, where the Reggio Approach developed. It is located about 2 hours southeast of Milan and an hour northwest of Bologna.

Research: Listening and observing children in order to understand what their words and actions convey about their interests.

Researcher: An aspect of a teacher's role in which she listens, observes, records, and hypothesizes, then brainstorms with colleagues to interpret what her observations imply about children's interests. The researcher tests hypotheses by presenting them to the children whose activity spurred them; if the children show further interest, it will likely lead to a project, although, as in any research, the outcome is not certain.

Rinaldi, Carlina: Long-time *pedagogista* and, after Malaguzzi's death, the philosophical spokesperson for the Reggio Schools.

Revisiting: Studying documentation with small groups of children. The process maintains their interest and focus on what they have done, and sparks ideas about how the work can continue.

Scaffolding: Adult intervention to support a child's attempt to understand.

Self-Regulated: A child who has developed sufficient internal control to stifle unfocused, impulsive, or disruptive behavior. It also may be called self-disciplined.

Significant Work: Classroom activities that are intentional, highly articulated, purposeful, absorbing, and responsive to a child's interest. It has potential to branch to other subjects directly or indirectly related, and yields work that is creative, complex, and original.

Sociocultural Theory: Theory of human development based on the belief that growth occurs as the result of relations with other humans in the context of a particular culture and using the tools of that culture. The theory places great weight on language as the most important tool in shaping development, and on the teacher's role as mediator between the child and the culture.

Studio, Studio Teacher: See *Atelier, Atelierista*.

Symbol System: A comprehensive way to represent groups of thoughts or actions in which a number of complex parts are inextricably related to one another to achieve particular goals; for example, language to represent meaning, alphabets to represent spoken sounds, notation to represent musical sound.

Transcendence: Going beyond the immediate stimulus and connecting it to other relevant events in the past or future.

Vecchi, Vea: For 20 years the *atelierista* in Diana School, one of the Reggio Preschools. With Malaguzzi, she helped to develop the function of the *atelier* and the role of the *atelierista*.

Vygotsky, Lev: Russian psychologist whose writing laid the foundation for sociocultural theory and focused the agenda for research on human development in the late 20th and early 21st centuries. He died at age 38 in 1934, and Soviet politics kept his ideas from reaching the West for several decades.

References

Barnett, W. S., Yarosz, D. J., Thomas, J., & Hornbeck, A. (2006). *Educational effectiveness of a Vygotskian approach to preschool education: A randomized trial.* New Brunswick, NJ: Rutgers University, National Institute for Early Education Research. Retrieved September 29, 2007, from http://neer.org/resources/research/ToolsoftheMind.pdf

Berk, L. E., & Winsler, A. (1995). *Scaffolding children's learning: Vygotsky and early childhood education.* Washington, DC: National Association for the Education of Young Children.

Bruner, C., & Copeman, A. (2003). *School readiness: Options for developing state baselines and benchmarks.* Des Moines, IA: State Early Childhood Policy Technical Assistance Network. Retrieved August 14, 2007, from http://www.finebynine.org/pdf/Baselines.pdf

Bruner, C., Floyd, S., & Copeman, A. (2005). *Seven things policy makers need to know about school readiness* [Briefing Papers]. Des Moines, IA: State Early Childhood Policy Technical Assistance Network. Retrieved August 14, 2007, from http://www.gettingready.org/matriarch/MultiPiecePage.asp_Q_PageID_E_206_A_PageName_E_SchoolReadiness

Bruner, J. (1996). *The culture of education.* Cambridge, MA: Harvard University Press.

Carpenter, E. G. (1973). *Eskimo realities.* New York: Holt, Rinehart and Winston.

Carroll, L. (1941). *Alice's adventures in wonderland.* New York: Heritage Press. (Original work published 1865)

Cherry, C. (1957). *On human communication.* Cambridge, MA: MIT Press.

Children's Defense Fund. (2002). *Mini green book.* Washington, DC. Retrieved May 23, 2005, from http://www.childrensdefensefund.org/pdf/minigreenbook.pdf

Corsaro, W., & Molinari, L. (2005). *I compagni: Understanding children's transition from preschool to elementary school.* New York: Teachers College Press.

Csikszentmihalyi, M. (1993). *The evolving self: A psychology for the third millennium.* New York: HarperCollins.

D'Amasio, A. R. (1994). *Descartes' error.* New York: Putnam.

Donovan, J. E. (2007). Really underage drinking: The epidemiology of children's alcohol use in the United States. *Prevention Science, 8,* 192–205. Retrieved September 27, 2007, from http://www.preventionresearch.org/September%202007%20Donovan%20Really%20Underage%20Alcohol%20FINAL.pdf

Edwards, C., Gandini, L., & Forman, G. (Eds.). (1993). *The hundred languages of children* (1st ed.). Norwood, NJ: Ablex.

Eisner, E. (2002). *The arts and the creation of mind.* New Haven, CT: Yale University Press.

Epstein, A., Schweinhart, L. J., DeBruin-Parecki, A., & Robin, K. B. (2004). *Preschool assessment: A guide to developing a balanced approach.* New Brunswick, NJ: Rutgers University, National Institute for Early Education Research. Retrieved August 10, 2007, from http://nieer.org/resources/policybriefs/7.pdf

Feuerstein, R. S., & Feuerstein, R. (2004). *User's guide to the theory and practice of the Feuerstein instrumental enrichment BASIC program.* Jerusalem: International Center for the Enhancement of Learning Potential.

Feuerstein, R., Feuerstein, R. S., Falik, L., & Rand, Y. (2002). *The dynamic assessment of cognitive modifiability.* Jerusalem: International Center for the Enhancement of Learning Potential.

Feuerstein, R., Feuerstein, R. S., Falik, L., & Rand, Y. (2006). *The Feuerstein instrumental enrichment program: Part I and Part II*. Jerusalem: International Center for the Enhancement of Learning Potential.

Forman, G. (1992). Research on early science education. In C. Seefeldt (Ed.), *The early childhood curriculum: A review of current research* (pp. 175–192). New York: Teachers College Press.

Gandini, L. (1993). History, ideas and basic philosophy: An interview with Lella Gandini. In C. Edwards, L. Gandini, & G. Forman (Eds.), *The hundred languages of children* (pp. 41–89). Norwood, NJ: Ablex.

Gardner, H. (1980). *Artful scribbles: The significance of children's drawings*. New York: Basic Books.

Gardner, H. (1983). *Frames of mind: The theory of multiple intelligences*. New York: Basic Books.

Gardner, H. (1993). *Creating minds: An anatomy of creativity*. New York: Basic Books.

Grehan, A. (2006, May 2). Using evaluation to improve and sustain literacy and educational programs [lecture of Mid-South Reads]. Memphis, TN.

Harr, J. (1995). *A civil action*. New York: Random House.

Hawkins, D. (1974). *The informed vision: Essays on learning and human nature*. New York: Agathon Press.

Hawkins, D. (1983). Nature closely observed. *Daedalus, 112*(2), 65–88.

Hendrick, J. (1994). *Total learning: Developmental curriculum for the young child*. New York: Macmillan.

KIDS COUNT. (2005). *Getting ready. Findings from the national school readiness indicators initiative: A 17 state partnership*. Providence, RI: Author. Retrieved August 8, 2007, from http://www.gettingready.org/matriarch/d.asp?PageID=303&PageName2=pdf hold&p=&PageName=Getting+Ready+%2D+Full+Report%2Epdf

Klein, L. G., & Knitzer, J. (2007, January). Promoting effective early learning: What every policymaker and educator should know. *Effective preschool curricula and teaching strategies*. Columbia University, National Center for Children in Poverty. Retrieved July 11, 2007, from http://nccp.org/publications/pub_695.html

Kunkel, D., Wilcox, B., Cantor, J., Palmer, E., Linn, S., & Dowrick, P. (2004). *Report of the APA task force on advertising and children: Psychological issues in the increasing commercialization of childhood*. American Psychological Association. Retrieved May 2, 2006, from http://www.apa.org/releases/childrenads.pdf

Lewin-Benham, A. (2006). *Possible schools: The Reggio Approach to urban education*. New York: Teachers College Press.

Malaguzzi, L. (1991). *The very little ones of silent pictures*. Reggio Emilia: Municipal Infant/Toddler Center.

Malaguzzi, L. (1993). History, ideas and philosophy (L. Gandini, Trans.). In C. Edwards, L. Gandini, G. Forman (Eds.), *The hundred languages of children* (1st ed., pp. 68–69). Norwood, NJ: Ablex.

Malkin, M. (2003, July 21). "Day care or toddler death centers?" BNET. Retrieved May 15, 2006, from http://www.findarticles.com/p/articles/mi_qa3827/is_200307/ai_n9244822/pg_1

Mix, K. S., Huttenlocher, J., & Levine, S. C. (2002). *Quantitative development in infancy and early childhood*. New York: Oxford University Press.

Montaigne, M. (ca. 1580). Of divine ordinances. In *Works, book 1*, Chapter 31.

Narrol, H. G., & Giblon, S. T. (2001). *The fourth "R": Uncovering hidden learning potential*. Baltimore: University Park Press.

National Association for the Education of Young Children. (1996). *Developmentally appropriate practice in early childhood programs serving children from birth through age 8*. Washington, DC: Author. Retrieved September 30, 2007, from http://www.naeyc.org/about/positions/daptoc.asp*

---

* From time to time NAEYC changes its Web site. Therefore, web addresses may differ from those supplied here.

National Association for the Education of Young Children. (2008a). *Accessing community resources.* Washington, DC: Author. Retrieved January 31, 2008, from http://www.naeyc.org/academy/standards/standard8/standard8B.asp

National Association for the Education of Young Children. (2008b). *Adapting curriculum, individualizing teaching, and informing program development.* Washington, DC: Author. Retrieved January 31, 2008, from http://www.naeyc.org/academy/standards/standard4/standard4D.asp

National Association for the Education of Young Children. (2008c). *Building and physical design.* Washington, DC: Author. Retrieved January 31, 2008, from http://www.naeyc.org/academy/standards/standard9/standard9C.asp

National Association for the Education of Young Children. (2008d). *Curriculum content area for cognitive development: Early literacy.* Washington, DC: Author. Retrieved January 31, 2008, from http://www.naeyc.org/academy/standards/standard2/standard2E.asp

National Association for the Education of Young Children. (2008e). *Curriculum: Essential characteristics.* Washington, DC: Author. Retrieved January 31, 2008, from http://www.naeyc.org/academy/standards/standard2/standard2A.asp

National Association for the Education of Young Children. (2008f). *Environmental health.* Washington, DC: Author. Retrieved January 31, 2008, from http://www.naeyc.org/academy/standards/standard9/standard9D.asp

National Association for the Education of Young Children. (2008g). *Maintaining a healthful environment.* Washington, DC: Author. Retrieved January 31, 2008, from http://www.naeyc.org/academy/standards/standard5/standard5C.asp

National Association for the Education of Young Children. (2008h). *Management policies and procedures.* Washington, DC: Author. Retrieved January 31, 2008, from http://www.naeyc.org/academy/standards/standard10/standard10B.asp

National Association for the Education of Young Children. (2008i). *NAEYC academy for early childhood program accreditation.* Washington, DC: Author. Retrieved January 31, 2008, from http://www.naeyc.org/academy/

National Association for the Education of Young Children. (2008j). *NAEYC early childhood program standards.* Washington, DC: Author. Retrieved January 31, 2008, from http://www.naeyc.org/academy/standards/

National Association for the Education of Young Children. (2008k). *Physical environment.* Washington, DC: Author. Retrieved January 31, 2008, from http://www.naeyc.org/academy/standards/standard9/

National Association for the Education of Young Children. (2008l). *Program evaluation, accountability, and continuous improvement.* Washington, DC: Author. Retrieved January 31, 2008, from http://www.naeyc.org/academy/standards/standard10/standard10F.asp

National Association for the Education of Young Children. (2008m). *Promoting and protecting children's health and controlling infectious disease.* Washington, DC: Author. Retrieved January 31, 2008, from http://www.naeyc.org/academy/standards/standard5/standard5A.asp

National Association for the Education of Young Children. (2008n). *Relationships.* Washington, DC: Author. Retrieved January 31, 2008, from http://www.naeyc.org/academy/standards/standard1/

National Association for the Education of Young Children. (n.d.a). *Table 1. Candidacy requirements.* Washington, DC: Author. Retrieved January 22, 2008, from http://www.naeyc.org/academy/table1.asp

National Association for the Education of Young Children. (n.d.b). *Critical facts about the early childhood workforce.* Washington, DC: Author. Retrieved September 30, 2007, from http://www.naeyc.org/ece/critical/facts3.asp#4

National Association for the Education of Young Children. (n.d.c). *The next era—a timeline.* Washington, DC: Author. Retrieved September 30, 2007, from http://www.naeyc.org/academy/HistoryNAEYCAccreditation.asp

National Center on Education and the Economy. (2007). *Tough choices or tough times: The report of the new Commission on the Skills of the American Workforce.* Washington, DC: Author.

NICHD Early Child Care Research Network. (2002). Direct and indirect effects of caregiving quality on young children's development. *Psychological Science, 13*(3), 199–206.

Ohri, M. (2007). Education and training market 2007: Key trends and dynamics. Outsell. Retrieved September 27, 2007, from http://www.outsellinc.com/store/products/501/

Parents United for the D.C. Public Schools. (2003). *D.C. public school funding: Myth and reality.* Retrieved September 23, 2007, from http://www.parentsunited4dc.org/mrfunding_report_i.htm

Perkins, D. (1986). *Knowledge as design.* Mahwah, NJ: Erlbaum.

Perkins, D. (1995). *Outsmarting IQ: The emerging science of learnable intelligence.* New York: Free Press.

Perkins, D., & Tishman, S. (2006). *Learning that matters: Toward a dispositional perspective on education and its research needs.* Cambridge, MA: Harvard Graduate School of Education.

Pinker, S. (1994). *The language instinct: How the mind creates language.* New York: HarperCollins.

Pinker, S. (1997). *How the mind works.* New York: Norton.

Pinker, S. (2002). *The blank slate: The modern denial of human nature.* New York: Penguin.

Policy Research Institute of the Region. (2006). Preschool teacher qualifications a vexing issue. *Regional Update.* Princeton, NJ: Princeton University. Retrieved July 25, 2007, from http://region.princeton.edu/issue_106.html

Presseisen, B., & Kozulin, A. (1994). Mediated learning: The contributions of Vygotsky and Feuerstein in theory and practice. In M. Ben-Hur (Ed.), *On Feuerstein's instrumental enrichment: A collection* (pp. 51–81). Palatine, IL: IRI/Skylight.

Rinaldi, C. (1992, June). The philosophy of the municipal preschools of Reggio Emilia [lecture]. Mt. Ida College, Newton Centre, MA.

Rinaldi, C. (2002). Pedagogy and furnishing. In *Atelier: Furnishings for young children.* Reggio Emilia: ISAFF.

Rinaldi, C. (2006). *In dialogue with Reggio Emilia: Listening, researching and learning.* London: Routledge.

Sacks, P. (1999). *Standardized minds: The high price of America's testing culture and what we can do to change it.* New York: Perseus.

Shin, E., & Spodek, B. (1991). *The relationship between children's play patterns and types of teacher intervention.* East Lansing, MI: National Center for Research on Teacher Learning. (ERIC Document Reproduction Service No. ED332803)

Vecchi, V. (2002). Grace and care as education. In *Atelier: Furnishings for young children.* Reggio Emilia: ISAFF.

Verne, J. (1992). *20,000 leagues under the sea* (M. G. Vogel, Ed.). New York: Baronet.

Weiss, H., Caspe, M., & Lopez, M. E. (2006, Spring). *Family involvement makes a difference* (Harvard Family Research Project No. 1). Retrieved March 22, 2007, from http://www.gse.harvard.edu/hfrp/projects/fine/resources/research/earlychildhood.html

Wharton, A. C., & Ford, H., Jr. (2007, October 28). Fixing broken dreams. *The Commercial Appeal,* pp. V1, V3.

Wilson, F. R. (1998). *The hand: How its use shapes the brain, language, and human culture.* New York: Pantheon Books.

Index

Entries appearing in the glossary are followed by "g" and those appearing in figures are followed by "f"

Photo by Rene Koopman

About the Author

Ann Lewin-Benham is an educator who has spent most of 4 decades developing programs for economically disadvantaged children and families. In the early 1970s in inner-city Washington, D.C., Ann directed one of the first corporate day care centers; in the poverty pockets of Arlington County, VA, she founded one of the first Montessori programs within a public school system; and she founded and administered Parkmont School, an alternative junior high school. In the mid-1970s she founded and for 20 years directed the Capital Children's Museum in Washington, D.C., locating the organization in a former riot corridor. There she also founded and directed Options School, a junior high school dropout prevention program, and the Model Early Learning Center (MELC), which is the subject of this book and her earlier book, *Possible Schools: The Reggio Approach to Urban Education*. The MELC, which opened in 1989, was one of the first charter schools and ran under contract to the District of Columbia Public Schools, which selected the children from oversubscribed Head Start sites. The MELC was accredited by the Municipal Preschools of Reggio Emilia. Ann is a graduate of Bryn Mawr College and lives in Memphis, TN, with her husband, Judge Robert Benham.

For more information, visit www.AnnLewin-Benham.com